£27·50

KING ALFRED'S COLLEGE
WINCHESTER

To be returned on or before the day marked
below:-

2 0 DEC 2002

2 6 APR 2004

− 9 NOV 2006

1 1 DEC 2006

15. MAR 96

02. DEC

− 6 OCT 1997

NIETZSCHE AND MODERN LITERATURE

Nietzsche and Modern Literature

Themes in Yeats, Rilke, Mann and Lawrence

Keith M. May

**MACMILLAN
PRESS**

First published 1988

Published by
THE MACMILLAN PRESS LTD
Houndmills, Basingstoke, Hampshire RG21 2XS
and London
Companies and representatives
throughout the world

Printed in Hong Kong

British Library Cataloguing in Publication Data
May, Keith M.
Nietzsche and modern literature: themes
in Yeats, Rilke, Mann and Lawrence.
1. Nietzsche, Friedrich — Influence
2. European literature — 20th century —
History and criticism 3. Philosophy in
literature
I. Title
809'.04   PN771
ISBN 0–333–39270–1

Contents

Acknowledgements

Acknowledgement is gratefully made to the following: Random House Inc. and Marianne Fallon, Permissions Editor, for permission to quote from *The Will to Power* by Friedrich Nietzsche, translated by Walter Kaufmann and R. J. Hollingdale, copyright ©1967 by Walter Kaufmann; Laurence Pollinger Limited and the estate of Mrs Frieda Lawrence Ravagli for permission to quote from D. H. Lawrence's *Lady Chatterley's Lover* and *Movements in European History*; Cambridge University Press for permission to quote from *The Letters of D. H. Lawrence*, General Editor James T. Boulton; Alfred A. Knopf, Inc. for permission to quote from D. H. Lawrence's *The Plumed Serpent* and from the following works of Thomas Mann: *Death in Venice, Doctor Faustus, Joseph and His Brothers, The Beloved Returns, The Magic Mountain* and *Tonio Kröger*, all translated by H. T. Lowe-Porter, and *Confessions of Felix Krull Confidence Man*, translated by Denver Lindley; Secker & Warburg Limited for permission to quote from the translations by H. T. Lowe-Porter of Thomas Mann's *Joseph and His Brothers, Tonio Kröger, Death in Venice, The Magic Mountain, Lotte in Weimar* and *Doctor Faustus*, and from the translation by Denver Lindley of Thomas Mann's *Confessions of Felix Krull Confidence Man*; Chatto & Windus: The Hogarth Press for permission to quote extracts from *Duino Elegies* by Rainer Maria Rilke, translated with introduction and commentary by J. B. Leishman and Stephen Spender. The lines from *Duino Elegies* by Rainer Maria Rilke, translated by J. B. Leishman and Stephen Spender, are reprinted with the permission of W. W. Norton & Company Inc., copyright 1939 by W. W. Norton & Company Inc., copyright renewed 1967 by Stephen Spender and J. B. Leishman.

Grateful acknowledgement is also made to: Viking Penguin Inc. for permission to quote from *Sons and Lovers* by D. H. Lawrence, copyright 1913 by Thomas Seltzer Inc. All rights reserved. Reprinted by permission of Viking Penguin Inc. From *The Rainbow* by D. H. Lawrence, copyright 1915 by D. H. Lawrence. Copyright renewed 1943 by Frieda Lawrence. Reprinted by permission of Viking Penguin Inc. From *Women in Love* by D. H. Lawrence, copyright 1920, 1922 by D. H. Lawrence, renewed 1948, 1950 by Frieda Lawrence. Reprinted by permission of Viking Penguin Inc.

From *Aaron's Rod* by D. H. Lawrence, copyright 1922 by Thomas Seltzer Inc. Copyright renewed 1950 by Frieda Lawrence. Reprinted by permission of Viking Penguin Inc. From *Kangaroo* by D. H. Lawrence, copyright 1923 by Thomas Seltzer Inc. Copyright renewed 1951 by Frieda Lawrence. Reprinted by permission of Viking Penguin Inc. To A. P. Watt on behalf of Michael B. Yeats and Macmillan, London, Limited for permission to quote from three works of W. B. Yeats: 'The Rose Tree', 'Two Songs from a Play' and 'Mohini Chatterjee'.

A selection from 'The Rose Tree' is reprinted with the permission of Macmillan Publishing Company from *Collected Poems* by W. B. Yeats, copyright 1924 by Macmillan Publishing Company, renewed 1952 by Bertha Georgie Yeats. A selection from 'Two Songs from a Play' is reprinted with the permission of Macmillan Publishing Company from *Collected Poems* by W. B. Yeats, copyright 1928 by Macmillan Publishing Company, renewed 1956 by Bertha Georgie Yeats. A selection from 'Mohini Chatterjee' is reprinted with the permission of Macmillan Publishing Company from *Collected Poems* by W. B. Yeats, copyright 1933 by Macmillan Publishing Company, renewed 1961 by Bertha Georgie Yeats.

Gratitude is also expressed for the use of the following works: Nancy Cardozo, *Maud Gonne: Lucky Eyes and a High Heart* (Gollancz, 1979); Gilles Deleuze, *Nietzsche and Philosophy*, translated by Hugh Tomlinson (Athlone, 1983); Richard Ellman, *The Identity of Yeats* (Faber & Faber, 1964, and Macmillan, 1954); Richard Ellman, *Yeats: The Man and the Masks* (Oxford University Press, 1979, Macmillan, 1948, and Faber & Faber, 1961); Romano Guardini, *Rilke's Duino Elegies*, translated by K. G. Knight (Darwin Finlayson, 1961); Martin Heidegger, *Nietzsche* Vol. I *The Will to Power as Art* and Vol. II *The Eternal Recurrence of the Same*, both volumes translated by David Farrell Krell (Harper & Row); T. R. Henn, *The Lonely Tower* (Methuen, 1965); Joseph Hone, *W. B. Yeats 1865–1939* (Penguin, 1971 and Macmillan, 1943); A. Norman Jeffares, *A New Commentary on the Poems of W. B. Yeats* (Macmillan, 1984); Walter Kaufmann, *From Shakespeare to Existentialism: An Original Study* (Princeton University Press, 1980); *Lawrence in Love: Letters to Louie Burrows*, edited and introduced by James T. Boulton (University of Nottingham, 1968); Thomas Mann's *Essays of Three Decades* and *Past Masters and Other Papers*, each translated by H. T. Lowe-Porter; *Thomas Mann Diaries 1918–1939*, selection and foreword by Herman Kesten, translated by Richard and Clara Winston (André Deutsch,

1983); *Last Essays*, translated by Richard and Clara Winston and Tania and James Stern (Secker & Warburg, 1959); *The Letters of Thomas Mann 1889–1955*, selected and translated by Richard and Clara Winston (Penguin, 1975); *Thomas Mann: A Collection of Critical Essays* (Prentice-Hall, 1964); Iris Murdoch, *The Sovereignty of Good* (Routledge & Kegan Paul, 1970); George Orwell, *Collected Essays* (Secker & Warburg, 1961); Rainer Maria Rilke, *The Notebook of Malte Laurids Brigge*, introduction by Stephen Spender (Oxford University Press, 1984); *Selected Letters of Rainer Maria Rilke 1902–1926*, translated by R. F. C. Hull (Macmillan, 1946); Arthur Schopenhauer, *The World as Will and Representation*, translation by E. F. J. Payne (Dover Publications, 1966, and The Falcon's Wing Press, 1958); *Works of Spinoza*, translated by R. H. M. Elwes (New York, Dover Publications, 1951); Joan Stambaugh, *Nietzsche's Thought of Eternal Return* (Johns Hopkins University Press, 1972); the following works of W. B. Yeats: *Autobiographies* (Macmillan, 1955), *Collected Poems* (Macmillan, 1969), *Essays and Introductions* Macmillan, New York, 1961), *Explorations* (Macmillan, New York, 1962), *Letters of W. B. Yeats* (Rupert Hart-Davis, 1954), *Memoirs* (Macmillan, 1972), *Pages from a Diary Written in Nineteen Hundred and Thirty* (Dublin, 1944), *The Variorum Edition of the Complete Plays of W. B. Yeats* (Macmillan, 1966), *A Vision* (Macmillan, 1962).

The author wishes to express special appreciation for the opportunity to make use of the following editions of Nietzsche's works: *Beyond Good and Evil: Prelude to a Philosophy of the Future*, translated with commentary by Walter Kaufmann (Vintage Books, Random House, 1966); *The Birth of Tragedy* and *The Case of Wagner*, translated with commentary by Walter Kaufmann (Vintage Books, Random House, 1967); *Daybreak: Thoughts On the Prejudices of Morality*, translated by R. J. Hollingdale, introduction by Michael Tanner (Cambridge University Press, 1982); *The Gay Science*, translated with commentary by Walter Kaufmann (Vintage Books, Random House, 1974); *On The Genealogy of Morals*, translated by Walter Kaufmann and R. J. Hollingdale, and *Ecce Homo*, translated with commentary by Walter Kaufmann (Vintage Books, Random House, 1967); *A Nietzsche Reader*, selected and translated by R. J. Hollingdale (Penguin, 1979); *Philosophy in the Tragic Age of the Greeks*, translated with introduction by Marianne Cowan (A Gateway Edition, Regnery Gateway, 1962); *Selected Letters of Friedrich Nietzsche*, translated by A. N. Ludovici, edited and introduced by O. Levy (Soho Book Company, 1985); *Thus Spoke*

Zarathustra: *A Book for Everyone and No One*, translated with introduction by R. J. Hollingdale (Penguin, 1980); *Twilight of the Idols* and *The Anti-Christ*, translated with introduction and commentary by R. J. Hollingdale (Penguin, 1978); *Unpublished Letters*, translated and edited by Karl F. Leidecker (Peter Owen, 1960, Philosophical Library USA, 1959); *Untimely Meditations*, translated by R. J. Hollingdale, introduction by J. P. Stern (Cambridge University Press, 1983).

1
Perspectives of Nietzsche

Nietzsche is the philosopher friendliest to art even though he pierces artists' masks. He goes behind appearances to motives, yet shows that appearances reflect motives. For example, Nietzsche points out that Euripides has the appearance of one fascinated by actual behaviour and is the wonderful observer among the earliest dramatists. But why was Euripides so fascinated? As a youth he sat among the spectators of Aeschylus and Sophocles uneasily aware that he, and perhaps he alone, could not understand the older authors. The performances bore little resemblance to Athenian reality and failed to represent the people who attended them. Why couldn't everyone else see this blatant falsification? So Euripides proceeded to write his tragedies in which the behaviour of the characters was familiar and, above all, intelligible. He introduced the everyday social man into the drama and, since he evidently despised the mass of spectators, wrote for two appreciative observers: himself as thinker rather than as poet, and the 'theoretical man', Socrates. In this fashion he paved the way for the New Comedy and strangled tragedy shortly after its birth. But that was his intention. We know Euripides as an eminent writer of tragedies, though in fact the spirit of tragedy was his prey. All Europe has been influenced by him to the present day, for we still believe that the phenomenal world is basic, whereas, so Nietzsche says, the ground of being is Dionysian, unindividualised and impenetrable.

Thus Nietzsche anatomises Euripides (in *The Birth of Tragedy*, sections 11–13) but he does not do so out of distaste. He probes the dramatist as he probes everything else; he goes behind the mask of psychological realism because he is himself the sharpest of all psychologists. But for Nietzsche to do this he has to know the mask in the way of an absorbed reader. It is necessary to empathise with Euripides. So Nietzsche successfully uses art as material for philosophy, because he greets it first as art.

The friendliness towards art, therefore, has nothing to do with veneration, but is connected with a belief that artists' productions

1

are no less trustworthy as guides for the conduct of our lives (and sometimes healthier) than the arguments of philosophy, the demonstrations of science and the certainties of revelation. Each of these fields has its characteristic weaknesses, and one weakness of the artist is that he is easily tempted to sacrifice an insight for the sake of an effect or out of laziness. ('On Gethsemane – The most painful thing a thinker can say to artists is: "Could ye not *watch* with me one hour?"'[1]) Just the same, artists at their most reliable deal with the actual world and do not prefer invisible spheres.

This is the virtue that Plato held to be a vice. It was harmful that poets were purely concerned with phenomena, the shadows cast by the fire on the wall of the cave. Plato's philosopher-rulers, fundamentally a sort of anti-poets, would be distinguished by their ability to see and delight in the essences of things. But to Nietzsche there are no essences, no Forms, no unseen intelligible principles. Therefore the artist's proper role is to assist in the shaping of this world, and though we might often remember that he is a liar, we should also remember that he does not normally pretend to tell the truth. Shakespeare, for example, has often enough been regarded as a truth-teller, though he, in the guise of Prospero, seems to have thought of himself as an enchanter. However, poets desert their phenomenalistic function from time to time, indeed in their 'highest flights' become 'glorifiers of humanity's religious and philosophical errors', as happened for instance when Dante wrote the *Divina Commedia*.[2]

But if artists are careless of the truth, how can we allow them, indeed encourage them, to affect our views of the world – as a rule by means of their elaborations upon established doctrines? Part of the answer is that we cannot 'correct' them without becoming artists ourselves or stop them without becoming tyrants. Every artist is an egoist almost by definition and in any event would not be able to do his work if he tried to see things 'objectively'. I mean that the artist, especially the greatly talented artist, promotes his own personal view of the world, his 'colouring', at all costs. If he is not original as a thinker, he is not a mish-mash of general opinions either. His vision must be a perspective. To this kind of argument Nietzsche's supportive response is to say that what we call the mind is and must ever be composed of perspectives, so that 'objectivity' refers just to a type of perspective whose distortions are at present hidden. Some perspectives should be seen as preferable to others, but not because they are nearer to transcendent truth. For example, the laws of physics offer a better perspective for modern people than primitive myth, though not on the grounds that they are literally objective.

To put the matter another way, a human subject cannot but see and think as a subject. He may not climb out of the prison of himself, or 'cleanse', as Blake puts it, 'the doors of perception'.[3] It follows that a painting, a product of human perception, never objectively represents the simplest thing. Neither does a photograph, the product of a mechanical process, since the thing-in-itself which the photograph apparently shows does not exist. 'Or is it to be supposed,' Nietzsche asks, 'that at that moment the things as it were engrave, counterfeit, photograph themselves by their own action on a purely passive medium?'[4]

Nietzsche means that even an unemotional and seemingly unslanted view of anything is still only a view. This is much clearer in the case of a sentient being, for it is plain that an objective view of a creature must somehow proceed from the subjectivity of an observer yet, impossibly, be made up of the subjectivity of the creature. In regard to things, it is tempting to say with Kant that they exist in themselves but are unknowable: however, what Nietzsche actually says is that the thing-in-itself is nonsense. There are only appearances and relationships.

> That things possess a constitution in themselves, quite apart from interpretation and subjectivity, is a quite idle hypothesis: it presupposes that interpretations and subjectivity are not essential, that a thing freed from all relationships would still be a thing.[5]

It is on account of this attitude, among others, that Nietzsche might be regarded as the poet's philosopher. He is not the philosopher's philosopher, though he could reasonably be seen as the philosopher of post-Einstein science. In effect he says to artists: 'Make your interpretations gladly and without obeisance to any pattern of meaning or morality that contradicts them.' In fact poets, or more broadly creative writers, have never much cared if they lived in a somewhat regulated society, provided they could reinterpret the rules. Perhaps even now writers prefer supposedly strict legislative or cultural rules that may in practice be broken. But for writers to be told by Nietzsche that there can be no creditable authority over them is perhaps unnerving. And it is certainly helpful for the writer to have some body of custom or belief to tilt against.

The poets and novelists discussed in this book seem to me the most considerable of those who have faced their world somewhat 'Nietzscheanly'. It goes without saying that they did not do so obsequiously: rather, three of them, Yeats, Rilke and Mann, saw what Nietzsche was driving at and accommodated his attitudes to their own. As for Lawrence, he was scarcely influenced by Nietzsche, but independently arrived at his own similar views on, especially, will to power.

The usual practice of critics is, understandably, to expound one or other of these four modernist writers with little or no reference to Nietzsche. But substantial aspects of their work grow much clearer when one does refer to the philosopher. Moreover, to mention some theme of Nietzsche in passing or in a footnote is likely to be misleading, since in that way neither the original thought nor its metamorphosis into a literary mode will be fully understood.

For these ideas are harder to grasp than they appear, and even more radical. When a Nietzschean insight dons the mantle of an image in Yeats or a setting in Mann it is thought to be more manageable, since it is now merely a piece of literature and need not be taken to heart. When a new idea masquerades as 'pure art' it may be officially ignored, even though it subterraneously eats away at old certainties. Generally speaking, Western literary works invite no positive commitment from anyone and simply contribute to a hopeless jumble of opinions; all the same, some few ideas (and Nietzsche's are notable in this respect) gather force decade by decade. Nietzsche himself remarks that new ideas gain currency by being assimilated to familiar attitudes: thus the Socratic plays of Euripides were not distinguished accurately enough from the plays of his predecessors. They were distinguished of course (and there was even a rumour that Socrates was their author) but no one seems to have grasped their essentially anti-Aeschylean and anti-Sophoclean import.[6]

This is the reason why the plan in this book is to cross academic boundaries and consider literature and philosophy side by side; for instance, to contemplate beyond-good-and-evil in Nietzsche and Mann. It is important, first of all, to appreciate the sheer novelty of certain attitudes. Second, these attitudes ought not to be confined to the sphere of learning, let alone to one branch of learning rather than another. At the outset, however, it is necessary to discuss a few pervasive features of Nietzsche, one of which we have already broached, namely his opinion of the status of 'truth'.

So far, then, we have noticed that Nietzsche is a sort of 'non-cognitivist' thinker who does not believe that truth transcends our thought-processes or that it can be objectively known. This amounts to saying, if we wish to put it so, that there is 'no truth'. Indeed, Nietzsche declares: 'There exists neither "spirit", nor reason, nor thinking, nor consciousness, nor soul, nor will, nor truth: all are fictions that are of no use.'[7]

But such an unqualified rejection of metaphysical assumptions does not mean a rejection of values. Oddly enough it does not mean a rejection of 'truth' in some sense, for Nietzsche often speaks of truth as if it were preferable to falsehood. Indeed, it is plain that the assertion 'There is no truth' is itself intended to be a truth. What Nietzsche has in mind is that human beings interpret everything as a matter of course: to perceive or to think about something is to interpret it. Nevertheless some interpretations are better than others because they exclude what we ought honestly to recognise as falsifications. Thus no one who frankly contemplates his own activities will be able to detect his spirit, reason, thinking, consciousness, soul or will. To say one 'thinks' is to simplify and therefore to falsify.

Fortunately (for this is a book-length topic of much complexity) John T. Wilcox's *Truth and Value in Nietzsche* deals exhaustively with the question of how Nietzsche both seeks truth and denies it.[8] Wilcox reaches the following conclusions: first, according to Nietzsche there are truths about truth itself (e.g. that it is fallible and provisional); second, there are certain large-scale truths (e.g. that man is purely a species of animal); and third, there are psychological truths (e.g. about the development of Christianity or the workings of pity).[9] As we have seen, these truths are still interpretations, but they are better interpretations than the obvious lies which they replace: for instance, that man is made in God's image or that the natural feeling of pity is also a virtue. If we now proceed to ask why some interpretations are better than others, Nietzsche's answer is that they affirm life rather than deny it. Here it must be understood that Nietzsche is not urging man to behave after the manner of a natural force or a lower animal. Man has a unique capacity for 'sublimating' his lower into higher impulses: that is the *natural* way for our species. We are not the talking animals so much as the sublimating animals, for speech is but a mode of sublimation.[10] If we look at cultural developments in this light we have the basis for a criterion of all human interpretations: false interpretations disown and denigrate their own natural sources. Note that it is never a matter of asking which of two interpretations promotes vigour the more, since there is a vigour of decadence too. No, we must look for signs that the artist or philosopher is a life-affirmer rather than a judge.

Nietzsche prefers to speak of 'strength' rather than 'vigour'. Here are some clear and consistent formulations of this quality.

The vigour of a mind, its *freedom* through strength and superior strength, is *proved* by scepticism.[11]

Freedom from any kind of conviction is part of the strength of his [the great man's] will... The need for faith, for anything unconditional in YES and NO is a proof of weakness.[12]

Everywhere else that the spirit is strong, mighty, and at work without counterfeit today, it does without ideals of any kind – the popular expression for this abstinence is 'atheism' – *except for its will to truth*. But this will, this *remnant* of an ideal, is, if you will believe me, this ideal itself in its strictest, most spiritual formulation, esoteric through and through, with all external additions abolished, and thus not so much its remnant as its *kernel*. Unconditional honest atheism ... is the awe-inspiring *catastrophe* of two thousand years of training in truthfulness that finally forbids itself the *lie involved in belief in God*.[13]

These remarks concern strength at present, not necessarily in earlier periods, and for modern people strength is indicated by atheism. The atheism must be complete and not of the partial or parodic variety that still believes in the moral law or entertains ideals of any kind. For an ideal is a token of God, while strength is the denial of everything that can be denied – except the will to truth. Now this remnant or kernel of an ideal (a remnant when we look to the past, a kernel when we look to the future) is the minimum from which new and sustainable values might grow. The matchless irony is that the will to truth is a result of the philosophy and faith (Socratism and Christianity) that have praised truth for over two thousand years. And now the strong in spirit see and reject the lies involved in these self-same teachings, and hence the teachings themselves.

Can we speak of our four authors as 'atheists' in accordance with this use of the word? Yeats was scarcely a sceptic, since in some curious fashion he believed in legendary Gaelic beings, or else he accepted them because they helped to express his system of values. He was certainly determined to preserve or reintroduce a sense of immaterial dimensions. But that is not what Nietzsche means by 'conviction' and 'faith'; indeed it is not what anyone normally means by those terms. So we must concede that Yeats at least was not what Nietzsche means by a 'great man'. For all that, Yeats's magical and pagan beliefs were precisely a denial of the one ideal God of Plato and Christianity.

Then, the search undertaken by some of Lawrence's characters is for *non-idealistic* meaning. Lawrence's 'new way to God' demands a new God who must be, as Lawrence repeatedly insists, a God of flesh and spirit, or of the spirit as flesh. Rilke is perhaps readily seen as an anti-idealist, since the *Duino Elegies* explicitly bring man down to earth and indeed trace idealism to its source in fear of death. Thomas Mann was sceptical about idealists, finding them comic or mischievous, and wanted to enhance our race by scientific rather than artlessly benevolent means. For instance, he attached great importance to experimental psychology. The chief point is that each of these 'Nietzschean' writers rejects God as truth and as the author of timeless morality. Therefore all four require what Nietzsche famously calls a 'revaluation of all values'.

Nietzsche says that atheism is the popular term for doing without ideals, meaning ideals of behaviour or character. Yeats scarcely concerns himself with moral questions in the familiar sense and indeed regards human beings in either a supra-moral or a fabulous light. He is tragic rather than moralistic. Rilke is avowedly anti-moral, believing that man should, on the contrary, strive for a feeling of kinship between himself and the rest of nature. He sees moralism as one form of consolation for pain, and thinks that suffering is the close relation of joy rather than its opposite. It is generally understood that Mann was preoccupied with merging so-called opposites: health and disease, art and philistinism and, perhaps above all, what we think of as goodness and wickedness. The God of the Joseph novels combines good and bad. Lawrence, for his part, recommended from first to last a God of infinite variety who should beckon each individual to a peculiar destiny. One of Lawrence's tasks was to distinguish such self-realisations from the coarse self-indulgence with which they were, and are, confused.

As we shall see, it is relevant to our four authors that Nietzsche denies the existence of opposites in the sphere of psychology. At the beginning of *Human All-Too-Human* he remarks that our race has made exactly the wrong assumption about this matter. We have implicitly argued as follows:

> . . . how can anything spring from its opposite? for instance, reason out of unreason, the sentient out of the dead, logic out of unlogic, disinterested contemplation out of covetous willing, life for others out of egoism, truth out of error. [14]

However, qualities have emerged and still emerge in just that fashion: for example, life for others and egoism are linked as a flower is linked to its roots. In the story of evolution the sentient has come out of the dead, and indeed life and death are related not as opposites but as alternating stages. (That is one of Rilke's themes.) Nietzsche contends that 'there are no opposites except in the usual exaggeration of the popular or metaphysical point of view'. [15] Elsewhere he says that 'between good and evil actions there is no difference of species, but at most of degree. Good actions are sublimated evil ones; evil actions are vulgarised and stupefied good ones.' [16] Two actual deeds are never opposites, though it is sometimes hard for us not to see them as such.

Nietzsche's overwhelming concern was always with values, or spiritual distinctions. He did not usually speak of opposites and we should be on guard against seeing radical opposition where there is only change and development. In *The Birth of Tragedy* Nietzsche discusses what Apollo and Dionysus meant to the Greeks. Those gods were regularly in conflict, yet at their most fruitful their strife was experienced by the spectators of tragedies as divine harmony. Apollo refers to man's power to make images, as in dreams and visual art, while Dionysus refers to non-imagistic self-expression, as in music. The two gods, or sets of psychological capacities, came to grips with each other in tragedy, Apollo barely mastering the formless Dionysian energies. Now our post-Freudian perceptions inform us that Apollo was never strictly the opposite of Dionysus but a 'higher' development of Dionysus, 'turning back', as it were, and mastering his own more rudimentary forces. Nietzsche himself refers to the Apollonian and Dionysian as antithetical *concepts*, suggesting, I suppose, that they are antithetical only as concepts, never in complex experience.

A strict antithesis is a purely linguistic and logical opposition. 'Big' is the opposite of 'little', though really there are only degrees of size. In theological history and in casual modern thought good is not only the opposite of evil but has no need of evil to complete and define itself. Nietzsche's argument amounts to saying, to the contrary, that Jekyll would not be Jekyll without the concealed Hyde qualities. All the qualities of this character shade into one another so that neither he nor anyone else is truly a 'dual personality'. Likewise Cordelia and Goneril are sisters in kind as well as by birth. This does not mean that Nietzsche would have us esteem the sisters equally (which would be nonsense and an ingenuous travesty of what Nietzsche intends) but that we should observe each of them moment by moment as neither angel nor devil but as a muddled, dynamic cluster of deeds. The two women should not be understood schematically in terms of absolute moral antagonism.

Similarly, the celebrated categories of master morality and slave morality are seldom in practice mutually exclusive. When Nietzsche begins to expound these moralities in *Beyond Good and Evil* he briefly digresses in the following words:

I add immediately that in all the higher and more mixed cultures there also appear attempts at mediation between these two moralities, and yet more often the interpenetration and mutual misunderstanding of both, and at times they occur directly alongside each other – even in the same human being, within a *single* soul.[17]

Nietzsche's own categories of master and slave morality are theoretical and therefore form an antithesis rarely found in life. Indeed, as Nietzsche shows in *On the Genealogy of Morals*, slave morality arose from *ressentiment* against the masters. It was conceived as an antithesis, but the slave, or rather the priest who set himself up as the slave's spokesman and guide, so created an artificial antithesis as a focus for his aspirations. The slave now felt himself to be good simply because he was not one of the 'bad' masters. In this way he became the reverse of a master. Nietzsche's discussion of this decisive historical process shows that he believed the antithesis to be contrived, a priestly fabrication disguising psychological realities.

Perhaps even the veriest 'slave-type' who venerates 'pity, the complaisant and obliging hand, the warm heart, patience, industry, humility and friendliness'[18] will once in a while behave with the joyous and reckless independence of a master (as distinct from the distrustful tyranny of a slave-become-master). Likewise the most complete master will have his moments when he apprehends only the 'morality of utility'.[19] How can an act be good, he will sometimes ask, unless it benefits someone? In such a fashion the mere notion of 'good' is a falsification of everyday psychology. Either language is at fault here or we are at fault for not trying hard enough to make our language subtler and more flexible – perhaps for failing even to notice its coarseness. At all events, Nietzsche remarks that '*language* . . . will not get over its awkwardness, and will continue to talk of opposites where there are only degrees and many subtleties of gradation'.[20]

It will later be shown, by implication when not explicitly, that Yeats, Rilke, Mann and Lawrence all thought in the same way as Nietzsche about this basic matter. The antithetical and paradoxical pattern in Yeats's thinking is not in the least a contradiction of Nietzsche but corresponds with the philosopher's view, much as Nietzsche's own references to Apollo and Dionysus are not self-contradictions. 'Blest souls are not composite', Yeats has his scholar-hero say in 'Michael Robartes and the Dancer', suggesting that 'ideally' there would be no ideals, because thought and argument, out of which ideals are made, would be subsumed in the flesh. All would be body and appearance, since materiality should express rather than affront spirituality. But note: the spirit should be taken into the body, not the other way round. Thus the spirit as a separate (Platonic or Christian) realm would die and only the flesh remain. But the flesh would then be more *erotically* beautiful than ever, because more radiant with spirit. For man is already erotic, while other animals merely copulate. Further, each advanced stage in an individual's life is seen by Yeats as a sublimation of elementary stages: 'I must lie down where all the ladders start/In the foul rag-and-bone shop of the heart.' Yeats appreciated that his own 'masterful images' had begun in 'A mound of refuse or the sweepings of a street'.[21]

In a yet more stark and startling fashion Rilke so thoroughly abandons antithesis that he regards death as transformation of life rather than its negation. Obviously there is nothing Christian about this, nothing to suggest life after death or even that 'our little life is rounded with a sleep'. On the contrary, Rilke thinks of death as the extinction of the individual which nevertheless gives him all his possible richness and meaning. Life 'goes into' death, or the visible side of life goes into the invisible (in Rilke's terminology), and this is purely a metamorphosis. Life flows into death, death flows into life, for all eternity. For Rilke meaning resides in the whole (the cosmos, infinity) and when we die we reach out to the infinite. (This seemingly mystical view is, as I hope to show, *materially* unassailable.)

Mann chiefly reconciles what we call 'good' and 'evil'. The best-known illustration of this is probably Hans Castorp's dream in Chapter 6 of *The Magic Mountain*. In a Mediterranean setting a number of handsome and tranquil people – perfect creatures in the Arcadian sense – seem aware that nearby two hags are dismembering and eating a baby. When the dream is over Hans feels that the beauty and the horror were part and parcel of each other, for 'Man is the lord of counter-positions'.[22] In other words, man rises above the counter-positions which his culture has taught him to detect. That is in fact an optimistic version of Nietzsche, for Nietzsche would say that the *Übermensch* will be capable of annihilating the counter-positions – for himself, not for mankind at large. Just the same, Mann renders something of Nietzsche's desideratum into a memorable fictional image.

Lawrence, admittedly, seems to make irreconcilable distinctions between his approved characters (an Ursula Brangwen, an Aaron Sisson, a Kate Leslie) and his unsatisfactory or 'wicked' people (for example, Gerald Crich, Loerke, Sir Clifford Chatterley). Nevertheless, the people in the wrong, through weakness or malice, are precisely people who are not whole and in fact fail to appreciate wholeness. Thus Lawrence's heroes and heroines are far from immaculate, for they contain and transcend the base impulses of the base people. Ursula, for example, has moments of pure hatred and destructiveness. Nor do these superior figures strive for immaculacy, which they see as an inorganic objective.

To make this topic clearer still, it might be sensible to draw two contrasts. First, let us recall that in such morally dualistic writers as Fielding and Dickens the paragons and villains are utterly distinct, never for a moment merging. They are locked in spiritual combat, each unable to imagine how his opponent feels. The second contrast is more pertinent today. Now there are many authors who superfically seem 'beyond good and evil' or incapable of value-distinctions of any sensible sort. That is not in the least what Nietzsche meant, though he predicted such 'weak nihilism'. Nor is it what our four authors advocated. Our contemporary nihilists have lost the God-given certainty of moral values and therefore assume that the mere notion of value is itself lost. They do not grasp that value is what one *creates*, without divine sanction or social approval.

To Nietzsche, then, 'good' and 'evil' are names which, in the way of all names, give unified existence to processes and self-contradictory bundles of activity. These bundles are essentially, not supererogatorily, linked to others. It is not a case of one self-subsistent entity being linked to another, but of so-called entities whirling from one partner to the next in a vast constitutive dance. The dance is not, so to speak, 'optional' for each of its elements: they do whatever they do because they are in the dance. What they do is what we like to call 'what they are', but in truth there is no such state of being. Nothing simply is and everything behaves. (This, by the way, is presumably what T. S. Eliot means in his Heraclitean phrase in 'Burnt Norton', 'And there is only the dance'.) Consequently the terms 'good' and 'bad' will serve here to illustrate what Nietzsche regards as the entire misguided assumption of men for millenia, the assumption that by naming something we acknowledge its independent or 'dance-free' existence.

The clearest exposition of Nietzsche's own views about ontology is his account of Heraclitus in sections 5 to 8 of *Philosophy in the Tragic Age of the Greeks*. Here Nietzsche expounds another man's philosophy and sees his subject as surpassing other pre-Socratic philosophers. Of the early philosophers, including Socrates himself, Nietzsche declares that 'All posterity has not made an essential contribution to them since.'[23] It is too early to say that Nietzsche succeeded in making an essential contribution in his doctrine of eternal return, but whether he did or not, eternal return is very like Heraclitus and may in fact be Heraclitus rephrased. Nietzsche remarks in *Ecce Homo* (written in 1888, twelve years after *Philosophy in the Tragic Age of the Greeks*) that eternal return 'might in the end have been taught already by Heraclitus'.[24]

Heraclitus, says Nietzsche, took two bold steps: first, he grasped that there is no other world lying behind our visible universe; and second, he saw that nothing, no object or quality, merely is, but continually grows, changes, withers and flows away on the ever-rolling stream. Never does it actually *exist* in the usual sense of the word.

> Louder than Anaximander, Heraclitus proclaimed: 'I see nothing other than becoming. Be not deceived. It is the fault of your myopia, not the nature of things, if you believe you see land somewhere in the ocean of coming-to-be and passing away. You use names for things as though they rigidly, persistently endured; yet even the stream into which you step a second time is not the one you stepped into before.'[25]

So Nietzsche paraphrases Heraclitus. The example of a stream is instantly convincing, though a more startling illustration would be provided by something we regard as solid and enduring, say a mighty mountain. Suppose one said 'That peak of Everest on which you gaze today is not the peak you saw before'. And this is what Heraclitus meant: the mountain is an activity rather than a mass, and we, the observers, are activities too. It is the fault of our myopia if we believe we see a static mountain and, similarly, there is no observer who remains as he was or, to put the matter another way, who exceeds the sum of his activities. We wrongly conceptualise ourselves as distinct from our doings. We and our doings coincide entirely, and indeed the subject, 'we', is just a linguistic imposition.

So far we have considered relations in space; what of relations in time? Just as space is the universal invisible arena in which things happen, so time is the measurable sequence of perceived happenings. Space and time are knowable because of their contents. Nietzsche points out that we know these dimensions intuitively. Every moment consumes its predecessor and is nothing more than that destructive act, since it has no duration. Thus everything in space and time has only a relative existence. But Heraclitus further believed that surmounting this incessant wavebeat and cosmic dance there is a One, namely the entirety of the dance. The One is the many, or to repeat Heraclitus' resounding utterance, 'The world is the game Zeus plays'.

These are philosophically primitive teachings upon which have rested several comparatively polished layers of doctrine: Platonism, the Hellenic anti-Platonic teachings, the successive stages of Christianity, science and scientific meliorism, and Marxism.

Nietzsche does not 'go back' to Heraclitus but in one way or another shows how these post-Heraclitean ideas – or, to shift the emphasis slightly, these anti-tragic attitudes – came into being. They have all been perspectives disguised as truth and certainly the Heraclitean view must also be a perspective. Nevertheless it is a *tragic* perspective and accordingly keeps the material nature of all things firmly in mind. Moreover, being tragic, Heraclitus' philosophy has even now the effect of dividing the strong from the weak. The strong cheerfully acknowledge it and the weak recoil in horror or argumentative denial.

Our four modern authors strive, alongside Nietzsche, to find modern ways of looking that develop rather than contradict this ancient awareness. When Lawrence speaks of God as flesh rather than spirit, this is roughly what he means. All that is is fundamentally flesh, from which has come the spirit, as a late and erring growth. Mann, too, sees the spirit as liable to error whenever it seeks to deny its material base. His solution is scientific in a broad and cultured sense. We must rely on knowledge rather than either faith or benevolence. He is a progressionist in a manner that Nietzsche never countenanced, but Mann, nevertheless, feels that reliable progress comes only from awareness of our earthly ties. Nietzsche likewise placed great store by scientific investigation.

Rilke is unmistakably Heraclitean and, especially, Nietzschean. The theme of the *Duino Elegies* is the reunification of man and nature, through man's taking into himself what he has hitherto perceived as 'out there', often indeed as alien. In other words we should not follow Plato by postulating essences and ideals but, on the contrary, take external nature into ourselves. And in Rilke there is no sense of being: 'For staying is nowhere' (nothing *is*, nothing remains), he declares in the First Elegy. Rilke's aim is a modest version of the aim of Nietzsche's Zarathustra: to experience a joy which wants the 'eternity of all things', wants life as it ineluctably is as opposed to an amended life of comfort and justice.

Finally Yeats, whom we shall shortly consider in detail, sought not improvement but acceptance of the world. What we may be tempted to think of as his 'romanticism' or, alternatively, his 'other-worldliness' still obscures his classical bent. Yeats is plainly and persistently hostile to bourgeois materialism, but the hostility is aristocratic. So far as he was concerned nothing was worse than a barbaric society and barbarism means absence or debasement of culture and lack of social discrimination. Yeats thought there must be what Nietzsche calls 'order of rank'. The poet could respect both aristocrats and peasants, but *as* aristocrats and peasants, not as potentially equal members of society. He saw order of rank as the bulwark of culture and the highest values, or even as their fertilising ground. For himself, once 'out of nature' he would take the form of a mechanical golden bird and sing to lords and ladies of Byzantium. He would not sing to the crowd and would not sing of essential change but only of the playthings of time. So Yeats rejected the invisible realm of Christianity, the kingdom of heaven, and the unfolding world of the dialectic. Several thinkers stiffened his purpose, but Nietzsche clarified and justified it by means of his uniquely shrewd understanding of human behaviour.

2
Yeats and Aristocracy

He cannot let anyone, except a friend, determine his life. For that
would be slavish; and this is why all flatterers are servile and
inferior people are flatterers.

Aristotle

Among Yeats's sources it is worthwhile to distinguish the few
authors who enchanted him from the many whose ideas or tales he
merely accepted. In *Autobiographies* he recalls:

I began [in the mid-eighties] occasionally telling people that one
should believe whatever has been believed in all countries and
periods, and only reject any part of it after much evidence,
instead of starting all over afresh and only believing what one
could prove.[1]

This continued to be Yeats's attitude. He would yield to positive
evidence but did not consider, for example, that the propositions
of theosophy needed to be proved. He was not constantly hostile
to science but wanted it confined to its proper sphere. Culture
ought not to be threatened by that extension of the scientific
method which asks for proof even in an area, such as theosophy,
where proof is out of the question.

Perhaps it was for a similar reason that he tended to disregard
the core and justification of Christianity, namely its moral teaching. For culture demands the evil that Christianity would have us
abjure. On the other hand the legendary features of Christianity,
the 'Bible stories', are themselves rich and fruitful. Yeats seems
always to have realised that 'perfection of the life'[2] is hostile to
perfection of the work; that purity in the full sense of *imitatio Christi*
means depreciation of culture. In choosing perfection of the work
he was hostile to social improvement as well. Or, to be precise, he
was one of those who regard the mere idea of progress in its
modern sense as barbaric. Despite his short-lived interest in

16

General Eoin O'Duffy's Blueshirt movement in the early thirties, he had not the outlook ascribed to him by Orwell 'of those who reach Fascism by the aristocratic route',[3] but he certainly assumed that there could be only a crumbling make-believe accommodation between culture and social equality.

In truth the test of a belief for Yeats was not, fundamentally, that a people somewhere has harboured it, but that a doctrine, a fable or a code of conduct has fostered a rounded, good-and-evil life. A Yeatsian belief therefore required colour, physicality and moral diversity. Perhaps, as in Yeats's reading of Plotinus (in 1926), our physical world might be regarded as territory to be crossed towards a spiritual sphere, but nevertheless the journey is all. Plotinus himself, according to Yeats, preferred the ugly Socrates to Socrates' beautiful thought.[4] This paradox pervades the unscientific, unprovable, absurd doctrines that Yeats entertained. Rosicrucianism, theosophy, spiritualism: each is 'other-worldly' in some fashion, but what must constantly have attracted the poet was the sense that an initiate is wholly in touch with nature. Conversely, science proper reduces all nature to quantifiable factors. Every respectable academic field is by definition exclusive. Christianity too is exclusive in its own equivocal way: that is to say, it humbles the sinner by loving and forgiving him. And what is left of the sinner when he has thus been humbled, when his sin has either been eliminated or become a source of guilt? He is now diminished – or so Yeats (like Nietzsche) believed. But the technical otherworldliness of theosophy excludes and denigrates nothing: one supposedly controls natural forces instead of trying to ignore them. Likewise the Rosicrucian, far from belittling nature, thinks he is privy to nature's commanding secrets. All along, then, Yeats was struggling to embrace the natural world, not to evade it. Certainly he wished to change some social developments of our century, because he thought them to be misguided. Although he generally welcomed artifice, he was against the artifice of equality.

Yeats wanted to arrange a marriage of heaven and hell or, better, to reintegrate them. He assumed with Blake and Shelley that what has been called evil at any period was then the fount of creativity. That is why Blake and Shelley were two of Yeats's teachers. Yeats tells us in *Essays and Introductions* that he found in middle age that it was Shelley and not Blake who had most shaped his life.[5] There is no mention of Nietzsche at this point, but it is certain that the German had a profound, if not exactly a shaping, influence upon him. Nietzsche came like a demon suddenly in September 1902. Otto Bohlmann points out in his *Yeats and Nietzsche* that the poet would have been aware of the philosopher by 1896,[6] but the chances are that he would have been aware of him only as a name and a misleading reputation. Nietzsche is still the thinker one 'knows about' for years, then by chance actually reads, and as early as the 1880s false and sinister ideas about what he stood for preceded him.

The evidence suggests that Yeats read Nietzsche from September 1902, when he received from John Quinn, a New York lawyer, copies of *The Case of Wagner*, *On the Genealogy of Morals* and *Thus Spoke Zarathustra*. At about the same time Yeats also obtained *Nietzsche as Critic, Philosopher, Poet and Prophet*, an anthology of Nietzsche's writings selected by Thomas Common and published in 1901. In a letter to Lady Gregory, undated but probably of late September 1902, Yeats explained that he had recently written to her in a rather scrappy way because he had been taken up with Nietzsche, 'that strong enchanter'.[7] The phrase was not hyperbolic, for Yeats was indeed spellbound by Nietzsche, and even thirty odd years later, towards the end of his life, he was still fascinated by the philosopher.

Along with Blake and Shelley, Nietzsche was never a mere serviceable source. His observations were scarcely accretions to Yeats's thought, for they strengthened and subtilised its foundations. As we shall see, Nietzsche gave form, justification and analytic meaning to certain vague shapes in the poet's mind. It is important to note the element of justification. From childhood a few people stir uneasily when they hear moralistic accounts of life, history and the nature of man. So overwhelming are these accounts – or more commonly the unspoken assumptions based upon them – that the doubter naturally feels he is misguided. But his eccentricity is simply that he sees moral criteria as interpretations and feelings while others see them as objective facts. Nietzsche supports the doubter and argues that it is about time the history of morality was investigated thoroughly, according to the strictest scholarly principles.

Nietzsche gives his support without drifting towards what he calls 'weak nihilism'. As we have seen, in preferring truth he knows he prefers the non-existent or the provisional. At the same time he draws the healthiest of distinctions between 'weak nihilism', which declares 'There are no general values, so I shall take the line of least resistance', and 'strong nihilism', which declares 'There are no general values, so I shall forgo *exacting* standards for myself alone'. (Zarathustra says that each of the 'wisest men' must become 'judge and avenger and victim of his own law'.[8])

There is far more to be said about this, in particular about the contrast between the affirmations of strong nihilism and the mesmerised reactions of the weak variety, but enough has been mentioned to clarify our approach to Yeats. Nietzsche, then, provided explanations for social and cultural phenomena that Yeats had simply, though unconventionally, observed. In this way Nietzsche showed, or seemed to show, the rightness of Yeats's observations. I mean of course the rightness in cognitive rather than moral terms. Yeats favoured social hierarchy. Did he then favour a sort of wickedness or the unjust pattern that gives rise to alienation and conflict? Yeats felt that social hierarchy was some-how bound up with culture, not just with a few types of culture but with all valuable types. Nietzsche did not postulate this same connection, as might any snob or apologist reactionary, but *incidentally* explained why to get rid of hierarchy is to make a desert.

Every enhancement of the type 'man' has so far been the work of an aristocratic society – and it will be so again and again – a society that believes in the long ladder of an order of rank and differences in values between man and man, and that needs slavery in some sense or other. Without that *pathos of distance* which grows out of the ingrained difference between strata – when the ruling caste constantly looks afar and looks down upon subjects and instruments and just as constantly produces obedience and command, keeping down and keeping at a distance – that other, more mysterious pathos could not have grown up either – the craving for an ever new widening of distances within the soul itself, the development of ever higher, rarer, more remote, further-stretching, more comprehensive states – in brief, simply the enhancement of the type 'man', the continual 'self-overcoming of man', to use a moral formula in a supra-moral sense.[9]

These remarks are already clear, yet we are so unaccustomed to such thinking that is is helpful to rephrase and enlarge upon them.

An obvious illustration of what Nietzsche means by enhancement of man is the widening and deepening of European capacities in the Renaissance, Yeats's favourite period. These developments were a reflection within artistic and adventurous souls of the 'pathos of distance' experienced by everyone in daily life. A prince saw the ranks of lesser people stretched out below him: the minor nobility, the burgesses and gentry, the yeomen, the urban craftsmen and labourers, the peasants, and at the bottom the canaille of vagabonds and criminals. The church stood aside with its own order of rank from supreme pontiff to novice. Each group, even the lowest, valued rank for its own sake, and classlessness was unconsidered or thought of, occasionally, as hideous. ('Take but degree away, untie that string. . .'.) This social variety was artificial, though it was widely understood to be a reflection of the physical universe itself. Now since separation or widening was the condition of society, it was in turn a spiritual condition and artists strove to produce images that should nearly break free from one another yet miraculously cohere. The artist encouraged tension in his works, a sense of images, characters and ideas straining away from one another, repelling one another, for his aim was to harmonise discordant elements. The greater the discord he could embrace the greater his achievement. He positively wanted a chaos to subdue. As Nietzsche says elsewhere, an artist of the grand style wills to become master of the chaos that he is.[10] The artist's own chaotic spirit was the immediate source of the artistic richness, but the ultimate origin was the hierarchical society, its distinctions and degrees, and the chasm between prince and beggar.

Two points should be made here. The first is that, if Nietzsche and Yeats are right, a choice presents itself: we may either have order of rank and the possibility of high culture, or something resembling social equality with the certainty of third-rate culture. The second point is that to both Yeats and Nietzsche order of rank was an order of qualitative distinctions, not an empty sequence as in modern business or bureaucracy. Each of them saw rank as the source of culture, and culture in turn as either the source or at least the mainstay of values. Neither man was in the usual sense an aesthete, taken up with every kind of beauty including the decadent; but for both beauty was the arena, so to speak, of estimable deeds. The negative object of poet and philosopher was to combat weak nihilism or to find a path through the nihilistic wastes; the positive object was to promote a value-laden form of life. The key difference is that Yeats wished to recover certain old values, while Nietzsche wished to discover new ones and so bring about a further 'enhancement of the type "man"'. Both however regarded the notion of social justice as a slow poison prepared by a sort of illusionists who thought of themselves as social realists.

To Yeats a levelled and 'perfected' society was more or less without meaning in itself, so that one could find meaning only by opposing the movement towards such a society. Just those who assimilate beauty to morality want to destroy a beautiful society. As the sixth of Yeats's seven sages says,

> Whether they knew or not,
> Goldsmith and Burke, Swift and the Bishop of Cloyne
> All hated Whiggery; but what is Whiggery?
> A levelling, rancorous, rational sort of mind
> That never looked out of the eye of a saint
> Or out of a drunkard's eye.[11]

These lines imply rather more than they state. Both saint and drunkard accept the non-rational because neither wishes to control the world. Whigs, on the contrary, bring everything to the bar of reason, since reason is the means of human dominance. The Whiggish assumption is that people are fundamentally alike and rational, that our differences are accidental and superfluous.

Was it not the rational bar, the bar of the dialectic in other words, that Yeats tilted against all his life? Nietzsche certainly did, and both men believed the dialectical method to be nothing more than a weapon in the service of the levelling sort of mind. Nietzsche says that 'the mob achieved victory with dialectics', a practice which before Socrates was considered ill-bred and indecent.[12] Yet here again that important difference between Yeats and Nietzsche emerges, since for Yeats there must be a replacement of our modern counting-house mores by values as old as Homer, while Nietzsche promised something utterly new, specifically Zarathustra's sign and 'great noontide'.

Yeats himself, never mind the critics, supposed his work of the eighties and nineties to represent an evasion of reality. On 14 March 1888 he wrote to Katharine Tynan that his poetry was 'almost all a flight into fairyland from the real world'.[13] Can we accept this, however? In 'The Song of the Happy Shepherd' the central distinction between 'the woods of Arcady' and 'Grey Truth' has been wrongly seen as a contrast between alluring dreams and the drab facts of life. The poem is rather an assertion that 'there is no truth/Saving in thine own heart' and further, in the words of the concluding line, that we should 'Dream, dream, for this is also sooth'. The prose argument of this anti-prosaic piece is that all so-called 'truth' is human (it is 'in thine own heart') and that dreams or fantasies are merely different truths from the truths of daily observation. Yeats is elevating one category of psychological behaviour, fantasy, above other categories such as everyday perceptions and obedience to convention. What he means is simply that 'the woods of Arcady' are of superior value to the 'Grey Truth' of late Victorianism. Both, however, are equally 'true' – or equally human inventions.

This is the constant, mildly Nietzschean theme of the poems in Yeats's first volume, *Crossways*, though Yeats had not yet encountered the German's work. Yeats is realistic and modern enough to assume that man's own soul organises and gives meaning to nature; that we must presume the universe as such (an impossible conception) to be a fecund, ravening chaos. Far from Wordsworthianly detecting a soul in nature corresponding to the human soul, Yeats explicitly denies such a connection. Thus in the 1880s Yeats anticipates something of the philosophical point of Sartre's *La Nausée*, published in 1938. In 'The Sad Shepherd' a sorrowful man speaks into a shell on the seashore, but his burden of sorrow does not fall away and the shell, says Yeats, 'Changed all he sang to inarticulate moan'. Man's thoughts and his seemingly magical words are his alone in the universe, very much as Sartre argues in *La Nausée*. For all that, as we may surmise, it is our task to make universal meanings, and everything depends upon the value in human terms of whatever meanings we make. In this fashion Yeats questions the value of the scientific-melioristic world picture.

I do not maintain that the young Yeats was fully aware of what he was doing, since he was obliged in his more pedestrian moments to accept the philosophic distinctions of his time: for example, the sharp distinction between objective knowledge and subjective experience. In the poetry, it seems, he already knows a strikingly modern thing: that gods do not make men, but men made gods to express their highest hopes at any period of history. Every creature and plant makes a god in its own image. 'The Indian Upon God' celebrates this insight, since Yeats presents the moorfowl, the lotus, the roebuck and the peacock as each having an appropriate god and seeing the environment accordingly. The peacock's domain has been created by a 'monstrous peacock' and man together with his colourless, spiritual God is, I suppose, an interloper there.

The *Crossways* poems often lament the narrow and sterile conceptions held by Europeans generally. Yeats's fairyland is a criticism of the dull streets of Dublin and London. He wishes to convince us that there is no stark divorce between so-called reality and so-called fantasy, but a flowing-together and countless nuances. Yeats's objection to 'reality' in the usual sense is that it is exclusive and low in value. He was alert to the difference between the scientifically proven and what he called 'monsters and marvels'.[14] In *Autobiographies* he recalls that a certain geologist, and therefore supposedly a man of science, rejected the young Yeats's Haeckel- and Huxley-based arguments, saying 'If I believed what you do, I could not live a moral life.'[15] Yeats always recognised that reality in the scientific-prosaic meaning must be informed with fantasy, or else surrounded by fantasy, for it to have any life at all. Science without 'the romance of science' is negligible, if not impossible, and the social sciences likewise owe their existence and nature to crusading zeal.

His own aim was inclusive: he wanted to combine as many diverse elements as he could. This was what Shakespeare had done, and not Shakespeare alone but many men of the Renaissance. Shakespeare perhaps almost achieved sanctity as a result of an imagination of terror and crime. Yeats once noted: 'I feel in *Hamlet*, as so often in Shakespeare, that I am in the presence of a soul lingering on the storm-beaten threshold of sanctity. Has not that threshold always been terrible and crime-haunted?'[16] That is part of the story, the vital 'evil' out of which sanctity may conceivably grow. Notice Yeats's characteristic assumption that we cannot have sanctity without crime, that a crimeless world would also be a world without the loftier virtues.

A related part of the same story is the unification of warring elements in Renaissance art: the fusing, for example, of harsh matter and verbal music. To couch foul deeds in fair language, as Elizabethan and Jacobean dramatists did, is exemplary, and such an achievement is not moral in the accepted sense but aesthetic. Accordingly Yeats asked Althea Gyles to design a cover for *The Secret Rose* (1897) which should express a unity of supposed opposites. Richard Ellman reproduces this design in black and white and describes it as follows: 'At its centre is a four-petalled rose joined to a cross, occupying a place just below the middle of a tree. The boughs of the tree resemble a serpent's folds; among them, just above the rose, are the kissing faces of a man and a woman.'[17]

In plain terms what does this design mean? It seems that the kissing people are the fruit of a serpentine or diabolic development. Further, the people and the serpent's folds together form a rose at the centre of which is a cross. Indeed the rose itself is also faintly cruciform. It is important not just to describe this concept of unity but also to grasp it in our own 1980s terms. I mean that the serpent must be taken to include whatever we now reject as 'socially unacceptable' or iniquitous. What is evil varies from civilisation to civilisation and period to period. Adultery was once evil, and so was blasphemy. Now such behaviour may be regrettable, but as a rule it is no longer evil. Today terrorism and frightful sadism are sometimes (by no means always) described as evil. Yeats, then, is saying that eroticism, romantic love and, finally, purity and beauty in all its forms, including the most spiritual, are knit together with the ghastliest crimes. The 'higher' love depends upon the 'lower' and the cross of Jesus grew out of sin. To put it another way, the rationalist's perfect world from which the bad is excluded and in which everyone co-operates joyfully is the fruit of error. For the rational is only a tiny growth in a huge jumble and utterly depends upon the jumble. Therefore the more rationally we live, the more languidly we live. 'Terrible beauty', as in 'Easter 1916', is only one form of beauty but it is a peculiarly intense and valuable form, unobtainable without the terror.

In fact the cross formed by the serpent is scarcely the cross of Christ, understood to represent the willed suffering of the Saviour and Man's redemption. The reason is this: Rosicrucianism seeks to incorporate even Jesus Himself into an all-embracing natural universe of spirit and flesh. When reading Rosicrucian texts and commentaries one seldom comes across anything expressed in a manner amenable to philosophy or even to common sense. Therefore what I am doing here is making a little sense out of a body of doctrine which claims to rise above orthodox discussion. The point is that, to the Rosicrucian, Jesus is no longer the Lord God but a subordinate character in a vast design which may be apprehended by us only as 'Eternal Beauty'. Nor is Eternal Beauty to be likened to Plato's Form of Beauty, since the latter is only one of several Forms, while the former is all-encompassing. Yeats's position was not in this respect Platonic, for he regarded 'beauty' as just our general term for particular things we find beautiful. Like other Rosicrucians and, more important, like Nietzsche, he took beauty to include and transcend charity, justice and the rest of the virtues. It might exclude every virtue and still be of the highest value. Beauty was precisely our harmonisation of elements which in our unaesthetic moments we perceive as discordant or simply insignificant.

It almost goes without saying that the story of Jesus was beautiful to Yeats. And Jesus was God rather than a moral teacher. I mean that Yeats was chiefly impressed by the God-man's death and resurrection, which defeated the mere health and sanity of Greece and Rome. Jesus showed the overmastering value of mystery, the fact that all our explanations and constructions are but human fairy tales disguised as extra-human facts. I suggest that to Yeats the story of Jesus transcended good and evil, so that Jesus was not the good who fights the evil but the God who annihilates that distinction. Yeats himself contrived to think of 'goodness', in either the Christian or the humanist sense, as a category of behaviour, no more valuable in itself than 'badness'. And both sorts of behaviour played their parts in a purely aesthetic universe: that is, a universe which may not be comprehended except aesthetically. How anti-Pascalian or anti-Kierkegaardian this is!

Yeats implicitly agreed with one of Nietzsche's most celebrated utterances: 'For it is only as an *aesthetic phenomenon* that existence and the world are eternally *justified*'.[18] Nietzsche's italicisation of 'justified' is interesting, for he intends to emphasise a sense of blamelessness. The world can be vindicated only when we see it in an aesthetic light – or, better, at such a time we no longer see any error or crime requiring vindication. No one reading the *Iliad* blames anybody. This does not mean that the arts are a means of glossing over guilt: it means that the arts at their best show up the folly and *self-indulgence* of guilt. Suffering now makes perfect sense – tragic sense, needless to say. Wickedness is now conformable. Take wickedness away – as is possible in dreams – and the aesthetic phenomenon which is the world is botched. Such a Yeatsian or Nietzschean vision is not dilettante but quite the reverse, the fruit of wholehearted engagement.

Yeats's attitudes were essentially unmoral. To take the best known example, when Yeats wrote about the fates of various republicans (in 'Easter 1916' and other poems in the volume *Michael Robartes and the Dancer*) he translated a fairly widespread public feeling into the terms of his own aesthetic vision. At the time most Irish people were out of sympathy with the rebels, whom they regarded less as heroes than as troublemakers.[19] Yeats was in Gloucestershire that Easter and a little later, in London, he wrote to Lady Gregory of the 'heroic, tragic lunacy of Sinn Fein'.[20] His feelings seem to have been similar to those of many Irish people, for they followed a course of surprise deepening to wonder and finally twisting into horror as the executions proceeded. He was neither more nor less outraged than many members of the public. So Yeats's own feelings traced a general pattern and his originality was imposed upon it.

'Easter 1916' makes three points: first, that the rebels had earlier seemed mediocre; second, that persistent single-mindedness is unnatural; and third, that the deaths have generated a terrible beauty. There is an elementary honesty in the poem, because while everyone knows that a tedious fool may turn into a martyr, few will admit as much, except in theoretical discussion. That is what I mean by Yeats's lack of morality: his perceptions are rarely blunted or perverted by considerations of justice. Beauty still predominates. Does not Yeats almost remark that the rebels were anyway moving towards spiritual death (since 'Too long a sacrifice/Can make a stone of the heart') and their physical deaths were therefore more valuable, *because more beautiful*, than their stony lives?

Yet it is exactly the beauty of such actions that changes the political and social climate. Thus the aesthetic need not be the merely aesthetic, and in fact it rarely is. Consider Yeats's representation of Patrick Pearse, the zealous schoolmaster, in the poem 'The Rose Tree'. In reality Pearse often talked of the need for the Irish to make a 'blood sacrifice'; in the poem these are his words:

> 'But where can we draw water,'
> Said Pearse to Connolly,
> 'When all the wells are parched away?
> O plain as plain can be
> There's nothing but our own red blood
> Can make a right Rose Tree.'

Yeats's Pearse does not speak of the wickedness of the English and his emphasis is upon refertilising Ireland. Yeats himself felt that Ireland needed fresh visions of beauty and it was only later that he came to believe that Pearse had rightly grasped the connection between 'blood sacrifice' and beauty. Or if this was partly a Yeatsian vision, then at least he was happy to attribute it entirely to the sacrificed Pearse.

Yeats cast an aesthetic light over the Rising and its aftermath, not to lie about them or soften them but to justify them in the sense Nietzsche had in mind. Such justification must transcend the partisan, so that the opposition is not wrong or evil and one's own champions are naturally flawed. Justification must of necessity be 'truthful': that is to say, no one in generations to come, when the dust has settled, must think it a piece of wish-fulfilment.

Let us for a moment compare this tiny piece of Irish history with a great war which we know only as a story, the Trojan War. The latter in Homer is frightful, thrilling, logically ridiculous, formally effective and sublime. To adapt a phrase of Nietzsche, the war with Troy was a festival play for the gods, [21] and it is a festival play for us as well, since we view it in a god-like manner, not without fervent sympathy, yet never for a moment wishing it away. We relish it even while we are moved by, say, Andromache's lament over Hector. Now if 'Easter 1916' describes Yeats's purified feelings about the Rising, his feelings with the dross of agitation removed, then he saw it like a sombre festival play. He sorrowed and rejoiced at the same time, in something of the spirit of an ancient tragic poet. Yeats's standard bears no relation, or an inverse relation, to notions of justice and human power over events. What matters is the fertilisation of the soul rather than any specific attainment. Therefore Yeats opposes the normal modern assumption that the soul reflects circumstances, the entire Marxian belief that the immaterial is simply a response to the concrete world. On the contrary, Yeats believes, the immaterial should shape and compose materiality, especially by means of art.

Another way of putting the matter is to say that Yeats always held to an aristocratic standard, though we should keep in mind that the phrase does not neatly refer to any actual aristocrat. The virtues of a sect or class must normally be above or beyond it. The aristocratic standard in Yeats has nothing to do with power over events and everything to do with power over oneself. It is still an aspiration, imperfectly realised as a rule. In Yeats's view the aristocrat is ideally able to form himself as a personality. He does not master events by making them turn out as he wishes (a bourgeois or proletarian ambition) but by playing his own chosen role in relation to them. Here is the explanation of Yeats's notion of personality and values. One's values are one's own as distinct from a social code; or, to be exact, the readiness to form values of one's own is the sign of nobility. The social code is not disregarded but is no more than the foundation on which the self-defining values rest. Further, one's peculiar personality should be an expression of one's peculiar values.

Yeats is triumphantly non-utilitarian in outlook. He appreciates aristocrats not so much on account of their day-to-day behaviour but because of their acceptance of what T. R. Henn calls the 'wasteful heroic virtues'.[22] An imagination of heroism is what matters: a desire to find persons, styles and deeds to look up to – in a fantasy world if not in the streets. Conversely, the sure sign of the mob is lack of respect for anyone, including oneself. But he who would be a hero has only to imagine heroism, as Richard Ellman points out: 'Yeats defiantly asserts his imagined self against futility, and to imagine heroism is to become a hero'.[23] If you picture Cuchulain to yourself strongly and consistently you become, not remotely Cuchulain of course, but one whose soul is elevated by Cuchulain-pictures, images of 'That amorous, violent man, renowned Cuchulain', as he is described in *The Only Jealousy of Emer*.

However, imagining heroism is not something anyone may readily do. To be able to apprehend a moral condition in subtle detail is already a gift, so that it is one thing to want to imagine heroism and another to do so. Such imagining is not itself the result of struggle, for it comes about either comfortably or not at all. An imagination of heroism is a consequence perhaps of childhood training, perhaps of undiscoverable childhood circumstances but in any case it is a mark of *undeserved* distinction. Nevertheless, in an aristocratic society the distinction is favoured, since such a society honours especially gifts that are not deserved – gifts of courage, beauty and artistic or athletic talent.

Yeats wanted remarkable people to celebrate and was therefore a poet for an aristocratic society (a born 'praise-singer'). He writes in 'Estrangement' that 'Those whom it is our business [artists' business] to cherish and celebrate are complete arcs'.[24] Thus Achilles is a complete arc and Homer is his celebrant. Today we tend to see Homer as the great one who depicted simple warriors, but Yeats's singularity was that he had something of Homer's celebratory attitude. He looked up to nature rather than down upon it and wanted, in a classical spirit, to eliminate the roughness of reality.

But of course aristocratic societies in general wish to surmount roughnesses or inadequacies, and are therefore characterised by courtesy, veneration, rivalry for honours and little regard for utility. For these reasons Yeats wanted such a society in which one is what one is. I refer to talents, not to social station. The great thing is to stop people desiring authority just because some others have authority. If one is cut out to be a boss, that is a different matter. Even an outlaw-shepherd such as Tamburlaine can end up as an emperor if (and only if) he has imperial qualities.

Yeats himself was the son of an unprosperous, if fashionable, portrait painter and his nature was that of a poet who sang partly in celebration and partly, as he puts it in 'To Ireland in the Coming Times', 'to sweeten Ireland's wrong'. He wrote not to remedy Ireland's wrong but to sweeten it. Ireland is a wronged country: that is to say, the Irish have for centuries regarded themselves in such a light. Yeats's characteristic aim in the 1890s was purely bardic: he was the poet of a wronged people and his object was to encourage them to relish the wrongness. In 'The Dedication to A Book of Stories Selected From the Irish Novelists' he defines his land as 'tragic Eire' and plainly has no wish to change its character. The standpoint may be expressed as a question: What would be the good of a politically victorious Ireland which had lost its specifically Irish culture, tinged – and often more than tinged – with melancholy? The only power that mattered to Yeats was cultural power. (Likewise Nietzsche argued that the military and political ascendancy of Bismarck's Germany over France could not match the cultural ascendancy of the French.[25])

Ireland is Cathleen Ni Houlihan, who in Yeats's play of 1902 demands a melancholy sacrifice from her champions and supporters, saying 'It is a hard service they take that help me'.[26] Ireland's pride is in the hardness of the sacrifice asked of her children or lovers. A merry Ireland seems nonsensical, and so does a cock-of-the-walk Ireland, a stranger to tears. Consequently Yeats did not wish to foster a people who should either resent their fate or undo themselves by becoming prosperous and vacuously cheerful in the modern style. His way was to take the wrongs of Ireland as they traditionally were and sweeten them. This is a tricky notion. Did Yeats misrepresent the aftermath of the Easter Rising? I think there is general agreement that he did not, while some others, ranters, fanatics and thoughtless people, did. Yeats sweetened, or beautified, the aftermath without misrepresenting it, and to do such things was his fate.

Consequently his regular disagreements with Maud Gonne were philosophical as well as personal, for while Yeats loved his fate and held that we should all do so, she strove to avoid her fate as a figure of unrivalled, self-sufficient beauty. She should have been not a fighter but an inspirer of fighters. A 'Ledaean body' is wasted when one spends one's time at public meetings or tightens one's flesh in anguish over political problems. In Nietzschean terms Maud Gonne had no *amor fati*. What does *amor fati* mean and how did Maud Gonne exemplify the lack of it? Here are Nietzsche's words:

> My formula for greatness in a human being is *amor fati*: that one wants nothing to be different, not forward, nor backward, not in all eternity. Not merely bear what is necessary, still less conceal it – all idealism is mendaciousness in the face of what is necessary – but love it.[27]

Fate is necessarily personal and necessarily bound up with one's social world. It is what one is in relation to whatever is taking place. Nietzsche therefore means that the 'great' human being positively loves his role and his time even if, for example, his role in political terms is to be a rebel. Then he loves rebellion, even as Nietzsche himself loved his grandly subversive, anti-Christian, Dionysian role, including the illnesses and the professional neglect that were the concomitants of that role. In short, the last thing a great human being is is bitter or resentful.

But Maud Gonne was almost desperately rancorous. Her natural fate, the fate she should have loved, was to reincarnate Cathleen Ni Houlihan (as she briefly and triumphantly did in the play) or else to focus republican aspirations, somewhat as Helen focused the aspirations of the Greeks. Maud Gonne's 'error', therefore, was to aid the cause in a strictly political way, organising meetings and making speeches. In Yeats's opinion she was wrong to loathe the enemy, England, and to regard the condition of Ireland as a sort of sickness that must be cured as the preliminary to a tolerable life.

Cathleen Ni Houlihan is inescapably a suffering figure, and proud to be so, not one who longs to be victorious. She is rejuvenated simply by the support of her champions. And Helen of Troy is never one to count her beauty subordinate to a political cause.

It is true that by 1908, in 'No Second Troy', Yeats ascribed Maud Gonne's lack of *amor fati* to a mismatch between her nature and her times:

> Why, what could she have done, being what she is?
> Was there another Troy for her to burn?

From a Nietzschean point of view, however, and really from a commonsense point of view, these famous lines are brilliantly disingenuous, because Maud Gonne's anger was not self-realisation but in part a product of self-evasion. Yeats usually despised the slavish self that automatically responds to circumstances, and such was Maud Gonne's personality, working against her pride and her sovereign beauty.

In old age she called Yeats 'lucky' for being able to 'escape into the freer life of the spirit beyond the limitations of time and space'.[28] That is one way of putting the matter and perhaps Yeats was lucky, but Maud Gonne too might, in theory, have lived the 'freer life of the spirit'; or, to say the least, Yeats's lifelong argument was that admirable people are people who can do so. They are aristocrats of the spirit if not by birth.

Yeats's ideal society consisted of a few aristocrats surrounded by many lesser folk, each of whom should be confidently developed in his own line. We recognise that Yeats revered the protestant landowning families of Ireland, especially as he understood them to have been in the eighteenth and early nineteenth centuries. Likewise he loved the Renaissance, destroyed in Britain, he said, by Cromwell ('The Curse of Cromwell'). His regard for Lady Gregory's Coole Park and the Gore-Booths' Lissadell; his enthusiasm for Swift, Berkeley, Goldsmith and Burke, each of whom despised notions of progress and equality; his hostility to the encroaching spheres of business and industry: these matters have been amply discussed by Yeats critics. It is important also to remember that Yeats's non-aristocratic figures are Shakespeareanly distinctive. The implication is that society should be a collection of robust eccentrics who do not seek to melt into the environment but stand square against it. There is no common good for which any of these individuals would sacrifice his nature and his vocation, since that would be to exchange the self for an abstraction.

On the other hand the new Ireland, a compound of shopkeeper mentality and bloody terror, is, as we say, 'conformist'. But consider a small sample of the characters Yeats either invents or recreates: Father O'Hart in 'The Ballad of Father O'Hart'; the hunter in 'The Ballad of the Foxhunter'; the jester in 'The Cap and Bells'; the fiddler in 'The Fiddler of Dooney'; Tom O'Roughley, that enemy of logic who thinks dying 'but a second wind'; Yeats's uncle when he returns to Sligo, in the poem 'In Memory of Alfred Pollexfen'; Red Hanrahan himself in all his wildness; Raftery, the blind poet; the 'affable irregular' of 'The Road at My Door'; the slut Crazy Jane who is wiser than the bishop; the quaintly and victoriously honourable Colonel Martin; the 'old bawd' Mary Moore in 'John Kinsella's Lament for Mrs Mary Moore' – but perhaps this brief list of singular characters is nevertheless long enough.

Mohini Chatterjee, the Brahmin whose teaching Yeats never ceased to respect, is given these words to say:

> I have been a king,
> I have been a slave,
> Nor is there anything
> Fool, rascal, knave
> That I have not been,
> And yet upon my breast
> A myriad heads have lain[29]

Mohini Chatterjee did say roughly the same in Dublin in the 1880s, so that Yeats absorbed from him an understanding of life as an endless, senseless pageant including no 'real' or imperative moral distinctions: one is simply fated to be oneself, good or bad. The way, said the Brahmin, was to refuse to reflect the outside world in one's thoughts or personality. That is an extreme variant of what Yeats always implicitly believed. (It is interesting, though not immediately relevant, that Nietzsche and Yeats both tended to view Christ as 'Asiatic', as the prophet of the indwelling kingdom of heaven.)

In the widest sense, therefore, Yeats's aristocratic beliefs entail seeing the personality as largely independent of events: his doctrine is pretty well the reverse of social determinism. Alex

Zwerdling, in his book *Yeats and the Heroic Ideal*, thoroughly examines this part of the Yeatsian web, taking care to distinguish the hero in Yeats (a solitary or wandering figure) from the aristocrat (essentially a member of a select group). From our point of view, the nearer Yeats moved towards simple admiration for aristocracy, the more he followed Ezra Pound into detestation of the urban masses, the less impressive he is as a thinker and even as a poet. This is not because his attitudes grow 'nasty', but because they are purely nostalgic – pleasant or even delectable but of no further consequence. Zwerdling assumes that the later Yeats, if not the earlier, believed that aristocracy would eventually come back in its old form, yet this is just the point that is not clear, for all the exegesis of recent years. Yeats wrote as follows in 1930:

> As for the rest, we wait till the world changes and its reflection changes in our mirror and an hieratical society returns, power descending from the few to the many, from the subtle to the gross, not because some man's policy has decreed it but because what is so overwhelming cannot be restrained. A new beginning, a new turn of the wheel.[30]

Did the mature Yeats imagine, for example, that at some time in the future elegant houses roughly comparable with the Gore-Booths' Lissadell would again be built, and beautiful girls much like the young Eva and Constance Gore-Booth would grace such houses with their presence (as those sisters timelessly appear in the poem 'In Memory of Eva Gore-Booth and Con Markiewicz')? But forms are never repeated, except as sterile copies. There have been so many hierarchical societies, none like the others except for the mere fact of social gradation. Bronze Age warriors, the patricians of Rome, the courtiers of Versailles: each group is distinctive. And if we say again that order of rank fosters culture, we should also emphasise that each order fosters its own characteristic culture.

It is likely that Yeats so regretted the decline of the Anglo-Irish landowners, each of whom had lived, so it seemed, 'rooted in one dear perpetual place',[31] that he cultivated a faith that their like would come again after the vilenesses of democracy. He might have tried to support such a faith by a certain understanding of Nietzsche's doctrine of eternal return (an understanding now

increasingly discounted by Nietzsche scholars) but he probably did
not think the matter out at all thoroughly. As a poet he was liable
to stop thinking whenever he came up against a fact unsuited to
his vision. Even if we take it that Yeats had in mind only
the contentions of *A Vision*, and especially the lunar phases and the
movements of the gyres, we should remember that any cyclical
understanding of history can only be an expedient, and that
'history' itself, as a branch of knowledge, is a construct. Yet so
openly didactic are some of Yeats's poems that they demand the
suspension of our disbelief and owe inextricable facets of their
beauty to dubious historical ideas. I mean not legends but the
question-begging history that Yeats was capable of.

Perhaps one small illustration will be enough, and certainly
there is no space for more. Phases 16 to 18 corresponding to the
eighth gyre, the period 1550 to 1650, are characterised by the
'awakening of sexual desire', as in Titian; the bursting forth of the
human personality, as in Shakespeare; an attempted return to the
synthesis of the Sistine ceiling, as in *Paradise Lost*; and a loss of
absolute Christian faith so that 'Christendom keeps a kind of
spectral unity'.[32] This reading of the period may be acceptable, and
plainly we should not quibble (saying, for instance, that sexual
desire had earlier 'awakened' in Ariosto). Further, we ought to
acknowledge that Yeats's swift analysis of Milton is impressive, for
he speaks not only of the Miltonic music and magnificence but also
of the unreality and 'cold rhetoric'.[33] Indeed *A Vision* as a whole
shows what a good critic of the arts Yeats was. The weakness of all
this lies partly in the emphases and partly in the attribution of
human affairs to phases of the moon. If one historical development
grows out of another, that process is better seen as dialectical, for
such changes may be observed in daily life and are thoroughly
understandable.

My purpose here is not the absurd one of faulting Yeats's
schemata but to comment on his tendency to draw parallels rather
than make distinctions. He wanted to contain his observations in
one great design, possibly because he could not measure them by a
moral yardstick. Things make sense if you divide them into right
and wrong, and if you do not, you may need another form of
organisation. Then, the usual way of making sense of history is by
seeing it as 'progress'; indeed, modern man is still supposed to be
the goal of the entire evolutionary process. But Yeats's patterns are
part of his overriding campaign against progress. He did not want

the old things to go; he feared above all a descent into barbarism, a smashing of native cultures on the Marxian grounds that all their varieties have depended upon vicious distinctions of class. (It is perhaps unnecessary to remark that putting culture into museums is a way of recording it, not preserving it.) Seen in this light, alienation, which Marx thinks of as a malady to be cured, Yeats thinks of as the only fertile ground of culture.

Yeats wanted old ways to return and believed they always had returned: Alexander's empire rose and fell, and about twelve hundred years later so did Charlemagne's. Most historians would be interested in the differences between these two chains of events, while Yeats is concerned simply with the fact of imperial rise and fall. Nietzsche himself is in some sense a rephrasing of the old heroic motif. He is a 'return' of Achilles.

> ... Eleven pass, and then
> Athene takes Achilles by the hair,
> Hector is in the dust, Nietzsche is born,
> Because the hero's crescent is the twelfth.[34]

In *A Vision* Nietzsche is Yeats's specific example of a Phase 12 man, and according to 'The Phases of the Moon' Achilles belongs to this phase as well. When Athene seizes Achilles' hair she prevents him from attacking his commander, Agamemnon, and by so doing initiates his long withdrawal from the fighting which ends only when he returns to kill Hector in revenge for Hector's killing of Patroclus. Athene's action is thus decisive and brings about the entire story. Now Phase 12 belongs to 'The Forerunner', a 'fragmentary and violent man'. The main point is that such a man 'overcomes himself' and has 'the greatest possible belief in the values created by personality'. He has 'immense energy' and is 'wrought to a frenzy of desire for truth of self'. At his best he is divorced from his circumstances and he is 'marble pure' rather than warm-hearted.[35]

It seems, then, that many or most heroes do not belong here. Achilles is discriminatingly chosen because though he is often passionate, he is scarcely ever sympathetic towards others. He is solitary, fated, conscious of a lonely destiny. Above all, his values are his own, related to the values of other Achaeans but by no means identical with them. Nietzsche could reasonably be said to

have these traits in common with Achilles. Both men desire 'truth
of self' at all costs and are therefore, in the most extreme and
perhaps admirable sense, 'anti-social'. Even so, consider the
obvious differences between a simple, if magnificent warrior,
capable of only elementary thought-processes, and an exquisitely
subtle thinker who called himself 'the opposite of a heroic
nature'.[36] At first sight Achilles and Nietzsche would seem to have
no point of similarity – until Yeats comes along and places the
similarity before our eyes.

Yeats's analogising bent is at its most audacious when in the play
The Resurrection he compares Christ with Dionysus. Dionysus is
usually thought of as the god furthest removed from Jesus, and in
modern times that is how Nietzsche pre-eminently thought of him.
Dionysus is orgiastic, uniting man with nature, while Christ is
precisely the God who transforms all nature from its cruel and
wanton reality into an indwelling kingdom of heaven. Thus
Dionysus retains man within nature and Jesus, conversely, takes
nature into man's own loving spirit. Nevertheless Dionysus, like
Christ Himself, dies and is resurrected.

> I saw a staring virgin stand
> Where holy Dionysus died,
> And tear the heart out of his side,
> And lay the heart upon her hand
> And bear that beating heart away;
> And then did all the Muses sing
> Of Magnus Annus at the spring,
> As though God's death were but a play.[37]

The still-beating heart of Dionysus was torn from his side by the
staring virgin (entranced Athene) and so he lives on in some
fashion. In course of time the Greeks and Romans created man-
centred worlds of reason, military prowess and artistic order. Then
God was born a man and died a real death, so that the smell of His
blood swept reason aside. Dionysus and Christ are thus alike as
divine intermediaries between man and the meaningless universe.
Perhaps indeed – so the impudent suggestion goes – they are
successive faces of one God. Man's own doings constantly pass
away after at best a momentary flame of glory.

Everything that man esteems
Endures a moment or a day.
Love's pleasure drives his love away,
The painter's brush consumes his dreams;
The herald's cry, the soldier's tread
Exhaust his glory and his might:
Whatever flames upon the night
Man's own resinous heart has fed.

Here is a yet more daring leap. Jesus and Dionysus are akin, since both are purely reminders that man and all his works are pointless. That is how the anti-humanist Yeats aspired to treat life: as a rapturous tragic festival, having no higher reality, no final justification, no purpose and no loving God. His poems would at best flame upon the night and they, like every conceivable perspective on the world, would be short-lived without 'truth'. This implies that Yeats's entire scheme is itself a semi-deliberate fiction or, as he put it in a letter of about 1910 to his father, 'The world being illusive one must be deluded in some way if one is to triumph in it.'[38] Strictly speaking, he meant by this that if one is to triumph one must produce and reach out towards a self-image. Nevertheless Yeats's patterns of thought, and especially the cyclical pattern of *A Vision*, were in a similar sense illusive: in other words, he made them up as means to his own special triumph.

Nietzsche would alternatively say: 'The world is independent of us and we know it only as our invention. We cannot actually change it any more than a few microbes can change a forest. Therefore we had better cling to Dionysus, who is the yea-sayer and brings tragic joy, rather than to Christ, who is the nay-sayer and replaces our terrestial reality with his sorrowful spirit.'

To whatever extent Christ and Dionysus are differentiated by Yeats, the poet's sense of divinity is in one interesting respect Nietzschean. His gods are not moralistic; nor are they examplars at all in the usual Western sense, but sacrificial figures whose death and rebirth keeps man in touch with his natural home from which he ever tries to stray. In Nietzsche's eyes that is true of Dionysus and quite untrue of Christ, but that is not my present point. Nothing gives the appearance of keeping nature at bay so much as man's faith, religious in its origins, that he is essentially apart from nature. That is why in modern, scientific times we tend to assume that all distressing personal destinies may in principle be transformed, and that pain is in principle curable. Christ Himself preached a purely psychological change for individuals, not a change in the environment or for society at large. But the modern notion is that the more we cling together, the less any creature can be singled out for suffering. Moreover, the popular idea of shared suffering is based on the fact that suffering may thus turn into a species of pleasure, albeit a melancholy species. In theory the suffering is apportioned and no one has more than 'his share'. Conversely an ancient tragic hero, such as Oedipus, would scarcely have imagined or even desired his suffering to be shareable: it was his lot and he was, if anything, jealous of it.

For these reasons a belief in God, or in many gods, preserves individuality and a certain sense of apartness, while the loss of God reinforces 'herd' feelings. Yeats knew this almost as well as Nietzsche, though he never expressed it so neatly. Nietzsche says that God used to be our 'unconditional sanction'[39] and in this particular sense Yeats's Christ is a different deity. Yeats was nevertheless aware of what had long been rising up in place of the sanctioning God. It is likely that he would have agreed with these comments of Nietzsche:

> Now suppose that belief in God has vanished: the question presents itself anew: 'who speaks?' – My answer, taken not from metaphysics but from animal physiology: *the herd instinct speaks*. It wants to be master: hence its 'though shalt!' – it will allow value to the individual only from the point of view of the whole, for the sake of the whole, it hates those who detach themselves – it turns the hatred of all individuals against them.[40]

God is or was in this fashion a protector against group authority, a guarantor that at least one will not be sucked into crowd movements waving meretricious moral banners. Yeats was constantly aware that the people's march would take such a form and expressed his awareness most fiercely in 'On the Boiler' (1939).

The poet always loathed mediocrity of mind, by which I mean not 'average intelligence' but the tendency at all intellectual levels to want to overcome that which cannot be overcome: the nature of things. We are clever enough to make use of nature, but that is altogether different. We may conceivably arrange matters so that no one needs to struggle overmuch, yet a feature of such a condition must surely be the rarity of joy. Nietzsche refers to the 'typical man' as fighting against evils 'as if one could dispense with them'.[41] Yeats had the same contempt for mediocrity and the same understanding that the total number of evils is never reduced. It is rather as if we destroy weeds and others grow in their place.

In accordance with this understanding Yeats detested, as did Nietzsche, the concept of a God who guarantees lowly and subordinate groups victory over their superiors. The victory might indeed be ultimate, that is to say, marking the end of time, the end of the experiment of creation, but what matters is the impudent assumption of its rightness. To be low is itself thought to be a sign of merit or at least a moral palliative. Coupled with this is the belief in modern times that a fair proportion of evils reside not so much in the superior group but in political power as such, and that political power can actually, if miraculously, be abolished.

To Yeats, God is not in the least an avenger or an equaliser (though vengeance of the ordinary human kind is not necessarily a bad thing). For his part, Nietzsche maintains that at the time of Christ Rome had ruled the West for two hundred years and subject peoples could not imagine how it would ever be possible to overthrow the empire. The culture and the very history of conquered races were treated by the conquerors as of no account. Accordingly, members of the subordinate groups came to worship the crucified God, the God whose death mocked the Roman imperium. In this way a grotesque genius born of despair taught people to exult in their own degradation – in filth and rags, in crucifixion and lingering suicide in catacombs. The Roman empire, or in other words the world as a whole, was now deemed ripe for destruction. Such a God who will one day destroy his own creation cannot be compared with the Greek Dionysus: therefore it is not this face of God that Yeats acknowledges. Yeats does not see mercy or forgiveness or, for that matter, judgement-day severity, but Godhood itself, assuring man that everything passes and everything returns.

Ideally, in Yeats's opinion, the poor and socially humble should not also be psychologically humble, but proud – as proud as Crazy Jane. They certainly should not resent their lords and masters, because the feeling of resentment is the sure mark of inferiority. Likewise, straining every nerve to climb a social or professional ladder confirms one's inferiority; or, as Nietzsche says in regard to promoted workers, to become 'a stopgap to fill a hole in human inventiveness' does not 'lift them from the *essence* of their miserable condition'. [42] So the promoted worker who is now a manager is still caught in the essence of his miserable condition, and the same applies even to a proletarian dictator (such as Stalin).

Money is only minimally important to the noble man. Yeats appreciated this and had no wish to become rich by selling his talent. I do not mean by prostituting it but by legitimately selling it. For, as Nietzsche says, one should not wish to make of one's genius a 'shopkeeper's affair'. [43] And wisdom should not be subordinated to cleverness or employed for material gain. In fact wisdom scarcely plans for material advancement at all. Yeats revered high social rank but did not regard it as a level to which a wise person deliberately climbs. Somewhat similarly, he thought money to be for sensible use and not in the least for prestige.

Yeats thought of power roughly as Nietzsche did, though not remotely to the same fruitful and all-explanatory purpose. (Will to power is discussed in some detail in Chapter 6.) Both men regarded power as creative ability, not at all the same thing as force or status. Thus Shakespeare had great power, while Elizabeth I had little or none. In fact the so-called power of a boss is commonly his compensation for lack of real power. Sometimes a politician or a soldier (Julius Caesar or Napoleon) may have the more adventurous kind of power, but that is rare. The feeling of power is a stretching of limbs and gusts of euphoria. Lady Gregory had power when she planted trees in Coole Park; Michelangelo had it as he worked at his 'David'; a gang of boys have it when they build a den on their holidays. The quality of the product is not the point, and indeed the product is valuable to the producer chiefly as the focus of his energies. Power is thus the entirely personal freedom to shape things, including words, ideas and one's own personality.

Nietzsche argues that 'Power which is attacked and defamed is worth more than impotence which is treated only with kindness.' [44] He means that the feeling of power outweighs all other considerations. Yeats's peasant or low-life figures are not treated with kindness and would normally resist such treatment as liable to restrict their self-created characters. And the impotent feel impotent even when they are technically secure: that is part of Nietzsche's point and I think Yeats would have agreed.

Both our subjects had a keen awareness of the difference

between personal and political strength. Nietzsche implies that political strength, when it is divorced from the private, inner will (as it often is), means that one is an actor, or worse: 'the imitation of an actor'.[45] The only role worth playing is a role chosen and invented for oneself alone, since the rest, the public or generally accessible roles, never suit anybody who has supervised his own development.

Political strength is a concomitant of weakness in the individual and cultural weakness in the state. Nietzsche thought German culture to be declining in the late nineteenth century just because the state was growing more powerful: 'After all, no one can spend more than he has – that is true of individuals, it is also true of nations. If one spends oneself on power, grand politics, economic affairs, world commerce, parliamentary institutions, military interests . . . then there will be a shortage in the other direction.'[46] As in other places, Nietzsche here offers an explanation for what Yeats intuitively grasped. I mean that Yeats believed Irish culture to be fertile so long as Irishmen did not worry overmuch about their country's political subordination. Further, like Nietzsche, he observed the humiliation inherent in giving priority to political power (and that was part of the reason for his continuing disagreement with Maud Gonne).

Yeats's play of 1904, *The King's Threshold*, is specifically concerned with the conflict between politics and poetry, and the question posed by the play is: Which of these activities yields the more honour? The poet, Seanchan, dies yet gains more honour than the King. Honour, it seems, is not reputation (though a person might rightly or wrongly have a reputation for honour) but a sort of private honesty of soul. Seanchan's (so-called) Oldest Pupil finally declares:

> Not what it leaves behind it in the light
> But what it carries with it to the dark
> Exalts the soul . . .

That is honour. The quality was always of the greatest importance to Yeats and we should note that it is anything but a general quality. We give a general name to something which by its nature takes the form of the singular individual: each person who 'has honour' has it in his own way.

Nietzsche makes no explicit comments along the same lines, but several of his aphorisms follow the same broad direction. Often such remarks reveal both the peculiar force and the fallacy of assaults upon the criterion of honour. Socrates himself could not understand this aristocratic concept. Nietzsche shows us repeatedly that dialectic – in the Socratic rather than the Hegelian sense – has always been destructive of honour, since honour cannot provide a reasoned justification for itself: it was bound to fall before the sword-thrusts of Socrates' questions.[47] But then, according to Nietzsche, even this prodigious thinker failed to understand that honour is admired *because* it is 'indefensible', in the sense of rising above argument and reason. Alternatively it is possible that Socrates did understand all this perfectly well and was driven to put honour on the defensive because – so Nietzsche speculates – human instincts were then at odds with one another and threatening to overwhelm Greek civilisation.[48] In such a fashion Socrates was possibly a saviour, though he cast a shadow over all succeeding generations.

Yeats detested what he, following Blake, called 'mathematical form', meaning the application to living beings of mathematical concepts, including the concept of equality.[49] Outside the realm of mathematics equality is plainly a metaphor. When we say that two people are of equal height or weight we are (properly) confining them to quantities, altogether ignoring their distinctive qualities. It might be better to say that we treat the quantities of height and weight as if they were not also, in living reality, qualities. Yeats *therefore* (not out of crude snobbery) hated the widespread modern belief that individual differences are either superficial or technical. The supposition is that visible differences (stature, colour, gender and so forth) are of the surface and other differences have to do with how well the individual has acquired a technical skill, such as using language or playing a game. In theory no differences are vital.

But to Yeats differences are pervasive and for the most part quite untechnical. More important, a difference is never a simple difference but a distinction of value. The latter-day ideal of 'equal but different' is absurd, since it camouflages the fact that equality means sameness. Naturally we may regard living beings as equal, but that is only to impose equality upon our original observations of inequality. The Yeatsian point is that each person has his own value and should reach after it. But that means that he cannot, in Nietzsche's phraseology, belong to the herd. Nietzsche is the pre-eminent preacher of this same attitude towards society, since he regularly opposes the belief that society should take precedence over each of its members. Similarly even the lowliest of Yeats's invented or borrowed figures, when he or she commands our approbation, feels above society. For each of them a virtue is not social but is one's own self-discovered quality. Nietzsche asserts such an attitude as a doctrine. 'A virtue', he writes, arguing against Kant, 'has to be *our* invention, *our* most personal defence and necessity: in any other sense it is merely a danger.'[50]

The thrust of this is clear but, once again, the doctrine is so unfamiliar today that some enlargement is called for. Nietzsche means that a public virtue with a public label (faith, hope, charity and the rest) is actually harmful. Or at least, Kantian virtues and the categorical imperative are harmful whenever they do not spring from one's private necessity. A public virtue is a contradiction in terms because a virtue belongs to one person only. Yeats desiderated a group, a society, a nation of such 'virtuous' individualists, none of whom would seek to impose his own virtue upon others but would be pleased (and perhaps also proud) to keep it to himself. In Yeats there are no attractive evangelists and no one wants others to imitate him. In 'Calvary' (1920) Yeats's Judas betrays Christ just because he will not be possessed by the Lord; likewise Lazarus is bitter because Christ has robbed him of his own death, his 'right to die', as we might nowadays call it. Insofar as God is the giver of specific laws (the commandments and the 'way' of the Sermon on the Mount) Yeats wanted to be free of God. And he wanted to be free of society as well, to the extent that aristocrats, artists and individualistic persons used to be free. He thought, with Nietzsche, that in modern times society has taken over from the legislative God as the grand despot.

'Herd animals', as Nietzsche zoologically calls them, the imitative ones, discover a lustreless kind of happiness in cultivating general qualities. No doubt, to be fair, there are also moments of euphoria in giving oneself over to the undifferentiated crowd. However, the most noble sort of person, for whom Nietzsche seeks, has the following characteristics:

> ... the feeling of heat in things that feel cold to everybody else; the discovery of values for which no scales have been invented yet; offering sacrifices on altars that are dedicated to an unknown god; a courage without any desire for honours; a self-sufficiency that overflows and gives to men and things.[51]

The ultimate noble man is therefore a singular being in this exact way. Approximating to him are such figures as Shakespeare's Brutus and the historical Mirabeau. According to Nietzsche Brutus is made of finer clay than Hamlet, since of all the characters in Shakespeare he has the highest regard for 'independence of the soul'.[52] 'The height at which he [Shakespeare] places Caesar is the finest honour that he could bestow on Brutus.'[53] This Brutus kills even such an outstanding man as Caesar for the sake of his soul's independence. Such seems to be the most sought-after quality in both Nietzsche and Yeats. And in Nietzsche at least, though in all probability this is true of Yeats also, independence of the soul is not simply given but is achieved, more or less strenuously. Nietzsche remarks (and we shall need to make further references to this interesting idea): *'What does your conscience say – ''You shall become the person you are''.'*[54]

Note that Nietzsche's conception of the conscience is completely personal and is thus quite different from the theological conscience, the Kantian conscience and the latter day 'social conscience'. Everyone should heed his own conscience and become what he alone is. There is no standard, no norm, except for members of the multitude who desire above all to lose themselves. Spirit in the Christian sense has normally assumed an impersonal, extrinsic form: it has approached purity because it has approached abstraction. 'Once spirit was God,' says Nietzsche, 'then it became man, and now it is even becoming mob.'[55]

Yeats's understanding was much the same. Both wanted to know what might become of spirit in the future. For Yeats, who was a complete conservative, spirit must sooner or later become man again, as it was in the Renaissance and the eighteenth century. To Nietzsche, the most thoroughgoing radical, it grew plain that man's value is confined to his function as bridge to the *Übermensch*, who is not a new species, still less a repetition of the variety 'great man', but *homo sapiens* with an entirely fresh psychology.

3

Rilke's Angels and the *Übermensch*

> Whatever has died has not fallen out of the universe. If it lives here, it changes here and is dissolved into its proper parts. These are elements of the universe and of you. And when these change they do not complain, so why should you?
>
> Marcus Aurelius

A useful preliminary is to ask ourselves whether we are to will the advent of the *Übermensch* as a radiant newcomer to the earth or to regard him as one who, in Nietzsche's own words, 'has existed often enough already'.[1] But the context of that remark in *The Anti-Christ* is an argument that the 'higher type' of man, the 'more valuable type', has been ousted by Christianity. Nietzsche is probably not talking specifically about the overman, who has earlier been adumbrated in *Thus Spoke Zarathustra* and of whom Zarathustra is the forerunner.

Walter Kaufmann assumes in the eleventh chapter of his *Nietzsche: Philosopher, Psychologist, Antichrist* that some historical persons fall into the category of overman. Nevertheless, Zarathustra tells his disciples, 'There has never yet been a Superman. I have seen them both naked, the greatest and the smallest man. They are still all-too-similar to one another. Truly, I found even the greatest man – all-too-human!'[2]

Here is no ambiguity, yet in *The Gay Science*, published in 1882, the year before the appearance of Parts One and Two of *Thus Spoke Zarathustra*, Nietzsche refers to 'the invention of gods, heroes and overmen of all kinds',[3] meaning overmen imagined by our forefathers. Why then does Zarathustra struggle so hard, and so *uniquely*, to work out what manner of being the overman will be? From the rapturous tones of *Zarathustra* and indeed from the straightforward meaning of the text one would assume that no one before Nietzsche had imagined the overman. 'Man is something that should be overcome', says Zarathustra in his first public speech,[4] and adds that man shall be a laughing stock to the overman as the ape is to man.

Kaufmann nevertheless believes that we should not take too seriously the assertion that the *Übermensch* has not lived as yet and argues that he is the man who overcomes himself, as Goethe overcame himself. Just the same, Nietzsche stresses in *Ecce Homo* the sheer novelty and rarefied height of *Thus spoke Zarathustra*, remarking 'that a Goethe, a Shakespeare, would be unable to breathe even for a moment in this tremendous passion and height.'[5] Nietzsche supposed that in *Zarathustra* he had thought on a new plane, perceiving man's life and history from an utterly fresh perspective. And that, of course, is the impression given by the work itself.

The imagined overman rises above Caesar, Shakespeare and Goethe not just in degree but absolutely. He rises above mythical creatures as well, for they were the inventions of people who sought consolation, explanation or aggrandisement. They – the Titans, the Olympian deities and the monster-slaying heroes – were, from one point of view, products of human weakness. From another point of view they were agents of human survival and development: it was necessary for our ancestors to think of Prometheus so that they might now and then behave somewhat Prometheanly.

It will be as well to mention here that Nietzsche never regards the overman as necessarily more intelligent than present-day human beings, since there is no question of a larger brain or a more complex nervous system. On the contrary, as we shall later see, the *Übermensch* has little need of specifically intellectual faculties and indeed the learned man or, as such a figure appears in *Thus Spoke Zarathustra*, the 'conscientious man of the spirit' is a sort of 'higher man' whom Zarathustra leaves behind.

The height of the *Übermensch* above man must be assessed in spiritual terms. The trouble is that our idea of spirituality is so informed by Platonism and Christianity that it may seem hard to think of a non-moral (or, as Nietzsche would say, 'moraline-free') spiritual condition. Yet clearly the spirituality before Plato – in Homer and Sappho, to take two obvious examples – had little to do with altruism, justice or asceticism. By 'spiritual' I simply mean connected with values transcending, though not excluding, the brutish and material. The overman will be anything but a simple brute and, though wonderfully higher than historical man, anything but an angel too.

The overman is neither an inevitable next stage nor a creature to be willed into being by an unconscious process, as Shaw's long-living people are fostered in *Back to Methuselah*. 'Man is a rope', says Zarathustra, 'fastened between animal and Superman – a rope over an abyss.'[6] So far the most remarkable people have been no more than that rope but they have typically longed for the other side of the abyss. These best people are 'higher men'. They are 'great despisers', giving of themselves in some fashion and wishing to be surpassed. They appreciate that they and the rest of mankind are inadequate. It is not that we are sinful in the eyes of God the Father, frail in the eyes of Jesus or piteous in the eyes of Mary, since the divine forms were themselves created out of our inadequacy. Man, being the deficient creature that he is, found it necessary to make a God in order both to judge and to justify himself. Therefore the 'great despisers' despise from their own perceptible vantage points and not through their dreams of a heavenly perspective. The best literary illustration of a higher man might well be Hamlet, as he, more than anyone else in his time or earlier, disdained mankind from a largely secular position.

Being a great despiser does not mean being an inveterate sneerer and mocker, for such a stance is petty and negative. The people Zarathustra loves despise because 'they are the great venerators and arrows of longing for the other bank'.[7] That is, they know that man as rope over the abyss has no justification but to get to the other side. The other side is no purer than the original animal side, because the notion of purity was always just a mode of longing not to be an animal at all. But the overman who will stand on that farther bank will assuredly be an animal, for what else could he be?

At this point, when we have at least begun to discard some false ideas about the overman, it would seem sensible to offer a positive definition or description. However, such an offering must depend upon our knowing what, in Nietzsche's view, is so wrong with man that he needs to be overcome – not just improved but overcome. After all, a widespread assumption at present is that humanity should be pitied and treated with irony, though not quite dismissed as hopeless. But Nietzsche foresaw this stage of nihilism and knew that it could not last. Nothing lasts, and man's inheritor, when he comes, must lack the weaknesses that have led to the present impasse.

These weaknesses – again, in Nietzsche's view – are other than the traditionally recognised ones: sins, social failings, absurdities and irrationalities. Indeed the weaknesses may not be judged by past criteria, because those criteria are part and parcel of the problem. Our race took a certain direction and has naturally always judged itself according to that direction. The overman will face the other way, so to speak, not in the childish sense of 'evil be thou my good' but rather in the sense, in Zarathustra's words, of wanting 'everything anew, everything eternal, everything chained, entwined together, everything in love'.[8] As we shall see, this doctrine, or vision, is opposed to all idealism, all traditionalism and all 'progress'. It is entirely original.

The way I propose to tackle this question is by first considering not Nietzsche himself, but Rilke's *Duino Elegies*, because these poems diagnose the malady in a distinctly Nietzschean fashion. We shall proceed towards the *Übermensch* proper by grasping something of Rilke's vision of humanity, to which his Angel and Nietzsche's conception are twin alternatives. The former seems meant to be unrealisable, while the latter is proposed (through Zarathustra) as a future possibility, or indeed as a being who must come because the dice are now so loaded in his favour.

It is true that over and above the natural differences of personality and attitude between the two men, Rilke's elegiac tones are foreign to Nietzsche's enterprise. It is also true that while Nietzsche is constantly a 'genealogist', one who explains by reference to growth and development, Rilke is not an explainer at all and thinks only of lasting conditions. Nevertheless, Rilke is the most philosophic of poets in the sense that no one else (not even the Epicurean Lucretius and certainly not Pope) has focused his attention so immediately and candidly upon the human situation itself. What is man? What is he doing here? These are Rilke's questions, or rather it is to these questions that he gives answers. The answers are similar to Nietzsche's, as if to suggest that anyone who refuses to set up ideals (man as heroic warrior, man as fallen angel, man as rational being, man as humanitarian neighbour, or even man as 'glory, jest and riddle of the world') must come to certain conclusions. It is the ideals that vary far more than the observable facts, even though the facts are scarcely 'objective' and can be approached in countless different ways.

According to Walter Kaufmann Rilke had in common with Nietzsche, first and foremost, 'his experience of his own historical situation'.[9] Both men felt cut off, unable to sustain themselves by the values of the past or by those common dreams of the future which are founded upon old values. In contrast, Marx fled into an imaginary future, and Kierkegaard and Dostoevsky were men of faith. Rilke and Nietzsche were alike, and perhaps alone, in seeing little in human culture but fallacy. Second, arising from this awareness of a historical dead end, Rilke like Nietzsche required a 'new honesty'.[10] We are in an unprecedented position which demands an unprecedented rejection of every discernible falsehood. Consequently Rilke's work is, Nietzscheanly, a 'complete repudiation of otherworldliness'.[11] There is no other world, even as the future of this world. That future must be yet another fantasy. Professor Kaufmann declares that 'Rilke accepts Zarathustra's challenge to remain faithful to the earth',[12] meaning neither a romanticised nor a scientific earth but merely the experienced world around us – albeit experienced ecstatically. Next and, for us, most important, the Angel of Rilke's *Duino Elegies* is 'the image or incarnation of the accomplishment of our striving, and his features thus merge with those of Nietzsche's *Übermensch*'.[13] The goal of the present chapter is to discover in what ways that is true. We must work carefully towards the goal, discerning en route not simply the features of Rilke's and Nietzsche's envisioned beings, but in addition the historical circumstances to which those beings are, as it were, 'solutions'. It is important to appreciate that unless one sees man's failings as Nietzsche and Rilke saw them one cannot apprehend the beings either. The beings are precisely what man has never been. They are not, nevertheless, reactions to man but, quite on the contrary, man as he would be if he himself were not entirely formed of defensive reactions to his environment.

Two further items should be added to this brief summary of a few of Kaufmann's observations. One is that he believes Rilke to resemble Nietzsche in exhorting us to 'live dangerously'.[14] The other is that he regards Rilke as weaker than Nietzsche, because the poet lacked 'ultimate honesty with himself'.[15] I too find that whenever there is a discrepancy between comparable attitudes of Rilke and Nietzsche, it is the poet who goes under.

Rilke was scarcely a disciple of Nietzsche and the question of influence is too obscure for sensible discussion. We know that Rilke enthusiastically read Nietzsche. Further, from the age of twenty-two onwards he was the intimate friend of Lou Andreas-Salomé, to whom Nietzsche had contemplated proposing in the early eighties, when Rilke was a boy. Rilke met Lou in 1897, at which time Nietzsche was insane and within three years of his death. In Rilke's letters there are very few references to Nietzsche, but one remark is worth noting: 'Nietzsche', he wrote to his wife, 'with whom we have all become slightly intoxicated, he [Hans Larson, a poet] has taken as a medicine and grown healthier from it.'[16] That is the most revealing of the few things we know by way of documentary fact. Rilke was one of those who, by 1904, had become 'slightly intoxicated' with Nietzsche.

The *Duino Elegies* were not written in consequence of that intoxication, but heady draughts of Nietzsche had long been Rilke's habit when he wrote the First Elegy in 1912. Rilke was entirely himself, standing aside from Nietzsche and from everyone else, yet he presumably felt that he and the philosopher were looking to the same stark future, which would be either a void or a new beginning. Rilke suddenly wrote the First Elegy in January 1912, when he was staying at the castle of Duino near Trieste, the property of the Princess Marie von Thurn und Taxis-Hohenlohe. The first poem, opening as it does with a declaration of an unbridgeable gulf between us and the Angels (they 'excel us in action to exactly the same degree that God is more active above them', Rilke commented in a letter[17]), is the start of a magnificent theme of man's lot, his attempts to overcome it and the impossibility of his ever doing so except, paradoxically, by welcoming it (*amor fati* in the largest sense, or tragic joy). Man is between the Angels and the animals; that is the whole explanation of his generic destiny.

Familiar though this may sound so far, Rilke's Angels are not insubstantial attendants of God but combine immensely heightened consciousness with the naturalness of animals. They are at home in the world, as a wild animal is at home, but are also comprehensively aware. They are perfected people, not in the sense of purity but as a rose is a perfected rosebud. Unlike a rose, however, they never wither and die. The being of each Angel is a constant state of becoming: that is, Angels are always moving, doing deeds, comprehending their surroundings, changing their natures (which are indeed so protean as to be describable only in general terms), but they never finally flourish or decay.

In one way it is seriously and even absurdly misleading to call Rilke an idealist, since he regularly implies that all ideals are false. Just the same, the Angels of the *Elegies* are themselves ideal, inaccessible 'birds of the soul' (Second Elegy, line 2) whose health defines our sickness.[18] Eventually the more we bear them in mind the better we shall see ourselves, but we should proceed by grasping Rilke's analysis of our limitations, punctuated by ever-clearer glimpses of the Angels. For the moment let us just note that the Angels are terrible to us because of what the poet calls their 'stronger existence' (First Elegy, line 4).

Below us, of course, are the animals. Yet the animals at least belong unquestioningly to nature. We, on the other hand, interpret the world: we have 'made' it or recreated it in our own image through every branch of culture, and now, says Rilke, 'we don't feel very securely at home/in this interpreted world' (lines 12–13). The animals are aware of our uneasiness. We sense from the watching eyes of a beast that it notices our unavoidable clumsiness and instinctual failure. We blunder as a matter of course, unlike lesser creatures, presumably because we regularly evade or try to outstrip our instincts. No one is completely unselfconscious, but is an animal ever remotely conscious of itself? Nietzsche makes some apposite remarks in *The Gay Science*: '*Animals as critics* – I fear that the animals consider man as a being like themselves that has lost in a most dangerous way its sound common sense; they consider him the insane animal, the laughing animal, the weeping animal, the miserable animal.'[19]

In addition, although objects are crudely apprehended by an animal, at least they appear in a straightforward fashion: they are good to eat; they cast a shadow; they are dangerous, and so on. But there are very few immediate (unmediated) realities for us and these are things encountered at random: for example, 'some tree on a slope' (line 14) and, it seems, always that 'mild disenchantress', the night (line 21). For although we do obviously interpret the night, it contrives to defeat our interpretations.

People in love 'only conceal their lot' (line 21), and in fact love in either a religious or a profane sense is no answer. We should endlessly strive for a sense of merging ourselves with whatever we perceive. But even this is a falsification of Rilke, for it is not a matter of 'merging ourselves': who are we that we have anything to contribute to the process? It is rather a matter of filling ourselves with externalities. To Rilke one is, or ought to be, nothing except an ability to receive the outside world, unimpaired and unrefined. This is a creative, not a passive activity, and it is most creative precisely when one's impression of the thing is freshly received. In the same vein, our feelings should be of a piece with our impressions and neither should be informed – which is to say warped – by doctrine. For what we term the 'mind' is a ragbag that confuses our original perceptions, with the result that we are normally divorced from what we observe.

In Rilke's extraordinary opinion worldly happenings and objects have need of us. Birds flying overhead, springtime each year, a star, a wave, the noise of a violin through a window: each of these is intrinsically incomplete. Our 'commission' is to make something of all such items, but without prejudgement. Thus we are to make of them what we already find them to be. An external thing is completed when it is transformed from its visible state (or, in general, its presence to the senses) into the invisibility of one's mental assimilation of it. We consummate the thing, so to speak, and that is our only proper function.

Rilke is possibly speaking of a process performed by wordless infants. If so, his belief is similar to that of the Wordsworth of the 'Immortality Ode'. Unlike Wordsworth, however, he is signally refusing to accept that 'soothing thoughts' must compensate us for the loss of the capacity as we grow up. On the contrary, it remains our Orphic role (unavoidable, though we have been avoiding it these thousands of years) to make the world invisible. Even the most remarkable people have failed to do this. The Hero lives his life to a purpose, which coincides with his death. That is the flowering of his deeds. So the Hero 'continues' after death, for 'even his setting/was a pretext for further existence, an ultimate birth' (lines 40–1). That is admirably said, since a hero lives as though impelled towards a particular death. The death gives him a 'further existence', not just a story for posterity, since Rilke has no use for stories as such, as 'mere' fictions; or for posterity. Everything past and future, fact and fiction, is all one, or at least these forms and dimensions endlessly flow together.

Another type of greatness is that of the great lover. Rilke's example is Gaspara Stampa, a sixteenth-century Italian girl loved and deserted by the Count Collatino di Collato. (In Part Two of *The Notebook of Malte Laurids Brigge* she is mentioned as one of those renowned female lovers whose 'laments have come down to us'.[20]) Such love encompasses and outstrips its object, as an arrow leaving a bowstring becomes 'something more than itself' (line 52). Rilke's point is that 'staying is nowhere' (line 52), and the great lover knows that the beloved is an occasion, not a terminus.

Nothing is a terminus, not even death. We should 'gently remove' (line 65) the impression of injustice that comes to us when we contemplate the youthfully dead. They have merely preceded us on their way through the universe. We draw 'too sharp distinctions' (line 80) between the living and the dead, for both are simply part of the 'eternal torrent' (line 84). Here it will be seen that Rilke is thinking of 'becoming' in Nietzsche's and Heraclitus' sense: he is assuming, without argument or explanation, that there is only unceasing motion and that no item in the stream may be circumscribed as 'being'. Indeed, I am again misrepresenting Rilke in speaking of distinct items.

The Second Elegy begins with a more elaborate account of the Angels. From one point of view they are substantial beings, because they constantly empty themselves into physical matter and are just as constantly replenished thereby. I do not see how it is possible to think of the Angels as divorced from matter, since Rilke does not conceive of spirit apart from flesh. Nor does an Angel have a character, as character is perforce limitation. Rather an Angel has a multitude of natures and therefore no 'nature' in the usual sense. The process of an Angel, or the process which constitutes an Angel, is a never-ending expiration and inspiration, outflow and inflow. We human beings are so much less because we 'evaporate' (line 18). We diminish in the material sense that our body cells are irreparably destroyed and we grow towards death. The handsomest people deteriorate. Our selves (mind-bodies) keep melting into our surroundings, hence into matter. Dust we are and unto dust we shall return, but not with the qualification that we shall be resurrected to eternal life through Christ. Rilke is talking about eternal transformation rather than eternal life. (Nietzsche's manner of saying something similar is impressive: 'The living is merely a type of what is dead, and a very rare type.'[21])

Lovers fancy that they confer eternity upon each other, that their bodies are rendered lasting through caresses. ('Eternity was in our lips and eyes', as Cleopatra says.) Nevertheless lovers inexorably change, or in other words slide away.

> Lovers, are you the same? When you lift yourselves
> up to each other's lips – drink unto drink:
> oh, how strangely the drinker eludes his part!

(lines 63–5)

No one and nothing simply survives, not even the Platonic Forms, which are, presumably, a set of words and a phase in civilisation. (How strangely and comprehensively is Rilke an elegist!)

There is something of Nietzsche's duality of Apollo and Dionysus in the Third Elegy. In a sense familiar to us through Freud and Jung it is, says Rilke, 'One thing to sing the beloved, another alas!/ that hidden guilty river-god of the blood' (lines 1–2). The sentiments and social transactions of romance are conspicuous, while beneath them seethes the gloomy god, Neptune, from whom the love-songs ultimately derive. A youth is aroused by a girl, a fledged and intricate individual, but she is just a focus for his ferocious energies. Above the youth, watching over him, are the women, his mother and his girl, while inwardly he harbours a 'night-space' (line 33). These women divert the 'floods of origin' within him (line 46). The upper agents are female, the lower male. The lower are more powerful by far and would be ghastly to behold, if they were not softened and prettified by the female agents. Paradoxically the youth is more attracted by the 'horror' than by the emollient women: it smiles at him more 'tenderly' (line 62) and he loves his 'interior jungle' (line 53). The object of a cherished girl should be to guide her youth 'close to the garden' (line 84). Note: not 'into the garden'. He is an accumulation of Caliban forebears and can at best be soothed, not spiritualised.

The failure of human instincts is crass and all but disastrous. We fly against the wind or across it and alight grotesquely on ponds. So Rilke says in effect at the opening of the Fourth Elegy. We are never free from the knowledge of weakness, while a lion is either splendidly alive or at death's door and there is no leonine middle way. We do not even know the 'shape' of one of our own feelings, 'but only that which forms it from outside' (line 18). According to Romano Guardini (whose study of the *Elegies* is rewarding, if pervaded, and even vexed, by his Christian objections to so much that the poet says) Rilke means in this reference to human feelings that 'Our experience only reaches our consciousness from without, namely through our proximity to whatever is alien or hostile to us.'[22] I stress this point because it will later be necessary to show that Nietzsche's *Übermensch* is characterised precisely by his lack of such human reactive feelings. That is, his creative joy embraces whatever would otherwise be experienced as alien or hostile. Rilke is surely right to see that at least a high proportion of our feelings are shaped by the hostile world. (He thinks this inevitable, while Nietzsche thinks it surmountable.)

We are both audience and actors at our own theatre. As a spectator each of us is dismayed by our own performance. One appears on stage not as an adroit dancer but as a 'bourgeois' (line 24), a lumpish, dutiful fellow. Our deeds and thoughts amount to inept role-playing. Even a doll or a puppet would seem preferable, since it has no disjointed inner life.

Rilke addresses his dead father who used to find the boy's nature bitterly displeasing. So far as Rilke was concerned, throughout his life, people were half dolls and half living creatures, or creatures with dolls' faces. Therefore a 'counterpoising angel' (line 55) was necessary to put them through their paces. Without the Angels, Rilke thought, there would be no play, nothing to watch. Only children and dying people lacked histrionic ways, and of these two exemplary categories, the first was in a hurry to grow up, or in other words to start posturing.

> O hours of childhood,
> hours when behind the figures there was more
> than the mere past, and when what lay before us
> was not the future!

(lines 65–8)

These interesting lines seem to mean that in childhood the 'figures' (of people in general, but especially of adults) embodied entirely personal pasts influencing present behaviour. The past in each instance was not the 'mere past' but the dynamic presence of the past in the present. Further, the immediately foreseeable future of a child, or at any rate the future as the 'coming holiday' or the 'examinations next week', is a far cry from the insurable, pensionable, drearily unspontaneous future of an adult. Thus the child lives more or less in the present and is relatively free-wheeling, relatively not a puppet.

The category of the dying is possibly easier to understand. What Rilke means is a good part of the point of Tolstoy's story 'The Death of Ivan Ilyich', which is a study of a man's freeing himself from theatricality and make-believe as he painfully dies. Life and death are still much the same for a child: his moments, whatever their qualities, are eternal. This means that each moment is neither isolable nor a link in a chain. Moments flow together and are eternal in the sense of 'timeless'. (Certainly we subject a moment to the 'time of chronometers', as T. S. Eliot calls it in 'The Dry Salvages', but time is not an intrinsic property of the moment.)

In the Fifth Elegy some street acrobats are described as a means of qualifying social life in general. Leishman and Spender remark that 'In many ways the acrobats, both in the exercise of their profession and in their relationships with one another, seem to Rilke symbolic of human activity as a whole.'[23] Perhaps, however, it is not so much a matter of symbolising as of *focusing*, because the acrobats reveal what is usually hidden. Rilke's own metaphor is precise: a performance by the acrobats at the centre of a period-ically changing group of onlookers is the 'pistil' around which a rose 'blooms and unblossoms' (line 21). Onlookers and performers thus share in the same fake-organic process.

For four months in 1915 Rilke lived in the Munich apartment of an absent woman friend, Hertha Koenig, who owned Picasso's picture *Les Saltimbanques*, which the poet called 'the loveliest of all Picassos'.[24] The painting is of six immobile figures against a vague landscape and a light, cloudy sky. Years earlier Rilke had seen the actual *saltimbanques*, and at the time of completing the Fifth Elegy (in 1922, about a week after writing what is now the Tenth Elegy) he told Lou Andreas-Salomé that these particular acrobats 'affected me so when I was first in Paris and have lain on me like a task ever since'.[25]

There is no very obvious relation between Rilke's account of a performance by the *saltimbanques* and Picasso's artifically frozen figures. The people in the poem are 'travellers' (line 1), as we all are, but slightly 'more fleeting than we ourselves' (line 2). In a certain sense they 'caricature' us, though they have no intention of caricaturing anyone. The effect is similar to that of glimpsing oneself strutting or slouching past a shop window, for Rilke's acrobats are seen, not coldly, but without the usual sort of cultural veneer.

The performers themselves and the shifting spectators are bored, but nobody realises as much. The cycle of a performance is a 'sham-fruit of boredom' (line 24). One pathetic fellow, big but 'shrivelled up in his massive hide' (line 29), beats a drum, since he is now too old to do anything else. In contrast a young athletic man does all the skilful tricks, and these (like much gymnasium work) are both clever and, frankly, dull. In further contrast a boy repeatedly climbs to the top of the group and repeatedly fails to keep his balance, falling like an unripe fruit. Every time he falls he is hurt, so that his feet tingle in anticipation well before they hit the ground. Tears come into the boy's eyes but he is not aware of them. He looks to his mother for consolation, yet she rarely responds.

Then there is a girl of about twelve who is 'mutely elided/by all the exquisite joys' (lines 65–6). Such joys pass her by, but she is so busy remaining composed, practising less the appearance of serenity than serenity itself, that she does not know what she is missing. She wills herself to be a placid show-piece: what is there to be unhappy about? The reality of these acrobats and the non-acrobatic people they dismally entertain (by extension, all of us) is camouflaged by the 'modiste Madam Lamort' (line 90), the death-concealing trappings of social life. Rilke probably means everything from fashion to the consolations of philosophy.

The alternative to this sheer inauthenticity (as we have complacently learned to call it) is at most a supposition, a 'place we know nothing about' (line 96) where lovers act with consummate skill and complete sincerity. They and their actions might, conceivably, coincide. And they might also be watched by a lively crowd who finally throw down 'coins of happiness' (line 105). In this situation there is no discrepancy between feeling and deed, between the individual and the environment. This dream is one illustration of Rilke's weakness in comparison with Nietzsche: the dream is enticing, so Rilke entertains it for at least the space of a closing stanza.

The Fifth Elegy expounds more graphically than the others how Rilke habitually saw his fellow men. He observed ugliness, pretence and self-maltreatment. This becomes plainer if one turns for a moment to *The Notebook of Malte Laurids Brigge* and reads, for example, the description of the waiting-room in the Saltpêtrière. Malte, representing the author, notices in detail the Zolaesque frightfulness of the hospital, but does so without Zola's habitual implication that such pain and fear should be rooted out. Nor is Rilke like Kafka in finding comedy and horror in absurdity. On the contrary, things are as they are, and there is not even a disguised complaint from the author. Stephen Spender suggests that *The Notebook of Malte Laurids Brigge* might well be called '*Portrait of the Artist as a Young Neurotic* (or, perhaps to update it further, *as a Young Existentialist*)',[26] but the fact is that Rilke, however neurotic, sees what is there, while the commoner sort of neurotic specifically and morbidly fantasises.

The exceptionally short Sixth Elegy is interesting in relation to Nietzsche, though its implications must be pursued, not here and now, but later in this chapter and in Chapters 5 and 6. Fig trees, says Rilke, scarcely flower at all, going almost straight to the fruiting stage. Conversely, we human beings linger in the flowering stage and then wake up one morning to find ourselves overripe and ready to fall. Heroes are different. 'These go plunging ahead' (line 18). Repeatedly the Hero 'takes himself off and enters the changed constellation' (line 23). For long enough Samson's mother was infertile, then she gave birth to him, the great one. He was a Hero even in the womb, for it was there that he chose himself out of the thousands of embryonic possibilities 'trying to be him' (line 35). He 'shattered columns' when he burst from his mother's body, even more than when he brought down the house at Gaza. Such a Hero smiles back at those who, loving him, would detain him.

No doubt we loiter through the phase of flowering, as Rilke says, but so do many plants, if not animals. We postpone ripeness until it is too late. Here Rilke must be referring to opportunities for self-fulfilment, the historical accidents that make a meaning of one's life, so that they do not seem accidents at all. On the other hand Samson knew exactly when to destroy the Philistines and, further, recognised at the same moment that such destruction was his destiny. Thus the Hero plunges ahead towards his death (as Rilke has already pointed out in the First Elegy).

Does the Hero choose himself in the womb and, if he does, doesn't everyone? Rilke means that individuality begins in the womb. Already one is oneself. Even if the individual later has a road-to-Damascus conversion and consequently a distinctive destiny, the seeds of that destiny were sown before birth. Not literally, perhaps; this is not necessarily a genetic process, but a sort of utterly unconscious self-selection takes place in the womb and the baby is born as a particularised person. This will seem nonsense to those who assume that character is the result of post-natal conditioning, but Rilke believes, to the contrary, that such conditioning generally obliterates original character.

Is it not likely that 'social pressures' instantly begin to deform the new-born piece of originality, and that the Hero resists those pressures? But why only the Hero, for Rilke himself was no Hero, and neither were most creative spirits. Shakespeare does not seem to have been heroic, yet he had a sense of his own fate that resisted the influences and obligations of Stratford and sent him to London. We must remember that 'fate' cannot be taken to mean a task imposed on the individual, in the way of ancient myth, but is an early act of self-will never renounced. From these brief remarks I hope it may be felt that Rilke's belief is important, if not unprecedented, but the message still needs a good deal of cognitive (as opposed to poetic) refinement.

As for Nietzsche, we shall later see that he thought of the self as a personality that lies *ahead* of the social character, a personality to be *achieved*. At first sight, therefore, it seems that Nietzsche did not regard the all-important self as pre-natal, but for all that he can only have meant that the self must be distinguished from various competing models. Certainly it is what is left when false, imitative selves have been stripped away. And perhaps the seeds are present in the womb. But how does one know the genuine from the spurious? Nietzsche's answer is that one simply does know, at any age, if a sprig of genuineness is still alive, for '*What does your conscience say?* – "You shall become the person you are".'[27] So one reaches out for whatever the sprig will grow into. But the paradox cannot be evaded: you have to strive to become what you initially elected to be. In Rilke only the Hero can do this (and he has no difficulty in so doing, whatever the incidental hardships of his journey), while in Nietzsche the one who follows his own path is merely an exception – a true 'original'.

The first twenty-nine lines of the Seventh Elegy have a fresh and rapturous tone. Up to now, throughout the *Elegies*, we might have been tempted to conclude that Rilke was counselling us to despise this life and 'be absolute for death'. But that is true only in a most unusual way, namely that for Rilke death was neither a meaningless negation, a cancelling-out, nor the gateway to another world. He did not imagine the dead to be somehow 'not dead', as in a child's picture of heaven or hell. On the contrary, Rilke assumed that at death everyone is decomposed into chemical substances and consciousness is naturally extinguished. Nevertheless to him death meant entry to another mode of existence. Not to non-existence, but to a fuller existence from which consciousness has excluded us. He regarded consciousness as a temporary gift, and not much of a gift, since we use it largely to estrange ourselves from nature, which is God.

Rilke was remarkable in this respect. He did not accept Jesus as

God but saw Him as a prophet who has actually taken us further away from God. Rilke was a theistic anti-Christian, as he makes plain in the famous 'Letter from a Young Worker' (written in February 1922, but never addressed or sent to anyone, and published posthumously). The letter asserts that Jesus was the grand repudiator of the earth, of the sense, of life itself. (This, of course, is Nietzsche's Christ as well.) Thus Jesus refutes Rilke's God, who is nothing more or less or other than what we must paradoxically call the 'spirit' of the material world. God is not behind or above the universe but *is* the universe, in all its beauty and destructiveness. It follows that man is included in the all-embracing spirit of God and that the spirit is part and parcel of materiality. Spirit and matter are not opposites; nor do they co-exist but, contrary to our traditions, coincide.

If anyone asks how this can be, since spirit is defined as other than matter, Rilke's implied response is that spirit is the human significance of matter. The universe without man would presumably be without spirit, but nevertheless man's spirit may only be exercised in conjunction with matter. It is what we make of things, and we make something of everything, however infertile it might be. 'The whole of creation, I feel,' Rilke writes in the letter, 'says this word [God] without thinking, if often out of profound meditation.'[28]

What does this mean? What can it possibly mean? One who wishes in a fit of literalness to deny that a tree or a cloud or a lump of igneous rock 'says' anything at all must assume that Rilke simply sees man as a creature of nature to whom, because he is conscious, nature in a manner 'speaks'. Thus a tree expresses itself to me, since I cannot, however hard I try, contemplate a meaningless tree – in other words, a 'voiceless' tree, a tree that utterly fails to communicate with me. It is no good saying that my experience of the tree excludes anything communicated by 'the tree itself': there can be no such thing in my experience as the tree itself.

To Rilke man's consciousness separates him from what he is conscious of. In looking at a tree I am too busy making up an imaginary or conceptualised tree to see the tree. Conversely, Jesus was one of those who have taught us to keep the world at a distance, reminding us always of 'toil and distress' and insisting on 'redeeming' us from the mere necessities of life.[29] But God has no use for a redeemer: God is the world from which Christ would redeem us. Unfortunately it is only now and again that Rilke can rapturously receive and venerate the actual. He does this at the beginning of the Seventh Elegy. He continues by insisting that when he 'calls' the lover, as he has just done, other girls also 'come and gather' from their graves (line 32), since a love-call cannot in practice be limited to one person, or even to living persons.

Destiny is no more than 'what's packed into childhood' (line 36). This means that destiny is not a circumstance to which one travels but an intensification of life at any time, though it is especially a property of childhood. Samson's death at Gaza was, in general terms, the sort of deed he had been doing all his life. It was historically significant for the Israelites and for us, but Samson did not think of his career as a mere preparation for that moment. So the Hero hurtles towards his death, not as a distant prospect but as an ever-present possibility. For most of us, however, the sense of personal, continuous destiny is lost as we grow up, because we are overwhelmed by social requirements and temptations.

Rilke now compares the early twentieth century with the past, to the disadvantage of modern times. Once men built 'permanent' houses, but now they build only 'invented' structures (line 53). It seems that invention is just a mode or a product of the fancy and it is unrelated to the natural sphere, with which we should fill ourselves. The cathedral of Chartres, anything but an invention in Rilke's sense, does not suffer much even in comparison with an Angel.

But, for goodness' sake, Rilke hastens to add, 'Don't think that I'm wooing!/Angel, even if I were, you'd never come . . .' (lines 86–7). The poet acknowledges that the intention of his poetry is, humanly, to fend off the Angel. He is so busy keeping Angels at bay that they cannot come nearer. An Angel, therefore, is not omnipotent, or perhaps one should say that an Angel cannot approach a man just as the omnipotent Christian God has no access to the heart of a hardened sinner.

So far in the *Elegies* Rilke has assumed without much elaboration that animals are at home in the world because they lack conscious awareness of it. We, on the contrary, name things and so separate ourselves from them. When a chimpanzee does human tricks or a mynah bird speaks, neither has any idea of what it is doing. Only an Angel both knows the world and is at one with it. Now, in the Eighth Elegy, Rilke explores animal nature. An animal's eyes are properly open, while ours entrap whatever they behold. A young child, too, has some of an animal's openness but is quickly 'turned round', as Rilke calls it, to the sphere of human codes. The animal has no concepts and no symbols: therefore its eyes gaze blankly and unimpededly at whatever is there. The eyes are blank because they are not 'compromised', as one might say, by prior knowledge, memory, understanding. And for the same reason they do emphatically *see*.

> ...the free animal
> has its decease perpetually behind it
> and God in front, and when it moves, it moves
> within eternity...

(lines 10–13)

'God in front' means the uninterpreted quality of things, which the animal faces. The reality of death is visible to an animal only now and then. The rest of the time, when the animal is not confronted by another's death, it is unaware of death and so 'has its decease perpetually behind it'. Death is hidden from the animal's sight. This is a favourable piece of ignorance since, when its time comes, the animal simply and willingly dies. Death is thus properly part of life and not a negation to be postponed or, as in the oldest of human dreams, to be replaced by some sort of conscious post-mortem existence.

Rilke is clearly implying that an animal's condition is, so far, part of what we should try for. The animal observes the open world of creation – endless, 'pointless' creation – and, as a corollary, has no notion of time or the *succession* of moments. Each moment is therefore 'eternal'. It is not apprehended by the animal as that which follows something or leads up to something. It is not a link in a chain and therefore lacks duration. The moment is eternal because it is timeless. Equally important is the fact that to an animal every moment is as important or valuable as every other moment. There is no sense of superiority and subordination. Consequently the animal lives in and for the moment, without prudence or perception of pattern. To an animal there is no pattern, while to human beings everything is patterned. Presumably we make patterns, for they are not objectively present.

There is only chaos, not 'for all eternity' as if chaos stretched out to the crack of doom (for there will never be a crack of doom either), but because every instant is chance, despite its necessarily following the preceding instant. Really there are two factors: every instant is a pure piece of chance and also unavoidably necessary. It was a piece of chance before it happened and a necessity afterwards. From the animal's point of view there is no before and after, anyway: there is only *now*. Therefore the now of every moment is necessary and necessarily part of infinity. No part of infinity is removable or replaceable, but each part falls into place contributing to the all-embracing chaos. Rilke's attitude here seems to me to resemble Nietzsche's. Both men saw the world as made up of a huge number of colliding and interacting forces. There is no design whatever, but even the tiniest event has its place. This is the greatest paradox: all is chaos and yet every motion of the chaos is linked *in its exact form* to the rest.

As it happens, Rilke implies, the animal is right about all this: that is how matters are, despite the history of human thought. The animal is right and doesn't know it; human beings are wrong and do not know it, and only Angels are right and know they are right. There is probably a close relation between Rilke's attitude here and Nietzsche's thought of Eternal Return. The latter, though, is still scarcely comprehended, for all the studies of the subject. That is as it must be because Nietzsche himself did not expound the doctrine clearly. To begin with, in August 1881, he received it as a sudden insight, and thereafter he returned to it again and again, but never cleared up the difficulties. In one of the best English studies of the insight Joan Stambaugh remarks, 'Thus, the thought of eternal return is *schwer* in the double sense of being extremely difficult and hard to think out, as well as weighty and momentous.'[30]

Later in this chapter, as we contemplate the *Übermensch* in comparison with Rilke's Angels, we must consider Eternal Return from one limited point of view, since the supreme creatures of both the philosopher and the poet differ from man precisely in their never-failing and (to us) miraculous grasp of eternity. Meanwhile let us note that the animals, for all their lack of human follies, convey a sense of sadness. This sense is, for once, not a product of our falsifying imaginations. The sad-looking horse is sad, not of course in the human way, but because it is never positively happy. Frisking in the meadow it is not cheerful; dying it is not sorrowful. It follows that, while animals do not make human errors of judgement and their earth is the actual earth, their lives are empty. They properly fill themselves with the environment but cannot properly exult in doing so. They are dull, frigid creatures who require to be charmed into significance by Orpheus. And who is Orpheus? He is not a specific, mythological poet but rather a general human capacity. For human beings must inescapably and Orphically confer significance upon all creation.

That indeed is the theme of the Ninth Elegy, completed at Muzot on 9 February 1922. Rilke asks and answers what one would carelessly suppose to be an unanswerable question:

> oh, why
> *have* to be human, and, shunning Destiny,
> long for Destiny

(lines 4–6)

Alternatively, why have to be non-human? Why live? The point is that human beings, alone of all beings, absolutely must justify their existence. The most incurable degenerate explains and justifies himself somehow. No doubt his self-justification is preposterous, but so is the self-justification of the hero, the artist and the saint.

We do not exist, says Rilke, for the sake of happiness, 'that precipitate profit of imminent loss' (line 8). It does not seem that Rilke means to deny the occurrence of joy, but to announce that happiness in any form is conditional upon loss. It is what we sometimes derive from transience; it is our way of profiting from things that pass or, commercially speaking, it is the profit we take before the business goes bankrupt. It is therefore a sort of illusion, but the melancholic who cannot be thus deluded is no more of a realist than the joyful person who can.

At any rate, happiness is not our *raison d'être* and should not be our goal. The destiny of everyone is to take in some fleeting portion of the world. We are here and that fact can never be erased. Our being here means, and means only, that certain events occur: if I were not here the events that befall me would not befall anyone. Even so elementary an experience as perceiving a tree is unique to me, for no one else sees the tree as I do.

Nevertheless my private experience is publicly named, for we all say 'tree'. We name things and so consummate them. That is all being human amounts to. A house, for instance, exists in an unrepeatable way because I perceive it and name it in an unrepeatable moment. No matter that we all say 'house', for the word is merely the public sign by means of which I suffer my peculiar experience of the thing. The fact to hold on to, however, is that my experience of the thing (*my* naming it) is what the thing exists for. Without me the thing would be unexperienced, unexpressed and inconsequential. Rilke means that the earth is meaningful and valuable only through each one of us alone. One life cannot replace another, because things are rendered meaningful only in singular, fleeting moments. Another moment, another person, another meaning: *there is no general meaning*.

A more elementary account of human existence can scarcely be imagined. What Rilke says is 'true', if anything is, and nothing more than Rilke's assertions could ever be proved to be true. Human beings are to be defined in terms neither of physiology nor of superior consciousness, but as the value-conferring animals. Alternatively, they give or perceive meaning. Of course the constant temptation is to give false meanings, to idolatrise. Rilke assumes that God is universal creation (not 'as a whole' but in specific forms) and that God requires man to recognise and praise Him.

From the complexities of the final elegy, the Tenth Elegy, there is only one essential point for us to consider: that pain and death are forever inescapable and, properly understood, are the entwined roots of rich and satisfying life. Just as to Rilke death is a metamorphosis rather than a negation, so pain and joy come from neighbouring sources and are bound together. We, however, live in the City of Pain, a place where pain is masked and unappreciated. Leishman characterises our habitation as follows:

> ... that half-life from which death, and all that is mysterious and inexplicable, is simply excluded; that life whose consolations are provided by conventional religion, and whose activities are the pursuit of happiness and the making of money; from which fear and misery are banished by distractions, and where suffering is regarded merely as an unfortunate accident.[31]

The City of Pain is much the same as Bunyan's Vanity Fair, except that now, in the twentieth century, there is more emphasis on money. Having presented us with this fairground city (complete with its fairground church) Rilke introduces us to a youth who is drawn further and further away from the booths and hoardings by a girl, a 'Lament'. She wears 'Pearls of Pain' (line 52) and is, presumably for that very reason, alluring to the youth. She takes him to a valley where he questions one of the older Laments. This second woman explains that she is a member of a vast family of suffering people whose line stretches back beyond the ancient civilisations. The family of Laments used to be rich and continues to be noble. Their forefathers worked mines in the mountains, from which one may still recover a lump of 'polished original pain' (line 59).

The older Lament now brings the youth to a distant gorge which is the 'source of Joy' (line 99). She leaves him and he ascends alone to the 'mountains of Primal Pain' (line 104). Primal Pain is strikingly different from our modern mode of more-or-less troublesome living, and even indeed from extreme modern suffering, because it is stark and undisguised. It is neither caused by events, nor is it itself for the sake of some cause or other. It will not be eliminated by future generations. It inexorably and permanently and pointlessly is. Apart from this, the gorge whence issues the stream of joy is in the foothills of the mountains of Primal Pain. Rilke can only mean something to the effect that pain is fundamental, woven into the writhings and blossomings of every life-form. We can minimise it only at a certain cost. That cost, it seems, is a like moderation of joy, a turning of joy into mild pleasure and spiritual infertility. For if great joy is what we sometimes feel in the absence of pain, it remains consequent upon pain. Rilke does not suggest that joy is simply relief, but rather that it is an intensification of emotion that can occur only in a general condition of heightened feelings, which condition naturally and perhaps primarily includes pain.

Rilke's concluding remark is typically pointed and paradoxical, a deliberate reversal of our normal assumptions.

> And we, who think of *ascending*
> happiness, then would feel
> the emotion that almost startles
> when happiness *falls*

(lines 110–13)

Happiness is a condition one receives rather than strives for. It is a gift, here contemplated in the image of fertilising rain or hanging catkins. Happiness is fertilisation and a passive, yet ecstatic, welcoming of what the earth offers.

Rilke is truly elegiac. We all realise that life without death is nonsense, but Rilke stresses that fact as no other modern poet does, because unlike others he offers no Christian or progressionist interpretation and does not fall back on either irony or helpless pity. To him death is not regrettable, and certainly not what it is to his commentator, Romano Guardini: a 'disgrace'. 'To be a person at all implies personality – that is, self-possession and responsibility for one's actions in a unity of mind and body. The destruction of this unity in death means ontological disgrace.'[32] This position of Guardini is the modern reversal or refutation of tragedy in a nutshell. Here we have the core of modern Christianity and the reason why even a sympathetic, learned exegetist cannot properly appreciate that rare quality of Rilke: the rejection of any belief that human beings have, or ought to have, powers that extricate them from the toils of nature.

Now we can discuss the qualities of Rilke's Angels. An Angel lacks the human weaknesses that are a large part of the matter of the *Duino Elegies*. He is an imaginary and presumably unrealisable being, whose being is, anyway, entirely composed of becoming. However we should not think of Angels as protean, for that suggests a changing of shape at will, capriciously. An Angel, on the other hand, inevitably (and joyously) changes to accommodate whatever portion of the world he is currently absorbing. He masters the earth not by caprice or wizardry but by taking it as he finds it.

He never-endingly 'takes in' the earth around him, then expels it to take in some other fragment. So if he is an ideal to Rilke, he is, in an unprecedented fashion, a 'realistic ideal'. For he never has ideas about what he incorporates: that is to say, he never subordinates a piece of materiality to an image of it. We, on the contrary, give a thing a name and thereby seek to master it. It is no longer an independent object (possibly housing a spirit, possibly dangerous), since we have appropriated it. And we appropriate it only by altering its nature, by falsifying it in some degree. But Angels welcome their original, fearless impressions of things and do not employ appropriative language.

Angels are supremely conscious, but this does not mean that they use reasoning intelligence, which, to Rilke, is no more than a means of humanising and falsifying things. An Angel is vastly more aware than even the cleverest person and for that very reason is not clever at all in the human way. The Angel does not think, but acts, continually acts. Nor is the Angel spirit as distinct from substance. He is the reverse, a shifting compound of material things made 'invisible'. He may possibly be described as a 'spirit' in a special sense, that is as one who readily makes material objects invisible, willingly receives them and so completes them. Thus the Angel is nothing if not natural. Or, if we decide to call him 'supernatural', we must remember that this means he complements rather than controls the natural sphere.

At first sight it might seem that an Angel has no personality because he is so changeable and accommodating, but if we imagine him as possessing unlimited negative capability, then no doubt he has personality. We do not think of Shakespeare as having less personality than Wordsworth because he had more negative capability. Angels are different in kind, but Rilke evidently thought of every Angel as distinguished from his fellows. We are forced to assume that the Angelic capacity to ingest the external world unimpaired does not mean that Angels receive things 'objectively'. In fact each Angel forms, or is composed of, his own characteristic impressions, but these impressions are not coloured by wishes or fears. The Angel knows no wishes or fears. He is afraid of nothing and accepts everything. Thus an Angel is malleable, not in the least rigid, but is nevertheless singular. He is himself, which automatically means that he is not an accommodating social entity.

Above all, and finally, the Angels are continually in touch with eternity. There is no line, no ascent or descent, no forwards or backwards, no circle or cycle, no 'progress' in the modern sense, no history, no beginning or end. Each instant is rich and, so one could guess, without sensible duration. Certainly its duration is not reckoned by the Angel. It seems also that the meaning of a moment is not influenced by reference to traditional patterns or to fashions. For the Angel, who consummates the meaning of the moment, is constantly creative. He does not try to match each moment to an historical pattern, although he knows, as no ordinary human being knows, that the nature of a passing event depends upon its exact place in a cosmic complex of events. All this means that the Angel is free to 'play with' the moment creatively. He shapes it even as he respects its given nature. He does not make it a reflection of his ego, since he has no ego. In fact he is empty and so shapes the moment disinterestedly, purely for the sake of creation.

Perhaps it will be helpful for us to think about Shakespeare. Shakespeare respected his source but did not feel bound by it to the extent of rubbing the shine off his creation, the play. Plutarch related that Antony and Cleopatra did such and such: very well, so they do in Shakespeare's play, but only on condition that the poetry and drama are not thereby marred. Nevertheless, Shakespeare does not make an Antony and Cleopatra to suit his private preferences, to advance a cause or even to fit a general moral scheme. They are in Shakespeare pretty much what they are in Plutarch. An Angel does this sort of thing and far, far more. Likewise Michelangelo fashions a David who – except for his size, itself 'heroic' – is conceivably, or even recognisably, the David of the Bible, but is a new creation just the same. Can the Angel, then, be imagined as a miraculously enhanced classical artist? I think he can in part and am sure that, at all events, he is not a crusading or resentful artist.

These are the ways in which a Rilkean Angel resembles Nietzsche's *Übermensch*. Both gladly play with the given world. Neither wishes to hurt anyone, although the Angel, at least, is not concerned if he does. Possibly the *Übermensch* will feel concern at times, for the last part of *Zarathustra* is not clear on this point. Neither is a 'legislator of the world', in Shelley's phrase, because their actions do not embody laws, even for themselves. There are no laws; or, rather, there is one all-embracing fact which we normal human beings might take to be a law, namely that the world is as it is. So, far from being ones who try to alter the nature of things, Rilke's and Nietzsche's alternatives to existing and historical humanity recreate the world according to its unalterable qualities. To offer the most striking illustration, every living thing goes through a metamorphosis which we call 'death': therefore neither Angel nor *Übermensch* imagines a deathless world, a paradise. The vital distinction between the two is that the Angel is a fantasy and the *Übermensch* a prophecy.

To some extent I am attributing characteristics to the Angels which Rilke does not mention. But these are characteristics an Angel must have in order to be a counterweight to man, as Rilke portrays man. Throughout the *Elegies* Rilke's diagnosis (or complaint) has been that people fail to empty themselves of egotism and cultural prejudices; that they reject or falsify nature; that they

wear dolls' faces instead of their own; that they are time-ridden;
and, above all, that they fear death. Angels, then, are or do the
reverse of these things. Even the Rilkean Hero is no more than the
best kind of human being, yet he falls far short of an Angel. We are
all exhorted to 'fling the emptiness' out of our arms (First Elegy,
line 22) so that some external thing might flow in. We should carry
out our commission whenever we perceive, for instance, a star; we
should let ourselves meet the world unshielded and, when
necessary, slip away from life.

> Early successes, favourites of fond Creation,
> ranges, summits, dawn-red ridges
> of all forthbringing, – pollen of blossoming godhead,
> junctures of light, corridors, stairways, thrones,
> chambers of essence, shields of felicity, tumults
> of stormily-rapturous feeling, and suddenly, separate,
> mirrors, drawing up again their own
> outstreamed beauty into their own faces.
>
> (Second Elegy, lines 10–18)

That is a description of the Angels and their exalted way which we
cannot hope to follow, but bearing Angels in mind presumably
gives us the best perspective on our lives.

Nietzsche's overman is the answer to man whom Zarathustra
hopes to herald. John the Baptist heralded the Saviour before he
knew what (not simply who but *what*) the Saviour would be.
Nietzsche, through Zarathustra, needs to work out what the
Übermensch will be. Doing this will help the man-above-men to
materialise. *Thus Spoke Zarathustra* portrays Zarathustra's dawning
appreciation of *Übermensch*-qualities. Nietzsche himself is crystal-
lising his awareness of these qualities as he goes along, though the
process is not laborious but ecstatic. (Nietzsche told Georg Brandes
that when writing the book he had been in a 'perfect condition of
one who is "inspired".'[33])

Towards the end of the work Zarathustra is confronted, one by
one, with the weaknesses in the best men, the 'higher men'. In
Part Four of *Thus Spoke Zarathustra* this mightiest of prophets

encounters a lesser prophet who is himself a higher man. The latter speaks of the 'great weariness' and teaches that 'It is all one, nothing is worth while, the world is without meaning, knowledge chokes.'[34] This prophet aims to seduce Zarathustra to pity for the higher men and soon Zarathustra manages to hear a cry of distress from the abysses near his mountain cave. This means that higher men (as opposed to the crowd or, as Nietzsche prefers to say, the 'mob') are now, in the modern period, desolate and might well excite pity.

What the prophet says is 'true'. Everything *is* illusion. The prophet, who probably resembles Schopenhauer, wants Zarathustra to accept nihilism in its most complete form and merely sympathise with certain exceptional beings who have actively sought a life of value. The prophet thus preys upon the last infirmity of Zarathustra's noble mind, a temptation to pity higher men. But such a course of action – or, rather, of torpor – will not do: it is the world ending with a whimper. Zarathustra must continue to accept that all is illusion but may be given value by acts of zestful creation. We cannot wait for value to descend again from heaven, for there is no heaven, no 'back world' as Nietzsche calls it.

The overman will not react against what he observes, will not make things in his own image, 'purify' them or confer spirituality upon them in the Platonic or neo-Platonic fashion. These are the all-too-human ways that our race has followed and they are obsolescent now. As a matter of fact Zarathustra started in Part One fully aware of the death of God and consequently of nihilism, but he has still been surprised now and then by the ignorance and cowardice of others. Throughout *Zarathustra* he learns as he teaches.

At this point it is possible that someone will believe, as the Nietzsche critic F. A. Lea has believed, that Nietzsche's doctrine may be reconciled up to a point with the gospels.[35] Nietzsche was convinced, on the contrary, that Jesus, in filling the world with His love, ignored realities. Jesus simply, if uniquely, replaced reality by His love. Thus he did not distinguish the qualities of people and things: all were weak and lovable. Nietzsche believed that Jesus initially found the world so intolerably vile that he was constrained to replace it by 'a merely "inner" world, a "real" world, an "eternal" world ... "The kingdom of God *is within you* ..." '.[36] The overman will be the supreme Antichrist because he will gladly give everything its due. Hostility, for instance, will remain hostility in his eyes. The aggressor will remain an aggressor and not be robbed of his aggression by the spirit of love.

Shortly after leaving the prophet, Zarathustra meets two kings driving before them a laden ass. The kings are the principle of social hierarchy and the belief in customary morality. They represent nobility in the sense of high rank and honourable ways as opposed to social climbing, money-making and other such pursuits of the rabble. Zarathustra finds the kings amusing and artless in their futile contempt for democratic assumptions. However, they are undoubtedly higher men, since they desiderate a noble society and quite accurately perceive some of the faults of our time. (Here, it will be appreciated, is a marked difference between Nietzsche and Yeats, for the latter, as we have seen, was a venerator of the highborn. Lady Gregory was 'regal' in this outmoded fashion.) Earlier the prophet rather cheekily announced that he would make his way to Zarathustra's cave and await Zarathustra's return at the end of the day. Now Zarathustra invites the kings, together with their ass (whose significance we shall later discuss), to wait for him in the same place, and this they are eager to do.

As the wanderer goes on his way he accidentally treads on a man lying camouflaged on the swampy ground. This is the 'man with the leeches' or, preferably, the 'conscientious man of the spirit'. 'Better to know nothing than half-know many things', he declares.[37] He is an impartial, scientific truth-seeker. The trouble with him is that he sacrifices his life for the sake of objective truth, never realising that such truth is only a perspective. Hence the leeches, which suck away his life-blood. Nevertheless this conscientious fellow is another higher man, for he despises propaganda, partiality, slipshod work and other barriers to science. He too stands above the mob, for all his grovelling in the mud, and is accordingly invited to Zarathustra's cave.

The sorcerer whom Zarathustra next encounters is, qua higher man, something of a puzzle at first. He wails at length about the torments that afflict him and calls God the 'cruellest huntsman' and the 'Hangman-god'.[38] Zarathustra is understandably disgusted with this man, but shortly comes to realise that the man seeks greatness by feigning pains he does not feel (which Nietzsche, after his earlier hero-worship of Wagner, came to believe to be Wagner's procedure). The sorcerer equates a certain brand of suffering with greatness and does not appreciate that while suffering is unavoidable it is, so to speak, 'nothing to boast of'. To be miserable even in a good cause, as a martyr may be, is not in itself a mark of greatness. And indeed 'greatness', according to Zarathustra, is *passé* as a concept.

Just the same, the sorcerer most earnestly wishes to be regarded as 'great': he fakes greatness because he is enough of a higher man to wish to be great. Gilles Deleuze, in his exceptionally illuminating *Nietzsche and Philosophy*, says that the sorcerer is the 'falsely tragic one',[39] which he evidently is, but for him to want to be tragic or to want to be thought tragic is a promising sign. At least it removes him from the mob, and one quality these higher men have in common is contempt for mediocrity and a longing for man to be surpassed. The sorcerer eventually confesses his spuriousness and says he also seeks Zarathustra. Consequently the sorcerer, too, is invited to the cave.

A man with a haggard face whom Zarathustra now finds sitting beside the path is the old pope who knows that God is dead but cannot let Him depart. It has always puzzled the old pope that God both loved man and judged him, for that is an impossible confluence of attitudes. It is no good our saying that by definition God can do it, since that means we must believe in an unbelievable God. The old pope has witnessed the whole process of Christianity from its beginning to the present day, and cannot shake it off. This man genuinely loved God, while the multitude merely pretended to do so or followed one another like cattle. Nevertheless the pope knows that a perfect God of love would perforce love 'beyond reward and punishment'.[40]

Towards the end of the great cycle of the Church the old pope grew disillusioned with Christianity, but did so as a loyal old retainer grows disillusioned with his master. It is his virtue as a higher man that he still needs a master and he accepts Zarathustra in this role, since Zarathustra is the most pious and godly of men. This is the point: Zarathustra wants the overman because he is too godly to be satisfied with man.

Zarathustra next enters the barren valley called 'Serpent's Death' where dwells an abominable man so ugly that Zarathustra is ashamed to look at him. This, the ugliest man, is the murderer of God, who now suffers unendurably not from the hatred of men but from their pity. However, he knows that pity is a vice, not a virtue: it is 'contrary to modesty'.[41] This monster of ugliness killed

God because God saw into his best-concealed corners, observed all his disgusting ways. So the man put himself in God's place and now hates himself as much as ever, because he knows that he is not remotely worthy of the place of God. Naturally he too seeks Zarathustra and consequently the overman who will relieve his guilt.

Shortly afterwards Zarathustra beholds a herd of cows in the midst of which, addressing the beasts, is the voluntary beggar. 'If we do not alter and become as cows,' declares this man, 'we shall not enter into the kingdom of heaven.'[42] Even this amiable idiot is a higher man, and not such an idiot either, for the antecedent of his belief was that he sought the kingdom of heaven on earth among the poor, only to find the poor no better than the rich. He is a Tolstoyan figure who has turned away from mankind altogether and now finds some solace among the innocent cows because they are at least incapable of greed, malice and pride.

Zarathustra seems to have met a fair variety of higher men, perhaps all the main types that manifest themselves in our time, but there is one remaining: his own shadow. The shadow may be thought of as a caricature of Zarathustra, or as his weakness. The shadow says, like Ivan Karamazov, 'Nothing is true, everything is permitted.'[43] He is roughly what some even quite thoughtful people still think Nietzsche meant by the overman: that is, a non-moral exploiter and mocker of his fellows. Yet this shadow is far from cheerful and the truth is that he is so composed of doubt that he has lost his function and goal. He doubts that he will ever find a function again. He is free to the point of emptiness. Zarathustra has the most important purpose of envisaging and preparing the ground for the *Übermensch*. Consequently the shadow, likewise, ought never to doubt that mankind will be superseded.

Finally in this catalogue of higher men we should return to the ass which the two kings drive before them, since this animal too is a caricature, not of Zarathustra but of the overman himself. The ass is this because it says 'Yes', or rather 'Ye-a', to everything. To understand the matter we must grasp what is essentially wrong with all the higher men and therefore (it goes without saying) with everyone else, everyone lower and undistinguished. What is wrong, in a word, is that they all see life as a *sphere to be solved and mastered*. They, like all the rest, want to be 'spared', says Zarathustra,[44] meaning that their attitudes are nostrums. They want to 'correct' life in order to match it to their own misshapen souls. That is why Zarathustra tells them (in a kindly enough fashion) 'And there is hidden mob in you too'.[45]

Even these higher men, striving with all their might to be heroes of culture, science or religion, are convinced that they or their progeny might, as it were, come out on top, having disciplined the world or distanced themselves from it. They are desperate now, it is true, and hence their delight when Zarathustra arrives. He will surely have the answer. But Zarathustra's answer is different from what any of them expected. From section eleven, 'The Greeting', to the penultimate section Zarathustra utters his final message to the higher men. Finally, in section twenty, 'The Sign', Zarathustra declares (to himself) that *his* day, his phase of the world, is beginning. A few elements of Zarathustra's discourse should be mentioned here, for they show how the projected *Übermensch* resembles Rilke's Angels.

Following Zarathustra a new breed of men, 'laughing lions', will come at some stage. Presumably these will be precursors of the overman and indicate what manner of individual he will be. A laughing lion is a man as natural and instinctual as a lion, who also treats everything, death included, joyfully. His laughter will be euphoric, not sneering, or when there is mockery, it will be entirely good-natured.

So Rilke's assumptions about animals, that they have 'God in front' and 'decease perpetually behind', apply to the overman as well. A lion is never afraid, one assumes, and is never joyful either, but the overman will combine fearlessness and joy. He will have the utter 'belongingness' of a lion in its habitat and Olympian playfulness into the bargain. The overman will in this way surpass not just our evasive modern ways, but even the sphere of tragedy as we encounter it in the ancients. He will be Dionysian: that is, one possessed of tragic joy. He will delight in tragic reality, delight in the given world, whereas even the grimmest of dramatic tragedies is a mode of 'making the best of things', a mode of solace.

To proceed from our present plight towards the advent of the overman, the higher men must acknowledge the abyss of nihilism and 'master it with pride', says Zarathustra. They must be prepared for great suffering and be honest at all costs. More important still, the higher men must shake off the 'spirit of gravity' which has beset their kind down the centuries and learn to 'dance': that is, to move physically and mentally in a sprightly manner. They must similarly learn to play with reality as though it were a game of dice; to be happy, uncaring gamblers.

There are possible misunderstandings, of course, one of which is typically the ass's error. The ass says 'Ye-a' to everything, which sounds admirably affirmative. But it is vital to say 'No' to some things, for example the things the higher men have always stood for: solemn striving, self-betterment, the ennobling effects of suffering, idolatries of all kinds. So the overman will be supremely but not universally affirmative. He will affirm everything natural but turn aside from consolatory attitudes, including tragedy when its ulterior motive is consolation. Another mistake is to assume that the higher men must abjure science. On the contrary, science at its best, its most purely empirical, is precisely not a form of consolation but a way in which man's courage conquers his fears. Science proper, devoted to nothing but knowledge, is vital, not because it is 'objective' but because it is courageous.

At the conclusion of these 'lectures' by Zarathustra the ugliest man declares: 'I am content for the first time to have lived my whole life.'[46] He continues by saying that now he is willing not only to die but to live his entire wretched life over again. At least for the moment he wills eternal return, or comes near to doing so. As I have mentioned earlier, we cannot here begin to do justice to the thought of eternal return, but for the purpose of comparing Rilke with Nietzsche we must bring into focus a view of human life which is at once a rough approximation to Nietzsche's insight and the way of the Angels. (The overman should be defined simply as the one who will live in the sure knowledge of eternal return.)

We ourselves stand in the moment, in every moment. The right manner of life is not to try to stand aside from the moment spectatorially but to take possession of the moment enthusiastically. The moment means the exact instant, not the general historical phase, though an infinity of past time, including what we classify and interpret as 'history', bears down upon each of us in the present. This has always been man's case, but never has he managed to face the instant without taking revenge for past griefs and humiliations. However, says Nietzsche, we cannot actually 'will backwards', or compensate in the present for old pains. Attempts at such compensation constitute all history and culture, for we have constantly tried to alter the past by our present (supposedly forward-looking) activities.

In Part Three of *Thus Spoke Zarathustra*, in the section called 'Of the Vision and the Riddle', Zarathustra fancies he sees a young shepherd writhing on the ground with a black snake hanging out of his mouth. The snake is the past which is choking the shepherd. Zarathustra cries out that the shepherd must bite off the snake's head, and this the shepherd does, to rise up no longer a mere man but a transformed, ecstatic being. We should aim to do likewise, or rather we should do it, at once. The past is not to be disowned, forgotten or palliated, for these are the procedures that choke us. On the contrary, the past must be wholly accepted, not just as that which happened but as that which we willed to happen. For unless we welcome the past (however hideous and however far removed from our personal liabilities it might be) we cannot welcome the present. The present, whatever it is, is a consequence of the past, all the past, including the repulsive parts. (Of course this is another kind of 'willing backwards', but a healthy kind.)

The black snake causing our convulsions is the guilt-ridden and vengeful presence of the past in the present. If we wholly accepted the past we could concentrate on creating the present afresh. Note: the past would not then have been cast aside; it would still be within us, as the headless body of the snake is within the shepherd. This is not a doctrine of wiping the slate. It is a doctrine of ceasing to feel either guilty or injured – even if we are 'guilty' or injured (as we obviously may be in a technical sense). Nevertheless, feeling guilty is also a way of clinging to the past, it is unadventurous and asphyxiating too. The new way that Nietzsche is recommending would not be 'happy', in the sense of painless, and indeed to dream of a painless future is just consolatory. The new way would be joyful and painful and, above all, *tragic* in the fullest sense, the sense in which man is rooted to the earth.

Insofar as this is eternal return Nietzsche means that man in such a guiltless, tragic, joyful spirit would be so in love with all vicissitudes (not fighting off the disagreeable ones) that he would make each moment afresh. Thus what would eternally return would be an unprecedented sort of positive creativity. (Up to now our procedures have been at best reactively creative or at worst mere slavish habit.) Therefore in such an admirable condition man would make a truly fresh future rather than a future which seeks to make up for the past and so drearily repeats the past. The point is that the future is bound to be a consequence of the past in any case, for, as Heidegger puts it:

If you allow your existence to drift in timorousness and

ignorance, with all the consequences these things have, then they will come again, and they will be that which already was. And if on the contrary you shape something supreme out of the next moment, as out of every moment, and if you note well and retain the consequences, then this moment will come again and will have been what already was. [47]

These words suggest to us the *modus vivendi* of both Rilke's Angels and the overman. Nevertheless there is an important difference between the two. If we accept the sequence prehistory, history and post-history, the overman will belong to the last. Angels, however, stand apart from history altogether and so differ from the overman even as they resemble him.

4
Mann: Beyond Good and Evil

The greatest souls are capable of the greatest vices, as well as the greatest virtues.

Descartes

In Mann's *The Tales of Jacob*, the first volume of *Joseph and His Brothers*, God is expressly regarded as beyond good and evil. The Prelude, 'Descent into Hell', is an account of biblical cosmology according to which, Mann states, there were in the beginning God Himself, soul and matter. Soul was the 'primevally human', and so for the purpose of reading the Joseph novels rightly we should imagine that some indescribable sort of human potential, some 'human stuff', existed before any species of plant or creature. Soul came to wish to impart form to matter, which was originally formless: 'the earth was without form and void', as we are told in Genesis. But the efforts of soul were futile until God sent spirit to act as soul's artificer and champion.

Now the sending of spirit was hotly opposed by God's entourage, the angels. They were hostile to God's creative plans, which is as much as to say that the angels, being immaculate, were hostile to creativity itself. That is the point: the purely good do not create and the act of creation is a worldly, as distinct from a heavenly, process. Creating means 'doing evil', as we say, for it is no more than a mode of living, in other words sinning. But the finished condition of angelic goodness is inevitably non-creative. For perfect goodness does not become or grow: it simply is, and is therefore altogether apart from existence and alien to worldly man.

Even so, God rises above goodness, even as he rises above sin. God made our world for a purpose:

He created the world; that is to say, by way of assisting the primitive human being He brought forth solid and permanent forms, in order that the soul might gratify physical desires upon these and engender man.[1]

79

Truly our place is not this world, for we belong with God, yet since we are here we ought at best to create. To create is not to escape from evil, but to do evil, and in the final analysis there is no better human alternative. God knows that we create as part of our worldly inheritance, though creation is distinct from goodness and opposed to it. Only God creates without sin, because God towers above sin. He is not simply good but soars over moral distinctions. When we fight against sin God Himself is not involved in the combat, for, after all, sin is merely our condition. In the eyes of God our world is a lively drama of good and bad and death, but it is not the be-all and end-all.

Mann emphasises that God Himself is the All.

> He was not the Good, but the All. And He was holy! Holy not because of goodness, but of life and excess of life; holy in majesty and terror, sinister, dangerous, and deadly, so that an omission, an error, the smallest negligence in one's bearing to Him, might have frightful consequences.[2]

This is, certainly, the God of Abraham, but if we remark that God's countenance changes in the course of the Bible and is far kindlier after the birth of Jesus, we might also appreciate that God remains the All and wears a different face according to the creative will of each inventive (and pious) generation.

According to Mann the Fall was not a decline into sin but a sudden access of consciousness. Most important, *the Fall was not contrary to the will of God*.

> We can, objectively considered, speak of a 'Fall' of the soul of the primeval light-man, only by over-emphasising the moral factor. The soul, certainly, has sinned against itself, frivolously sacrificing its original blissful and peaceful state – but not against God in the sense of offending any prohibition of His in its passional enterprise, for such a prohibition, at least according to the doctrine we have received, was not issued.[3]

Sin is therefore harmful to the soul but not 'against God'. Our human sense of sin is a means (and hitherto the principal means) of giving meaning to our lives. To give meaning is an enterprise peculiar to man and constitutive of man (compare Rilke) in which God has assisted us down the ages. It follows that God transcends good and evil, for they are no more than elements in the drama He has set in motion.

But what is good and what is evil depends upon the creative spirit of the age. This is not 'moral relativism', to use the fashionable phrase, and by definition it is not nihilistic. In Mann's presentation the heroes of the Old Testament are heroes because they give new shapes to goodness and wickedness. Jacob and Joseph both work, or live, in a quasi-artistic manner to effect changes in notions of morality. Each is creative. To 'create' does not mean to devise in order to gratify one's whims but to reach out, in defiance of distractions, towards a vague and private goal. That is exactly the way of Jacob and Joseph.

For example, Joseph resists the conspicuous charms of Potiphar's wife. He regards her as taboo, not because she is married (to a eunuch, after all) but for a number of other reasons, and he would think himself lost if he yielded to her. Potiphar's wife, Mut-em-enet, is a painted, perfumed aristocrat, fawned upon since childhood by slaves and lesser concubines. Endlessly she attends to her smooth brown skin, her shining nails and her artificially bright eyes. She also lusts after Joseph, her husband's steward, with all the morbid passion of her ultra-sensual, prison-house world.

The story of Joseph's time in Potiphar's house takes up Chapters 4 to 6 of *Joseph in Egypt* (the third volume) and Mut's pursuit of him takes up chapter 6, entitled 'the Smitten One'. She is one of Mann's best realised characters, who seems to us scarcely wicked but, rather, ill-starred and degenerative, as Mann implies in the Foreword of 1948 when he speaks of his 'humanisation' of Potiphar's wife. Frenziedly she has Joseph thrown into prison after he has torn himself away from her clutches, but even this is understandable.

In fact Joseph rejects Mut for seven reasons which Mann recounts in the chapter 'Of Joseph's Chastity'. To summarise: Joseph's celebrated chastity is compounded of his sense of betrothal to God, his loyalty to Jacob and a spiritual reaction against that association of dissoluteness and death which seems to him peculiarly Egyptian. Joseph's God is of the spirit and will be betrayed if Joseph makes love to Potiphar's wife. Joseph thinks of himself as a chosen being, a man with a distinct destiny which somehow involves a reunion with Jacob. Joseph constantly waits, or even expects, to return home and thus *incidentally* helps to mould the history of all the Israelites. The fate of Israel crystallises around his personal desires. He never tells himself in so many words that his fate and that of his people are bound together, but his yearning for Jacob is in its effects a racial yearning. Joseph fulfils himself by working his way home to his people, and in so doing he consolidates the identity and history of his race.

Joseph thus says 'No' to Egyptian death and 'Yes' to Jewish life. That is why he rejects Mut: she would detain and compromise him utterly. So we gather that sin is not behaviour specifically prohibited by God but is what a creative person, an artist such as Joseph, assumes to be hateful to God. Sin is what Joseph's God deplores but not what God Himself deplores. God has no preferential view of morality. Joseph is a man of destiny because he seeks his own destiny and eschews everything that would decisively block his path. In this way the story of Joseph and Mut-em-enet illustrates what I believe to be beyond good and evil in Mann, for Mann is plainly on high, seeing the tale from beyond the moral as well as the physical confines of the characters. Nor is this simply because they are ancient Jewish characters, since it is a peculiarity of Mann, as we shall see, that he does the same with modern figures in other novels and stories. To him a composition is complete only when it synthesises good and evil.

No one in *Joseph and His Brothers* is or aspires to be good in the New Testament sense. The immaculacy of Jesus is undreamt of and the injunctions of Paul lie far in the future. It is worth noting here that in *Beyond Good and Evil* Nietzsche praises the grandeur of the Old Testament and remarks that to have 'glued' the 'small-souled' New Testament to the Old is 'perhaps the greatest audacity and "sin against the spirit" that literary Europe has on its conscience'.[4]

In Mann's version of these tales altruism is not even a theory. The admired people are those who make a law first for themselves and consequently for everyone else. The chapter called 'The Great Hoaxing' in Book Four of *The Tales of Jacob* is a plausible account of the ousting of Esau by Rebecca and Jacob. Jacob trembles with terror at the prospect of being caught out and cursed by Isaac instead of blessed, but he cares nothing about the badness of his behaviour. As readers we take self-interested tricks for granted and scarcely feel disposed to make ethical judgments. For instance, when Jacob at Laban's house finds that he has been tricked into sleeping with Leah instead of Rachel he regards Laban as a 'wolf-man', but we are given little sense of the uncle's wickedness. The story, like all the stories in this quartet of novels, is scarcely moralistic but contributes to what is, after all, a majestic comedy.

Jacob's 'virtue' in the ancient pre-moral sense, his special meritorious gift, is his capacity for musing: he associates images and ideas from widely varied (and indeed what we think of as 'opposite') spheres. But Jacob's musing leads in turn to the plainer virtue of resolution. He is thus a hero and steadfastly maintains the patriarchal line. Rachel is his chosen bride in whom his seed, which is to be as the 'dust of the earth' (Genesis), must germinate.

As for Joseph, he is profoundly self-centred. We understand why his brothers beat him and throw him into the pit, for who would not be maddened by this spoilt darling with his coat of many colours? Mann interestingly says of Joseph that he made an 'assumption that everybody loved him more than themselves'.[5] 'Piety', Mann elsewhere writes, 'is the subjectivation of the outer world, its concentration upon the self and its salvation'.[6] In this 'pious' fashion Joseph sees others as contributors to his story and perhaps sees even God as his personal God.

The father, Jacob, is a meditative man while Joseph, at least when young, is a charming self-loving exploiter of his handsomeness and cleverness. And both are ultimately determined by that natural sensuality of the Old Testament which bursts forth in 'The Song of Solomon'. For even the chaste Joseph *quite knowingly* directs his sexual impulses into spiritual channels. He deliberately 'lives a story' by which means, in the years after his marriage to Asenath as well as in the long years before, he devotes a good measure of his sexual energy to a spiritual end. Of the two men, Jacob is more obviously an artist-visionary and Joseph an artist-administrator, but both are notably creative.

The emphasis in *Joseph and His Brothers* is upon making fertile use of circumstances. The two heroes create new meanings out of their vicissitudes. Mann is never 'moral' in the usual restricted sense, the sense in which the reader is abreast of the author in knowing right from wrong. Thus the 'song of Joseph', as Mann happily calls the four united novels, may serve as our first clue to Mann's work as a whole. All along, from Hanno's love of music in *Buddenbrooks* to Leverkühn's pact with the devil in *Doctor Faustus*, Mann is of the devil's party and knows it. But he is of that persuasion not in order to defy goodness but to reach out for a greater harmony. Privately he referred to himself as 'a man of balance'. He wrote in a letter to Karl Kerényi, 'I am a man of balance. I instinctively lean to the left when the boat threatens to capsize on the right.'[7] This seems a merely reasonable attitude, but in Mann's literary practice it meant that he instinctively leaned towards bad when the boat threatened to capsize on the side of good. Clearly, though, he could not simply override goodness as a scoundrel does. Mann's moral ambivalence is one of the most conspicuous features of his works and it has been discussed a thousand times, but I do not think it has been satisfactorily defined.

In the first stage of his career, at the turn of the century, Mann inched his way towards his proper leading theme, the theme he would come to make his own. That is why the youthful masterpiece *Buddenbrooks* cannot be thoroughly understood as a tale of the decline of a prosperous bourgeois family, ending with the death of the last male heir, the sickly, music-loving Hanno. Nor should we rest content with seeing this novel as a familiar sort of contest between the overbearing world of commerce and the beautiful sphere of art. If it were such a novel the author's stance, if not his conspicuous tones, would be satirical – as *Madame Bovary* is a satire and, more crudely, *The Man of Property*.

Buddenbrooks is rightly never called a satire because it is a more honest, by which I mean a more comprehensive, study of bourgeois ways than perhaps any in that long sequence of writings by disaffected bourgeois sons and daughters. In comparison Balzac and Flaubert are plainly unfair: that is to say, morally selective. Nevertheless there can be little of importance that anyone wishes to say against the bourgeoisie that Mann has not *inadvertently* contrived to say. However, he says such things less from hostility than from a liking for facts. Later on, especially in *Doctor Faustus* but also, to a degree, in *Lotte in Weimar*, Mann sometimes overloads his works with information, while here the proportion seems right. The result is that *Buddenbrooks* impresses us as an accurate picture of north-German mercantile society in the nineteenth century.

Old Johann Buddenbrooks, for example, is a man whom Balzac, Flaubert or Zola would present as either unpleasant or misguided. And we can plainly see the traits of Johann that would have been painted blacker by another hand. Nor does Mann conceal Johann's philistinism, sharp practice, self-will and *Schadenfreude*. Yet Johann is not at all vile in the author's eyes but merely interesting, a subject to pin down. No one hostile to old Johann could see him so roundedly, and in truth the young Thomas Mann wished to come to terms with the bourgeoisie; not to yield to them but to acknowledge them completely, warts and all, and then (but only then) master them through art.

The problem for Mann was that he regarded this venture as dangerous and conceivably fatal. Earlier authors had seen nothing especially risky in assailing the bourgeoisie, and indeed such had been the sport of artists since the 1830s. On the other hand, Mann is the one major author to distance himself from the bourgeoisie out of artistic and philosophic need rather than enmity. Mann's childhood was happy and in that sense he may be said to have 'loved' his family and acquaintances whom he depicted in this first novel.[8] Therefore, while he nicely observed their so-called faults, he did not condemn these as faults. He was not, so to speak, against sin and he portrayed his family accurately because his specific *non-moral* vocation demanded that he should.

For this reason alone the artist's distancing himself from bourgeois society was apprehended by Mann as morbid and deathly. Society, whatever its failings, amounts to health and 'goodness' in the eyes of one who has been happy and socially integrated as a child. Society is a coherence and the artist, along with outlaws and other misfits, threatens that coherence. Therefore the figures in *Buddenbrooks* who fall away from society, notably Thomas and his son Hanno, are doomed. Thomas has a fatal stroke after a painful visit to the dentist. Somehow this is scarcely an accident, since his life has been deteriorating for some time: the family grain business is falling behind competitors; Thomas's mother, the Frau Consul, has died; his wife, Gerda, is involved in a suspect friendship with an infantry lieutenant; and he has come to long for easeful death in consequence of reading part of Schopenhauer's *The World as Will and Idea*. Young Hanno, after a night of enchantment at a performance of *Lohengrin* followed by a normally wretched day at school, sickens and dies of typhoid fever.

Thomas and Hanno die because in moving away from society they disintegrate. Society is not only a coherence of individuals but cohesive for each individual. He is mentally and morally intact to the extent that he is a member of the group. But to pursue truth one must separate oneself from the group, since social morality and truthfulness are not the same, are hardly even neighbours. Mann's picture of Lübeck society in the nineteenth century, I repeat, appears to us accurate and reasonably comprehensive, in other words a product of yea-saying; but in order to produce that picture he needed to hold himself aloof.

To Mann the Buddenbrook faults were venial while damnable vices boiled down to one vice: coldly exploiting the social group or, alternatively, the very same 'noble objectivity' which Rilke found in *Buddenbrooks*.[9] That, however, is a narrow view of the matter. Comprehensively speaking, whatever threatens the social citadel is immoral. The threat varies in relation to the historical nature of the citadel, but he who stands outside its walls is the immoral one. He may be calmly exploitative or wild and reckless; all that counts is the wilful self-exclusion. But at this stage of his career Mann was concerned in a limited fashion with the goodness of the bour-geoisie and the badness of straying from them.

Such is the significance of Tonio Kröger's celebrated declaration of regard for his social class in the novella that bears his name. *Tonio Kröger* was published in *Tristan*, two years after *Buddenbrooks*, and here Mann frankly confronted his own problem for the first time. Tonio confides to Lisabeta Ivanovna, his Russian painter friend, his belief that the artist must stand apart from the rest of humanity.

> The artist must be unhuman, extra-human; he must stand in a queer aloof relationship to our humanity; only so is he in a position, I ought to say only so would he be tempted, to represent it, to present it, to portray it to good effect.[10]

When Tonio has finished his lengthy self-analysis Lisabeta rather depressingly tells him that he is a 'bourgeois *manqué*'. At the close of the story Tonio confirms her observation. He is 'an artist with a bad conscience'. He writes to her as follows:

> I stand between two worlds. I am at home in neither, and I suffer in consequence. You artists call me a *bourgeois*, and the *bourgeois* try to arrest me . . . I don't know which makes me feel worse. The *bourgeois* are stupid; but you adorers of the beautiful, who call me phlegmatic and without aspirations, you ought to realize that there is a way of being an artist that goes so deep and is so much a matter of origins and destinies that no longing seems to it sweeter and more worth knowing than longing after the bliss of the commonplace.[11]

Ordinarily a good artist is not bourgeois, whatever the social class of his upbringing, and for that very reason he misrepresents bourgeois people. He does so ignorantly and with a clear conscience. He identifies with his feelings about the bourgeois, not with their feelings about themselves. Thus the normally experienced reality of small-town Normandy in the mid-nineteenth century must have been qualitatively different from Flaubert's portrait in *Madame Bovary*, which is of course the height of 'realism'. Such a manner of life felt otherwise to the actual doctors and chemists and dreaming housewives. But Mann wanted to feel as a bourgeois feels. Flaubert empathised with Emma Bovary, but only because she was a figure devised out of his own passive and dreaming personality. Conversely Mann wished to 'go out of himself' in order to see the world through the eyes of a Thomas Buddenbrook, for instance. In *Tonio Kröger* he apprehends this aspiration, this longing indeed, as the root of his capacity as an artist. It is an irremovable trait, essential to his artistry. For all that, his vocation as an artist estranges him from the non-artistic community. However, Mann evidently senses the 'damnable' possibilities of his vocation, for it cuts him off from the legions of the good, the unquestioning bourgeoisie. 'Damnation', let us keep in mind, has to do with being rejected, exiled.

Here it is probably necessary to emphasise two points. First, the usual estimate of the bourgeoisie as narrow, unimaginative, complacent and so on should be resisted in this context. I mean simply that bourgeois people naturally provide a positive criterion for anyone happily brought up in their midst. Second, it will today be easy for many readers to view Mann's creative dilemma as obsolescent. But the point is that there is always an orthodoxy of attitudes and behaviour, even when it takes the form of widespread tolerance, for then control and discipline edge towards the wicked side. So far Mann has recognised the orthodoxy of bourgeois customs, while later he concentrates on the orthodoxy of faith in beneficent progress. He is dialectical as a matter of course; his nature demands that he takes the antithesis into account, not sparingly but with enthusiasm. Nevertheless, let us note here a point that must be developed later: utter crassness, Nazi crassness, the assumption that louts should sweep aside creative intelligence (albeit wicked creative intelligence) never enters Mann's public writing and enters the diaries and letters only for the purpose of being dismissed as self-evident nonsense.

Death in Venice, which Mann referred to as 'next of kin' to *Tonio Kröger* in terms of 'youthful lyric bloom',[12] strikes a different note, however, from the earlier writings in that civilised values of a subtle sort are themselves now set in place as mere attitudes by means of which we manage our lives. They have no higher sanction and no surer foundation. They are not remotely 'true' and match our experience only to the extent that we fearfully or cannily fail to experience whatever would contradict them. Here is an important development in Mann's career. To begin with he saw the principal opposition as between social and family order on the one hand and art, specifically music, on the other: the socio-moral, that is to say, versus the beauty which the socio-moral tends to exclude. But now, at the stage of *Death in Venice*, art occupies the positive pole while ranged against it are nothing less than bestiality and putrefaction. Aschenbach's nightmare is composed of foul animal forms.

> His senses reeled in the steam of panting bodies, the acrid stench from the goats, the odour as of stagnant waters – and another, too familiar smell – of wounds, uncleanness and disease. . . . But now the dreamer was in them and of them, the stranger god was his own. Yes, it was he who was flinging himself upon the animals, who bit and tore and swallowed smoking gobbets of flesh – while on the trampled moss there now began the rites in honour of the god, an orgy of promiscuous embraces – and in his very soul he tasted the bestial degradation of his fall.[13]

Mann thus implies that Aschenbach's writing, especially in its later phase, has held at bay the slobbering, slavering, rank and fleshly chaos of the natural. In this way Aschenbach has merely behaved humanly, since human beings must sublimate their instincts and art is an elaborate mode of sublimation. Nevertheless, art at its best concedes the precariousness of its accomplishment. Shakespeare does this in the figure of Caliban and in *Titus Andronicus*, *Measure for Measure* and *King Lear*, to mention the plainest instances. The Greek dramatists were obviously aware of chaos, as were Homer, Dante and Goethe. Indeed such awareness at its keenest might well be the touchstone of the best literature.

Throughout his career Aschenbach has seemed to face this great challenge. Up to middle age he treated of 'the heroism born of weakness',[14] the emblem of which is Sebastian with the arrows piercing his flesh. In that phase Aschenbach venerated a heroism of knowledge that defies, or even destroys, the simpler, stupider heroism of faith. But in middle age he 'made a right-about-face',[15] having concluded that knowledge blunts the 'noble and active mind'.[16] It is not clear whether Mann himself, Mann the ironic narrator, regards this conclusion as necessarily an error. He comments upon it as follows:

> And yet: this moral fibre surviving the hampering and disinte- grating effect of knowledge, does it not result in a dangerous simplification, in a tendency to equate the world and the human soul, and thus to strengthen the hold of the evil, the forbidden and the ethically impossible?[17]

On the face of it, then, Aschenbach first pursued knowledge but abandoned that pursuit on the grounds that it blunts the noble and active mind. Were those grounds false? Three of Mann's teachers, Goethe, Nietzsche and Freud, would all have declared them to be so. Nietzsche writes in *The Gay Science* of 'the great passion of the seeker after knowledge who lives and must live continually in the thundercloud of the highest problems and the heaviest respon- sibilities'.[18] Such a passion might confound the mind, even to the point of madness, but would scarcely blunt it.

What it seems we should read into *Death in Venice* is as follows: Aschenbach was first on the right track, or he would have been if he had valued knowledge more than the heroism involved in obtaining it. But in fact at all stages of his much-honoured career he valued effort for its own sake. Not effort for the sake of knowledge or, later, effort to keep knowledge at bay, but effort as sufficient unto itself, as the *way*. It is this way that leads to the disintegration: to the mortuary chapel in Munich, the vexations en route to the hotel in Venice and, supremely, Tadzio, the beautiful boy, and the epidemic of Asian cholera. (These and other incidents of the story all took place, exactly as Mann describes them, in 1911 when he, his wife and Heinrich Mann spent some time in Venice.[19])

It is clear that Aschenbach's ethic of struggle has been not excessive, but finally and for all the intelligence involved in it, *blind*. Aschenbach youthfully turned himself into a hero in defiance of his frail constitution. To be exact, he fashioned a sort of heroism out of his own unheroic nervous system. Therefore, since his doctrine has been one of effort, his fate, his form of corruption, turns out to be a yielding, even to death. This seems to be psychologically valid, but for our purposes it chiefly demonstrates that the infamy of an individual, or a society, or an entire civilisation, is whatever the chosen virtue rejects. Thus the infamy of a martial epoch is shame or dishonour; the infamy of a compassionate age is, of course, callousness. To Aschenbach the virtue is self-control and the vice self-abandonment. Mann was by now reaching our for completeness, a Goethean objective, a manner of writing that should encompass pro and contra, high and low – as good and as evil as he could artistically embrace.

The novel in which he does this most explicitly is not in fact *Doctor Faustus* but *The Magic Mountain*. The latter is a novel of ideas and is perhaps supreme in that admittedly sparse category. What makes it supreme – if I am not overpraising it – is that the ideas are exceptionally well formulated, and at the same time permeate the narrative and sensuous particulars of the work. The ideas and the concrete details do not merely overlap but interfuse. And of course the novel is full-blooded: ideas are made flesh. The 'talkers', as Mann called them, Settembrini and Naphta, are memorably men of ideas, while the personalities of others, especially Clavdia Chauchat and Pieter Peeperkorn, imply that ideas are always inferior and derivative. Mme Chauchat is one of the most palpable people in modern fiction, a Slavonic refutation of all theory, all idealism.

As must be well known, the title of this novel and its fundamental argument are Nietzsche's. The philosopher writes as follows in *The Birth of Tragedy*:

> If heroes like Goethe and Schiller could not succeed in breaking open the enchanted gate which leads into the Hellenic magic mountain; if with their most daunting striving they could not go beyond the longing gaze which Goethe's Iphigenia casts from barbaric Tauris to her home across the ocean, what could the epigones of such heroes hope for – unless, amid the mystic tones of reawakened tragic music, the gate should open for them suddenly of its own accord, from an entirely different side, quite overlooked in all previous cultural endeavours.[20]

Briefly, in writing the novel Mann referred to the Hellenic magic mountain which he believed, following Nietzsche, to have been formed by the Apollonian containment of Dionysian forces. I should say 'the bare containment' or even 'the apparent containment', for Nietzsche remarks that 'In the total effect of tragedy the

Dionysian predominates once again.'[21] Then, *The Birth of Tragedy* closes with the mention of a dream of Ionic colonnades and harmonious people whom the dreamer recognises and declares to be venerators of Dionysus – pretty much Hans Castorp's dream in Chapter 6, 'Snow'.

The fundamental argument of *The Magic Mountain* is that the world has for long enough exhibited two forces ranged against each other. This antagonism may be labelled as enlightenment and progress versus blood and terror. Most of the reasoning one hears is naturally for the first force, since the second is by definition irrational. Nevertheless the second seems to be the only means of reinforcing a dualism of body and spirit for which many people yearn. Let us look at this opposition in a little more detail.

Settembrini is a monist who argues with unrivalled lucidity that man is the apogee of nature, that he is what millions of cosmic years have worked up to. To be precise, man's rational spirit holds that place in the scheme of things, and when we shake off the detritus of the past, nature will be as it were fulfilled. Thus man and nature, spirit and flesh, will *properly* come together in man at his harmonious best.

Settembrini's conversation is, according to him (and we must agree), 'plastic': that is, he moulds his raw material elegantly. The world is his material and so he sees the world itself as manipulable. Nevertheless, death is 'the inviolable condition of life'[22] and man's spirit must (after the manner of Socrates) accept that fact. But disease and pain are errors to be eradicated. Certainly, says Settembrini, he prefers 'an intelligent ailing person to a consumptive idiot',[23] and Hans Castorp (who is at this stage becoming something of a pupil) should have no truck with the view that disease has dignity, a view which 'comes down to us from a past seething with superstition'.[24] It is now our noble task to steer mankind away from the superstitious ages. Much later the humanist tells Hans that 'Disease and despair are often only forms of depravity.'[25] Health of mind and body is morally right, while sickness is, to a degree, moral as well as physical degeneration. Analysis of all kinds, physiological and psychological, can be on the one hand an 'instrument of enlightenment' and on the other hand a practice 'allied to the grave and its unsavoury anatomy'.[26]

This superb talker is a member of the International League for the Organisation of Progress, whose members are compiling a massive work entitled *The Sociology of Suffering*. In his diary Mann called Settembrini's exposition at this point a 'comic bit of rationalism',[27] as indeed it is, but the comedy lies in the assured exposition of what many people hesitantly think. Settembrini believes that 'almost all individual suffering is due to disease of the social organism'.[28] In general the League exists to aid individuals towards self-realisation, and that is also Settembrini's vocation. One bad feature of the Berghof, he remarks, is that there is 'too much Asia' there, too many 'Muscovite and Mongolian types'[29] caught in the toils of nature, unlike Europeans to whom the natural scale is subordinate.

Such faith in progress seems facile to us (the period of the novel is 1907 to 1914) but, nevertheless, Settembrini voices no more than the unspoken and unexamined assumptions of modern man. His creed is the post-Renaissance thesis, the good of the post-Renaissance world. It was Mann's intention that readers would find it all mildly absurd, and so they do, but only a tiny number of people have any alternative understanding of their lives. Mann himself outside the realm of fiction made similar assumptions. Nor is Settembrini shallow: he merely has greater faith (and far greater articulacy) than one normally encounters. Take away the residual belief in progress and for many despair must follow. Indeed, that is fitfully happening even now, the world over.

However, *The Magic Mountain* is celebrated for its clash and variety of philosophies, so that Settembrini's is only the good which Mann seeks to qualify. It is qualified, first, by the boisterous scientism of Hofrat Behrens, to whom life is *'une destruction organique'*. 'Living', he says, 'consists in dying' (a somewhat Rilkean conception arrived at via biochemistry).[30] Alternatively, according to Mynheer Peeperkorn, the retired Dutch tea-planter for whom the author's own partiality was, he supposed, plain for all to see,[31] life is a 'sprawling female with swelling breasts close to each other, great soft belly between her haunches, slender arms, bulging thighs, half-closed eyes'.[32] To Peeperkorn life is to be *taken*, and taken emotionally. There is, certainly, something anciently noble and as it were 'extra-moral' about this figure.

No doubt it is incorrect to speak of Clavdia Chauchat as having a 'philosophy', for she is too lazy, indifferent and (shrewdly) unintellectual for that. Nevertheless, her 'anti-philosophy' is a sub-variant of Peeperkorn's stance. She moves between amused contempt for European mores (in fact for social reality as a whole) and esteem for a hero when she meets one. For long enough she appears nihilistic, then her dignified comportment with Peeper-korn, her 'protector', and with Hans Castorp, her young admirer, discloses certain undefined values of her own.

But the starkest challenge to Settembrini's faith is the faith of Naphta. In the sixteenth century Naphta's way would have seemed to many terrifyingly right, one 'extreme' of Christianity, of course, but scarcely an error or a brutality. At that time Settembrini's ideas would have seemed blasphemously wrong. In our time the positions have been reversed and Naphta is the bad one. He enters the novel only in Chapter 6, about halfway through, and from then until his suicide after the abortive pistol duel with Settembrini he is the antagonist. Naphta's beliefs are calculatedly a demolition of optimism, even though he is a Marxist as well as a Jesuit. Mann has found the perfect antithesis: this exquisitely clever, malign man who keeps an ugly fourteenth-century pietà in his room; who wishes to hurt people as a means of saving them; and who regards the historical function of the proletariat as the shedding of bourgeois blood, the striking of terror into bourgeois hearts for the purpose of reminding them of the human separation from God. Naphta is literally a terrorist and is thoroughly modern in that sense. For some of our contemporary terrorists, especially the more intelligent specimens in Germany, see their activities not simply as means to a better society but as spurs to the soul of listless modern man. Naphta is also a confirmed dualist who regards God, the ultimate reality, as forever removed from our discernible realities. He believes, therefore, that 'Whatever profits man, that is the truth',[33] meaning that scientific truths of nature are of no account, since they take us no further towards salvation.

Settembrini is intellectually inferior to Naphta, and also more likeable. Naphta is distasteful but fascinating. Settembrini exemplifies and mildly travesties the good of modern ethics. I do not mean ethics as propounded by philosophers but rather the ethics of the market place (though the two categories overlap). Naphta exemplifies what even modern liberals with their dislike of the concept of evil nevertheless regard as evil. Mann's implication is that antitheses are artificial and mutually dependent. Settembrini and Naphta are 'extremists', Mann remarks, presumably because neither accepts the primacy of muddled, healthy living.

Both creeds are classifiably historical and therefore wrong in Mann's eyes. His synthesis seems meant to be 'a-historical', a kind of honourable attitude esteemed in classical periods and still esteemed by us today. No doubt such an attitude is in fact historical in a very wide sense, but not in the limited fashion of other characters' attitudes in *The Magic Mountain*. But above all the attitude is earthly and impressive in its utter lack of idealism. Conversely, Settembrini aims to 'improve' the earth and Naphta to intensify earth's pains. Mann has now come upon his own rightful doctrine, namely that we should, in Zarathustra's words, 'remain true to the earth'.[34]

This does not mean to be 'bad' necessarily, to be animalistic, except in the sense that one must be a human animal without any lingering Christian regret that one cannot be more purely spiritual. However, it does mean that one needs to resist narrowness – narrow perspectives and prescriptions – simply because such self-limitation is the result of contrivance. We train ourselves to be narrow, or are so trained. Thus an artless child is ignorant rather than narrow and might well be willing to widen his vision. On the other hand a Settembrini who refuses, in the modern humanist style, to acknowledge the Naphta-components of human nature (or, more precisely, regards them as atavisms to be expelled by reason) is wilfully narrow.

At the start of his career Mann resisted the narrowness of the bourgeoisie and of the usual artist's estimate of the bourgeoisie: in the nineteenth century especially it was a deliberately limited vantage-point. Next, Mann wished to know both Aschenbach's iron self-control and the chaos that Aschenbach had devoted his life to controlling. At least Mann included images of chaos. Therefore Mann was both Aschenbach and the greater-than-Aschenbach who wrote the story. By 'greater' I mean more comprehensive, more supple and accommodating. By the early twenties, at the time of writing *The Magic Mountain*, Mann succeeded in jointly appreciating the ideal of progress and the idealisation of endless suffering. *The Magic Mountain* suggests to us that both are contrived ideals, the first arising from hatred of pain and the second from love of pain. It is not clear that either alternative is better than the other, for Mann himself, through Peeperkorn and through his own good-naturedly ironic style, seems to express a 'reasonable' distaste for pain, so to speak, and a Rilke-like awareness that some sort of natural suffering is a vital ingredient of our sense of significance.

In addition, at this period Mann was sharply conscious of the nature and shortcomings of theorising. But true to dialectical form

Mann also saw what it means to disdain theorising, either in the rare manner of Peeperkorn or in the commoner manner of Clavdia Chauchat. For even Peeperkorn is faintly comic and Clavdia has her obvious faults. Mann apparently aspires to see all and therefore no sooner thinks of a principle than he thinks of an opposing principle. The most interesting illustration of this is *Lotte in Weimar*, in which even the all-embracing Goethe barely retains our sympathy in contrast to the lovable heroine, Charlotte Kestner. Up to now, however, and despite Naphta's analyses, Mann has not confronted plain destructiveness: he has not done what Shakespeare did in creating Iago.

Is Cipolla in *Mario and the Magician* 'evil' according to Mann's own criterion? I think he is, simply because the magician appears to be the complete nihilist. That is, he aspires to station himself apart from the creature manifold of the world and bring about general desiccation. His desire is to make the organic inorganic. Is he therefore God's antagonist, even as God is contemplated in the Joseph novels? If he is, then, miraculously, he is a fragment of God antagonistic to the whole. He is a worm of loveless opposition, and yet even this annihilating worm is a piece of the all-embracing God. Here is Nietzsche's comment on what I take to be the type of Cipolla.

> *The perfect nihilist* – The nihilist's eye idealizes in the direction of ugliness and is unfaithful to his memories: it allows them to drop, lose their leaves; it does not guard them against the corpselike pallor that weakness pours out over what is distant and gone. And what he does not do for himself, he also does not do for the whole past of mankind: he lets it drop.[35]

What Nietzsche means is this: the nihilist forgets the good bits of his life; he lets his joyful memories go as a tree loses its leaves. Then a blight spreads over his past and it is all a desert. Likewise he drains history of richness, making it a parched and pallid tract.

So far as we can judge, Cipolla is in this way composed of rejection. He sees little in the world except that which he can bend to his will. But his will also is empty: it is a purposeless instrument. Cipolla does not even attempt to be attractive, as if he wants his audience to 'see through' the snares of charm and beauty. He is hunchbacked and his manner is cross-grained, sneeringly proud and self-satisfied. He has broken, saw-edged teeth and a metallic voice.

Just as some ugly persons seem determined to deny beauty, Cipolla wishes to make everything base by in no way modifying or concealing his own baseness. In effect he declares to the audience: 'I shall bring every one of you down to my level, but there demonstrate the superiority of my will.' Thus if a member of the audience has a touch of style or seems to depend upon a sentiment (say of patriotism) or, as in the case of Mario, is actually and fervently in love, Cipolla reveals the superficiality of the enhancing feature. What he seems to demonstrate is that all are fundamentally equal and *therefore of no value*. Mario's beloved Silvestra is merely flesh and blood, as is the foul Cipolla himself. Cipolla brings out the nihilism inherent in the ideal of equality.

At this point it is necessary to ask how far in both Mann and Nietzsche evil and nihilism are equated. In Nietzsche evil is historical and the term has a clear etymology. The notion of evil was invented by priests speaking on behalf of their slave-peoples to combat aristocratic oppressors. Thus evil is the quality of a master seen from the point of view of a slave. The slave himself is good simply and solely because he is the reverse of an evil master. On the other hand, part of what Nietzsche meant by nihilism is the denial of differentiating values. No one is more valuable than anyone else; that is one aspect of the nihilistic attitude. It is clearly connected with the slave's apprehension of himself as good. All slaves are equally good (equally beloved of God) and even the evil masters might congregate on the slave-plateau, if only they would shed their pretensions to superiority.

To Nietzsche what is undesirable (to put is mildly) is precisely nihilism. Nevertheless nihilism is the modern norm and had better be positively welcomed by higher men as the soil in which a revaluation of values might germinate. The old values are dead or dying and may not be reinvigorated: therefore, sooner or later, new prophets will light upon new (and more fully) human standards. As for evil, that old priestly valuation had better be discarded as we come increasingly to recognise that it was and is merely a way of rejecting whatever cannot be creatively absorbed. In the past the hiving-off, the rejection, was itself a creative act, but now the act is repetitious and sterile.

Conversely, in Thomas Mann there seems to be what we might call a 'creative confusion' between evil and nihilism. Perhaps indeed the two terms are thoroughly equated. If in Mann evil is assimilated to nihilism then perhaps he should be seen as undertaking the revaluation of values that Nietzsche heralded. To Mann evil consists in denial, exclusion, cutting out. This is plainest, perhaps, in the essay 'Goethe's *Faust*' (1938). According to Mann Goethe stands up for life through his character, Faust. Life is 'the healing creative force' (Goethe's words) to which Mephistopheles opposes the 'cold devil's fist'. Mephistopheles is specifically nihilistic, in the grandest possible sense that he wishes to end life itself, to make a barren universe. But Mephistopheles is also a projection of Goethe, expressing Goethe's own 'rebellion, denial and critical bitterness'.[36] This means, I suggest, that in Mann evil 'in itself' is purely destructive, though it may be used creatively. A creator must turn his own evil tendencies into elements of a comprehensive good. Thus Goethe's own spirit of denial would have been mere evil left to itself. To begin with it was evil, but when Goethe transferred this spirit into Mephistopheles it became an indispensable part of the good, or life-enhancing, *Faust*. Mann might be imagined giving us the following advice: 'Neither deny evil nor succumb to it, but acknowledge it and make it succumb to you.'

Goethe as Mann depicts him in *Lotte in Weimar* turns all his experiences to creative account and that is why he is capable of distressing Lotte. She is momentarily hurt and bewildered when she appreciates the complete difference between Goethe and herself: he, in a word, *passes on*, taking his experiences up into an ever-growing pattern, while she remembers and values the past for its own sake. Their youthful love affair went into *The Sorrows of Young Werther* and then Goethe proceeded to his next phase. Goethe takes every happening, every feeling, every person, and his own personality into the bargain, to be essentially mobile. There is 'nothing other than becoming', as Nietzsche says, paraphrasing Heraclitus.[37] 'Life is but change of form,' Goethe tells Lotte as they take their last ride together in his landau, 'oneness in many, permanence in change.'[38]

Goethe informs Lotte that she thinks of herself as the moth that flew into his flame, but she should understand that he himself is flame, candle and moth. Once he sacrificed her, but he continually sacrifices himself. If Lotte were to object that she never offered herself for sacrifice, he might well reply that sacrifice is all, that living is sacrificing – of self and others. Mann's Goethe exploits people, but exploits himself most of all. In Chapter 7 of *Lotte in Weimar*, which is substantially an interior monologue, Goethe reflects in his sententious way that art is not moral but ruthless; that mind is a 'product of life' in which life 'truly lives';[39] and that he has 'never heard of a crime I could not have committed'.[40]

Generally the scores of aphorisms and sentiments in this chapter betoken a supremely creative, non-moral, non-reformist, catholic Goethe, but the most notable observation from our immediate point of view is that the poet has never heard of a crime he could not have committed. This is a questionable assertion. Do we not usually suppose, for example, that Shakespeare fully understood the murders of Duncan and Desdemona but could not himself have committed them? That is, we feel that Shakespeare was too imaginative (not simply too moral) to perpetrate a gross killing. An actual killer is a lesser – a narrower, simpler-minded – sort of person. Yet Mann's Goethe means that no deed is too atrocious for him.

The truth surely is that Mann's Goethe includes the mentality of a criminal but could not be reduced to that pitch. What Mann does not reckon with here is that brutal deeds are done by people who fail adequately to imagine them. And Goethe's imagination would never falter for the duration of a planned or relished murder. Here is a measure not so much of Goethe as of our subject, Thomas Mann. His Goethian aspiration was to contain everything, but to do so only in a world of images. In such a world he could comprehend (subsume and understand) the sanguine amorality of a Felix Krull and the satanic coldness of an Adrian Leverkühn. These two characters reflect their creator in some fashion, the first light-heartedly and the second with a deadly seriousness leavened only by the narrator's scrupulous style. But the reflection in each case is of Mann's personal preoccupations and, therefore, of Mann's nature at its core.

However, Mann's private attitude towards *Confessions of Felix Krull Confidence Man* while he was continuing the forty-year-old fragment after the second world war was one of constant misgiving. He was writing a comic yarn: what a way to end a distinguished career! As early as 1948 he wrote to Erika Mann that *Felix Krull* 'consists of nothing but pranks',[41] and in 1954 he asked Erika, 'Is it right for a man to celebrate his eightieth birthday with such compromising jokes?' 'What's wanted', he continued, 'less than weary wantonness?'[42]

Yet in the thirties, in the Preface to *Stories of Three Decades*, he mentioned the existing fragment, *Felix Krull*, in much more favourable terms. It was there that he declared: '*Felix Krull*, like *Royal Highness*, is in essence the story of an artist; in it the element of the unreal and illusional passes frankly over into the criminal.'[43] A certain entry in the *Diaries* may be regarded as an amplification of the same idea.

'Art is a microscope that the artist focuses on the secrets of his own soul, and that then *reveals to men the secrets common to them all*.' [These are Tolstoy's words; Mann continues.] Very good. – *The Confidence Man*, for example, means exactly this.[44]

It appears that for two or three decades Mann was quite equable about *Felix Krull* and then, presumably because of the Nazis and the insistent question of the artist's social responsibilities, saw the work in a different light.

Thus he was often torn between his artistic aspirations and his social conscience. In *Felix Krull* he seems to assert from first to last, from Felix's opening evocation of an irresponsible golden child-hood to his adventures with Zouzou and Dona Maria Pia in Lisbon, that life might be an enchanting game. That is what Mann meant in the letter to Erika by 'weary wantonness'. But this stunted novel is not weary to us, the readers, and is it even wanton? Everyone appreciates that the comedy makes a serious point.

The serious lesson, according to T. E. Apter, is that the 'essence of the human spirit is frivolity'.[45] That does seem to get the measure of the work and yet the author apparently never realised as much. From his letters and *Diary* remarks we grasp that he did not appreciate the significance of displaying human nature as incurably feckless, histrionic and, above all, *pointless*. Mann's consistent suggestion in *Felix Krull* is not that people cover inner reality by outer show, but that every human activity above the zoological level partakes of show. It is probable that the words of Professor Kuckuck to Felix as they travel together to Lisbon convey Mann's own premiss. It is this: humankind is nothing but a form of being, and being, in turn, is purely an inconsequential develop-ment in an eternity of nothingness. Being, says Kuckuck, is an interlude between Nothingness and Nothingness.

The organic world is ephemeral and progress futility in the end.

There was progress, Kuckuck said . . . without doubt there was pro-gress from Pithecanthropus erectus to Newton and Shakespeare had been a long and definitely upward path. But as with the rest of Nature, so too in the world of men everything was always present at the same time, every condition of culture and morality, everything from the earliest to the latest, from the silliest to the wisest, from the most primitive, sodden, barbaric to the highest and most delicately evolved – all this continued to exist side by side in the world, yes, often indeed the finest became tired of itself and infatuated with the primitive and sank drunkenly into barbarism.[46]

However, such progress as this, from Pithecanthropus erectus to Newton and Shakespeare, will come to naught, since Nothingness in the sense of the inorganic is the one recurring cosmic condition. So it appears that man's concerns are pieces of fantasy, self-preserving or species-preserving devices. They might turn out to be species-destroying devices, but at all events they are no more universal than man himself. Therefore, if we fault Felix Krull for his none-too-scrupulous *joi de vivre*, we do so from a social standpoint only.

Felix samples life, knowing nothing of either despair or rapture. Quite otherwise, Adrian Leverkühn of *Doctor Faustus* reaches the depths if not the heights. So we understand not solely from his final, hideous condition but also because the devil candidly foretells Adrian's future when the pair of them have their one and only conversation. Here we must pay attention to the theme of evil in *Doctor Faustus*: that is, we must separate the evil colouring of the novel from the numerous prosaic details. *Doctor Faustus* clarifies Mann's lifelong preoccupation with the relation of good to evil and of both to the realm of art. Not surprisingly, perhaps, it is Satan who explains these relations with common sense and candour.

Leverkühn is reminded that in the early twentieth century music has fallen into a morass of technicality. It has grown aridly self-conscious, as the devil explains. 'It comes down to this, that his [the artist's] compositions are nothing more than solutions of that kind; nothing but the solving of technical puzzles. Art becomes critique.'[47] Satan offers what is needed now: 'shining, sparkling, vainglorious unreflectiveness'.[48] Art in general needs this quality, and not art alone but the whole of human life. The devil liberates, restores the ancient, pitiless euphoria. Adrian is told that the bane of the modern world is a finicking, morbid self-consciousness and a burden of duties. This condition is quite different from aesthetic regulation, which must be observed before there can be aesthetic beauty. On the other hand, moral rules inhibit life and may inhibit art.

Now what is the price to pay for the satanic life? It is easy to reply that one must be damned, but what on earth, in modern times, can be meant by that Middle English term? Leverkühn asks this pressing question and is told the simple truth. The penalty for Adrian will be emotional coldness, inability to love another. Anyone he does care for will be ruined. Adrian thinks such damnation is no great matter, since he is unloving by nature. The point seems to be that selection by the devil is either foreordained or takes place in youth, so that the apparent temptation we are now considering is just a ratification. As for eternity in hell, that ghastliest product of the priestly imagination, Adrian hopes that he will be able to free himself by a final moment of contrition. He is sceptical or inattentive when the devil tells him that he is too subtle to be contrite.

Mann is connecting creativity with the absence of love. The more one loves, the less impressive one's creations must be, though of course there are many unloving individuals who have no aspirations to creativity. Hell is the loveless sphere. To trace the subject in ordinary ethical terms, Mann means that to create in art (or science or philosophy) one must to a degree disregard the needs of others. People must be viewed as material for one's compositions or else ignorable creatures. There are echoes of Kierkegaard in Mann's attitude here and of course reflections of the entire modern world-picture, in which art, along with everything else, is in theory subordinated to ethics. But Adrian is more than a selfish genius, for he is also a sacrificial figure. Though he does not care for people, he wishes to revitalise music for the sake of the world at large. At the very end his appearance is Christlike and, as we shall see, Mann reconciles good and evil by not resisting evil. Just the same, it would be false to liken Leverkühn's non-resistance to Christ's.

It is part of Leverkühn's sacrifice that he infects himself with syphilis, in the belief or the hope, according to Zeitblom, the narrator, that such 'daemonic' intercourse will provide a 'deathly unchaining of chemical change in his nature'.[49] Zeitblom means that Adrian evidently decided to alter the chemistry of his body so as to elevate his musical talent. Nietzsche, who was Mann's main teacher in this matter, constantly associated his own achievements with sickness. In *Ecce Homo*, for instance, speaking of his production of *The Dawn* (or *Daybreak*), Nietzsche refers to 'that sweetening and spiritualization which is almost inseparably connected with an extreme poverty of blood and muscle'.[50]

As is well known, Mann supposed that he had taken the episode of Leverkühn's visit to the prostitute Esmeralda from Nietzsche's life. In February 1865 Nietzsche, then a student, went to Cologne sightseeing and, having asked a street porter to take him to a restaurant, was taken to a brothel instead. He fled in embarrassment and fear. Nietzsche recounted this incident to his fellow-student Paul Deussen and, so far as we know, said no more about it. Mann, however, concludes in the essay 'Nietzsche's Philosophy in the Light of Recent History' that Nietzsche must have returned to Cologne a year later and this time 'contracted the disease (some say deliberately, as self-punishment) which was to destroy his life but also to intensify it enormously'.[51] Now this is speculation and may well be untrue, as Nietzsche's latest biographer, Ronald Hayman, makes plain.[52] At this point Mann almost comically displays the literary man's propensity to convert supposition into solid fact.

Certainly much in Nietzsche's life and thought was important for Mann's work generally and for Mann's theme of Faustus. The novelist's admiration for Nietzsche here finds its fullest expression. But Mann's attitude is also thoroughly ambivalent, so that Leverkühn is both hero and dreadful warning. I do not imply that Leverkühn is meant to resemble Nietzsche in personality or accomplishments, which he plainly does not. Rather it is that Leverkühn puts music before ethics and Nietzsche regarded such a precedence as healthy in principle. Leverkühn is not a villain-hero in the ordinary way but one who courts evil on our behalf as well as his own. Without doubt Adrian is of heroic stature, and in truth the last chapter of *Doctor Faustus* takes us beyond good and evil in a certain sense. For there Mann's Faustus is confirmed as awe-inspiring because he has devilishly (inhumanly, mercilessly) enlarged human capacities.

Mann's argument in the essay 'Nietzsche's Philosophy in the Light of Recent History' is far cruder. He sees Nietzsche as a 'Hamlet-figure' who became 'the mouthpiece and advocate of blatant force, of the callous conscience, of Evil itself'.[53] Mann does not recognise that Nietzsche (truly like Hamlet) 'gave mankind up', as it were, because he found insufficient difference between the highest and the lowest. Mann's implication in this late essay is that we should simply accept the primacy of goodness and pursue truth, if we wish, behind that virtuous stockade. But Mann assumes that the pursuit of truth must always be a means of fortifying goodness, whereas the entire point of such a pursuit is that no one can know where it will lead. Nietzsche had long before appreciated that this tendency in modern thought is just a disguised form of theism. God and the universal good are one and the same, so that if one dies the other dies too. It is not so easy to get out of the modern trap as Mann sometimes fancied, though he more than others faced the difficulties in his imaginative writings.

In *Doctor Faustus* Leverkühn's behaviour is scarcely repellent but in some sense sublime. At least we are meant to be appalled, not contemptuous. Zeitblom observes his friend with pity, horror and veneration. Nor is there any doubt that the supposedly wicked Leverkühn is of greater stature than the good and reasonable Zeitblom. Adrian's giving himself to the devil consists of a consolation or an intensification of his native coldness. So he is enabled to reach beyond mere technicality in music. His final work, the symphonic cantata called 'The Lamentation of Dr Faustus', is described by Zeitblom in the following words:

> No, this dark tone-poem permits up to the very end no consolation, appeasement, transfiguration. But take our artist paradox: grant that expressiveness – expression as lament – is the issue of the whole construction: then may we not parallel with it another, a religious one, and say too (though only in the lowest whisper) that out of the sheerly irremediable hope might germinate? It would be but a hope beyond hopelessness, the transcendence of despair – not betrayal to her, but the miracle that passes belief.[54]

Zeitblom's speculation here is the measure of his friend's fiendish achievement. Leverkühn has soared beyond technique to a dark night of the soul and in that extreme condition disclosed the possibility of a miracle of acceptance. Leverkühn has reached this height – or abysmal depth – by ignoring the needs of others and treating the social question as a fashionable irrelevance.

Around him, as his work proceeds, human life is generally debased or diseased. Clarissa Rodde, a failure as an actress, is seduced by a lawyer who then tries to blackmail her into becoming his regular mistress when she is about to marry an upright businessman. She poisons herself in a hotel room. Her sister, Inez Institoris, a morphine addict who thinks of life as an 'ignoble fetter', [55] shoots Rudi Schwerdtfeger on a Munich tram and is seized, insane, by fellow-passengers. Adrian's little nephew Nepomuk, nicknamed Echo, a 'fairy princeling' as a baby, dies in screaming agony of meningitis. Since Leverkühn has grown attached to Echo he now sees himself as the boy's torturer and murderer. This is the occasion of Leverkühn's hysterical revolt against Satan, whom he calls 'scum, filth, excrement'. [56] Consequently Adrian sets out to 'take back' the goodness of Beethoven's Ninth Symphony and so composes 'The Lamentation of Dr Faustus'. This cantata is the breakthrough in which Leverkühn, on behalf of his period in history, uses the devil to beat the devil. The only way to conquer Satan, so the composer finally explains to friends, is to welcome him, knowing him to be scum, filth and excrement. Evil may be turned around when one *knowingly* takes it to one's heart. Leverkühn makes the following remark: 'But an one invite the divil as guest, to pass beyond all this and get to the break-through, he chargeth his soul and taketh the guilt of the time upon his own shoulders, so that he is damned.' [57]

This has little to do with Christ's unique message, 'Resist not evil', since Leverkühn is advocating co-operation with the devil in order to enter the kingdom of art, not the kingdom of heaven. Nevertheless, here is Mann's final way both of bringing art and life into a mutually enriching relation and of uniting evil with good. For surely to take guilt upon one's own shoulders is both evil and commendable. And only a hell-bound hero, a martyr who will never be claimed by God, may do this on our behalf.

At the end, though, Mann does not see what he readily saw as late as *Lotte in Weimar*: that life itself is innocent. We cannot know 'life itself'; indeed the phrase is strictly meaningless because such a vast and forever unknown reality dwarfs our human grasp. The reality, a set of forces, stands apart from culture, while morality (any conceivable morality) is a piece of culture. Mann seems to have discerned the following relation: on the one side ascending life, the devil, meaningful art, suffering; and on the other side descending life, empty art, morality, consolation for suffering. According to *Doctor Faustus* these two sets of relations may be caused to converge. According to some earlier writings, especially

The Magic Mountain, Joseph and His Brothers and *Lotte in Weimar,* the
first set should simply and robustly annihilate the second.

Nietzsche's influence upon Thomas Mann, though considerable,
cannot be traced or described with any precision. It can be roughly
traced, of course. In the *Diaries* there are nineteen references to
Nietzsche, the first made in 1918 and the last in 1938. All references
are either neutral or favourable. A most interesting observation
occurs under 16 January 1936. A writer had claimed that there were
only superficial differences between Nietzsche and National Social-
ism. Mann angrily commented as follows:

> But Nietzsche, who stood for utmost 'intellectual rectitude', for
> the Dionysian will to know, who smiled at Faust for being a
> 'tragedy of knowledge' because he knew better, who was ready
> to endure every suffering caused by the truth and for the sake of
> truth – this man they want to claim in connection with myths of
> action of a mass appeal roughly of the level of the most
> degenerate popular dirty songs.[58]

And yet only eleven years later, at the time of 'Nietzsche's
Philosophy in the Light of Recent History', Mann's attitude
towards the philosopher had grown nearer to the attitude he
despised in 1936. Here is what presumably happened.

Throughout much of his adult life Mann was fascinated by
Nietzsche, seeing him as possibly a philosopher of the first rank
and for sure an unparalleled observer of his fellow men. Then the
devastation produced by the Nazis changed Mann's estimate in
part. Like many others he became convinced that evil must be
placed beyond the pale, not contemplated. He now assumed that
the liberal contemplation of evil – for example, its analysis in
intellectual terms – is potentially dangerous for the human race.
The enquiry Mann had himself conducted in *Doctor Faustus* (and let
us not forget that *Doctor Faustus* is an enquiry, a spiritual
adventure) he now saw as essentially removed from the reality of
corpses and torture chambers. Zeitblom's horrified references to
the war do not alter this essence, which has to do with the paradox
of Leverkühn as wicked martyr.

Nietzsche had seemingly bridged the gap between reflection and physical action, between philosophy and social reality. But it was Nietzsche's cardinal error, according to Mann, that he heaped abuse upon the 'theoretical man' while himself being 'this theoretical man, *par excellence*'.[59] My contention is, to the contrary, that despite some polemical tricks Nietzsche meant what he said and knew in flesh and blood terms what his ideas portended – not encouraged, but simply portended. For some of Nietzsche's most resonant remarks are prophecies rather than recommendations.

That is why he scorned the dualism of good and evil. Rather, he scorned the weakness that once produced the dualism; saw what purpose (or *whose* purpose) it served, and sensed that it was petering out. Nietzsche knew of course that people do frightful things, but regarded moral classification as interpretative, not factual. Then, the interpretations, good and evil, are psychological dodges: that is to say, ways of averting our gaze from psychological realities. The clearest statement of Nietzsche's thought on this subject is not in *Beyond Good and Evil* but in *The Will to Power*. For once we shall need a long quotation.

> The demand is that man should castrate himself of those instincts with which he can be an enemy, can cause harm, can be angry, can demand revenge —
>
> This unnaturalness corresponds, then, to that dualistic conception of a merely good and a merely evil creature (God, spirit, man); in the former are summarized all the positive, in the latter all the negative forces, intentions, states. —
>
> Such a manner of valuing believes itself to be 'idealistic'; it does not doubt that, in the conception of 'the good', it has posited a supreme *desideratum*. At its peak, it imagines a state in which all that is evil is annulled and in which only good creatures actually remain. It does not even consider it settled that this antithesis of good and evil is conditional on the existence of both; on the contrary, the latter should vanish and the former remain, the one has a right to exist, the other ought not to be there at all —
>
> What is it really that desires this? —
>
> Much labor has been expended in all ages, and especially in the Christian ages, to reduce mankind to this half-sided efficiency, to the 'good': even today there is no lack of those deformed and weakened by the church for whom this object coincides with 'humanization' in general, or with the 'will of God', or with

'salvation of the soul'. The essential demand here is that mankind should do nothing evil, that it should under no circumstances do harm or desire to do harm. The way to achieve this is: the castration of all possibility of enmity, the unhinging of all the instincts of *ressentiment*, 'peace of soul' as a chronic disease.

This mode of thought, with which a definite type of man is bred, starts from an absurd presupposition: it takes good and evil for realities that contradict one another (not as complementary value concepts, which would be the truth), it advises taking the side of the good, it desires that the good should renounce and oppose the evil down to its ultimate roots – it therewith actually denies life, which has in all its instincts both Yes and No. Not that it grasps this: it dreams, on the contrary, that it is getting back to wholeness, to unity, to strength of life: it thinks it will be a state of redemption when the inner anarchy, the unrest between those opposing value drives, is at last put an end to. — Perhaps there has never before been a more dangerous ideology, a greater mischief *in psychologicis*, than this will to good: one has reared the most repellent type, the unfree man, the bigot; one has taught that only as a bigot is one on the right path to godhood, only the bigot's way is God's way.[60]

These words are most important not only for an understanding of Nietzsche's phrase 'beyond good and evil', but for a general grasp of his peculiar way of philosophising. They are notes, since *The Will to Power* consists of notes. The remarks help to illustrate how Nietzsche did his thinking: he made psychological observations as a matter of course and aimed to change common views which ran counter to such primary observations. For example, everyone spoke of the 'will' as a mental agent or faculty. But Nietzsche could not discern this celebrated will in either his own or anyone else's make-up.[61] Therefore he concluded that the will is a fiction (as Gilbert Ryle concludes in *The Concept of Mind*).

Now in the above words from *The Will to Power* we can see how Nietzsche pondered the question of good and evil. It was not a question arising in a discipline called 'Ethics', still less a matter of spontaneous feelings, but rather a social injunction to pour one complex set of actions into the category 'good' and another, equally complex set into the category 'evil'. It was further decreed that the two sets should be opposites. Thus the good-and-evil schema was artificial, *and not even a sound device for reducing our harmful, or evil, tendencies.* Ancient scriptures and modern moralists alike urge that we should overcome our harmful impulses. But this would be to castrate ourselves, because such urges are constituents of health. We could create nothing without our harmfulness. The idea that one might be harmlessly vigorous or vigorously harmless is misguided, since the activities of a species or an individual cannot but encroach upon the ways of others. So doing harm is inescapable for all creatures.

If doing harm is roughly what we mean by evil, then the belief that evil might be eliminated is wrong. So is the contemporary assumption that evil is 'caused' – by injustice or oppression. For the implicit belief here is that the very roots of evil may be plucked out, one by one, until there are none left. The modern moralist declares as fervently as his ancient forebears that accepting evil is a disgrace. As moral beings we must at least deplore wickedness. Fighting evil, the moralist argues, may not often be profitable, but there is no decent alternative. This last, common assumption rests (I believe) upon a merely theoretical recognition of the durability of evil. The shadowy thesis is that humanity might gradually shake off harmful impulses.

Nietzsche agrees that we need some sort of value discrimination, but not that we must entertain mutually exclusive categories of good and evil. He is certain that 'many actions called immoral ought to be avoided and resisted and that many called moral ought to be done and encouraged'.[62] Nietzsche's point here is that morality and immorality are blanket terms which misrepresent our actual and often singular motivations. The reasons for our behaviour might profitably be seen as other than the moral ones we commonly ascribe to them. We might say, for instance, that to hate another is bad, not on the grounds that hatred is contrary to a commandment but because it is psychically crippling. Likewise systematic persecution is either a sickening debauch or else a quasi-mechanical, barely human practice. Then a latter-day terrorist, whatever his avowed motives, must inevitably be or become a spiritual cretin. In offering these illustrations I too am simplifying, but at least I am looking for improvements on the murky or thoughtless epithet 'evil'.

In this regard, as in all others, Nietzsche recommended acuity and intellectual courage. He believed that those qualities should take precedence over all others. Morality should therefore be seen as subordinate, not primary: the first requirement was to see and think as honestly as possible. For example, it is commonly assumed that we should aim for 'peace of soul', but why should we do so? Indeed that aim is dangerous, for such peace brings 'chronic disease'. No matter how we wriggle round the point, peace soon becomes infirmity. Peace is necessary and desirable at intervals, but as a lasting condition it would be disastrous.

Life 'has in all its instincts both Yes and No'. These words mean that any force embraces some things and rejects others. An individual is a force or a collection of forces and must therefore welcome bits of the environment and deny other bits. The bits he denies have to be fought in some fashion; man himself must say Yes and No. But what he repels is not so much 'wrong' as unassimilable. It is neither 'wrong in itself' nor the antithesis of the right. Accepting and rejecting is, properly, a matter of nuances, not of absolute distinctions. An individual is obliged as a condition of life both to love and to combat other individuals. If this fundamental requirement is the 'war of every man against every man', then that war is not a mere Hobbesian doctrine but a supra-doctrinal state. In fact, however, the war, like all wars, entails alliances, loyalties, motions of love and momentary reconciliations.

The bigot is one type of unfree man. He is en route to godhood because he knows *sans peur et sans doute* what is right and what is wrong. He has devised rules not just for himself but for all. But good is never universal good and evil never universal evil. Or rather no two deeds are actually the same, and to speak of moral degrees is still misleading. The belief that deeds may be categorically evil is no longer a priestly but a democratic prejudice. To say this is not to open the door to atrocity: it is to try to see everything, atrocity included, in the clearest light.

Today, after twentieth-century vilenesses or in the midst of them, speaking as Nietzsche spoke seems to some people sinister, foolish or anachronistic. So Thomas Mann came to believe: the century had put Nietzsche out of court. But Mann contrived to hold that opinion only by means of an ingenious final novel which tended to refute his earlier writings. Indeed it might be said to refute itself, since it concerns the career of a wicked saviour. Then there was the late Nietzsche essay in which the philosopher was seen as unacceptably aesthetical. History, thought Mann, had crushed such pretensions.

However, let us consider another possibility for a moment. It is this: Nietzsche's view of good and evil is now surreptitiously and *irreversibly* creeping over mankind, although few acknowledge as much. Perhaps it is here that we find the essential history of our post-war period, the history that cannot be wished or engineered away. Nietzsche's view might thus be less an argument and more a flight of understanding.

5

Lawrence: How One Becomes What One Is

> Everything, in so far as it is in itself, endeavours to persist in its own being.
>
> Spinoza

Lawrence's writings seek to demonstrate that becoming what one is is supremely valuable and arduous. It is *the* value, the one factor that separates Lawrence's heroes and heroines from the rest of his characters. These best people have a hard time, for they are not like Rilke's Heroes, whose destiny is assured and unquestioned from the beginning. None the less, Lawrence's admired ones are incapable of wandering all their lives along a populous highway, but must sooner or later make off down a side track. Indeed it would be better to say that they force their way into the trackless forest.

As for Nietzsche, he too maintains that self-becoming is an exploration, a series of goals, each indescribable until one has reached it and is pressing on to the next, 'for your true nature lies, not concealed deep within you, but immeasurably high above you, or at least above that which you usually take yourself to be'.[1] Both Nietzsche and Lawrence see the majority as incapable of this vital progress. And both regard plans for a co-operative society, in which people respect each other's ways, as disguised plans for a standardised society in which distinctions are ornamental. Here it will be convenient for a change to deal with the philosopher's theory first and to put the artist aside for a few pages. The reason is that Nietzsche's view of self-becoming is closely allied to his theory of will to power, and the latter in turn is the foundation of both the Nietzschean and the Lawrentian vision. Lawrence intuitively saw power as Nietzsche saw it.

'Will to power', then, is Nietzsche's cardinal term, used by him to refer to the principle of all being. *'This world is the will to power — and nothing besides!* And you yourselves are also this will to power —

111

and nothing besides!'[2] The world, the totality of all things, is nothing but will to power, so that whenever people seek to differentiate themselves from the physical universe (as, for example, by regarding their natures as essentially spiritual) they are only doing in a human fashion what non-human beings do in their varied fashions – exercising will to power. A person's spiritual aspirations and a plant's growth through the soil are alike modes of self-fulfilment. And the self is a powerful will.

At this point I should make it plain that the argument I am briefly expounding is Nietzsche's adaptation of the central idea of Schopenhauer. It was Schopenhauer who first argued for the universality of will. 'Therefore,' he wrote in *The World as Will and Representation*, 'in this sense I teach that the inner nature of everything is *will*, and I call the will the thing-in-itself.'[3] The argument is thus over a hundred and fifty years old, but it is unfamiliar at present and many people might well feel uncomfortable thinking in Schopenhaurian terms – which seem, nevertheless, to be supported rather than refuted by Einsteinian physics. But let us continue to consider what these terms of Schopenhauer and Nietzsche are.

Will to power is what being is. There is not first being which is then sometimes informed by will to power. Will to power is being and being is will to power. As Heidegger puts it, 'Will to power is never the willing of a particular actual entity. It involves the Being and the essence of beings: it is this itself.'[4] As we remarked earlier, being is actually becoming, since nothing exists unchangingly.[5] It appears that Nietzsche saw inorganic substances as once-organic or potentially organic substances at present stabilised. To say that something is 'stabilised' amounts to saying that no force within the substance may *at this moment* dominate the others. Nothing is currently happening because the indwelling forces are exactly balanced against one another. Equilibrium is stasis and is no healthier in the body politic than in the physical body. However, stasis is evidence not of the enduring absence of will to power, or of its enduring negation, but of its temporary quiescence. Einstein once made this point when discussing the theory of relativity: he remarked that 'inert mass is nothing else than latent energy'.[6]

Will to power emphatically does not mean appetite for power or pursuit of power. In fact each term – 'will', 'to' and 'power' – needs comment here. First, it may be helpful if we briefly think of will as drive or energy, for then the universal application that Nietzsche intends will be easier to assimilate. It is not that Nietzsche takes the non-mechanical quality out of will but rather that he restores that quality to all forms of energy. The philosopher lies behind Freud in believing that conscious will is at best the rationalised upper residue of unconscious will. Further than that, Nietzsche attributes will to every force in nature, since he believes that everything non-mechanistic is informed by will. For instance, a breeze whipping along a shoreline, bending trees, rocking boats, causing people to totter: such a breeze undoubtedly has drive or energy. But since will is never properly conscious, why do we not say that the breeze has or *is* will?

The breeze is not a mere force, or if it is a mere force, how may we define force?

> The notorious concept 'force', by means of which our physicists have created God and the World, still needs to be completed: an inner will must be ascribed to it, which I designate as 'will to power', i.e., as an insatiable desire to manifest power; or as the employment and exercise of power, as a creative drive, etc. [7]

Nietzsche implies that, for example, when we call a breeze a 'force' we must bear in mind that force is not necessarily or normally mechanical. We tend wrongly to regard a breeze as quasi-mechanical, but of course a breeze is not a mechanism, not a machine at all, for it does 'what it likes' and not what it has been engineered to do. The breeze is neither more nor less than what it does of its own accord.

For anything to act of its own accord is to be or display what we normally understand as 'will'. We should not deny will to the breeze on the grounds that the breeze doesn't know what it is doing, or doesn't plan its doings, or is forced into them by atmospheric conditions. Such grounds apply to creatures also, including human beings. Even the elevated consciousness of a person is nothing but the application of words to original libido. And libido, in turn, is no more than a form of that molecular activity which we share with everything else. The differences are stages, not gaps or jumps.

An individual is therefore a cluster of drives forming a distinctive core. The core is will to power. Like the breeze, however, the individual is not will to obtain power, for power is what he already is. As we have seen, the 'power' of the phrase 'will to power' is a property of every element in creation. We ourselves exercise power and are power in all our actions. As Gilles Deleuze neatly puts it, 'The will to power is thus ascribed to force, but in a very special way: it is both a complement of force and something internal to it.'[8] Deleuze means and makes clear in four illuminating pages that each force both has and contains its own self-defining, irreplaceable power. Power in a general sense is plainly an abstraction. Political power or the power attached to any recognised social role is a slave-substitute for genuine power. The latter is entirely personal and may neither be conferred nor removed by others.

So far, then, we can say that 'will to power' means drive to show or exercise one's own peculiar power. Each of us is to be defined as a *specific* 'insatiable desire to manifest power; or as the employment and exercise of power, as a creative drive, etc'. Finally, therefore, the preposition in the term 'will to power' bears no connotation of seeking or aspiring, but abbreviates the phrase 'to the exercise of'. We will to exercise the power that we already happen to be.

Now it is clear that exercising one's personal power entails conflict with others. How could it not do so? Without the conflict there would be no power and, in practical terms, the less conflict the less power. Yet the majority look for frictionless conflict and do this by disowning themselves. The procedure is to cover one's face with a mask chosen from a large but standardised batch and to strive (successfully as a rule) to mould one's native features to the mask. The millrace of one's unique will to power thus flows into a broad and sluggish stream. It loses much of its character and special force, but it still exists in a diffused and weakened form. The individual now feels that he has some political power, recognised power, though his personal power is dissipated. Among the masked people there is a formularistic sort of conflict. These people do not fight for themselves personally but in some public cause. One hears many arguments and each is empty, inapplicable to any single individual. The debators are, above all, reasonable, ready to yield to a majority view, which can be no more than an agreed formula. Naturally the formula is sterile. All this procedure is gone through in order to avoid actual wounds and intensity of life.

By this means the weak defeat the strong and have progressively done so down the ages. The weak nullify themselves and imagine that the strong may do the same. A weak man, Nietzsche says in effect, is like a lamb regarding an eagle and thinking to itself, 'That

frightful bird would be acceptable if only it behaved like a lamb.'
The lamb fails to appreciate that predatoriness is not accidental but
essential to the eagle-nature.

Nietzsche does not suggest that *homo sapiens* is necessarily a
predator. He means that a strong person retains his ability,
whatever it is, while the numerous weak allow themselves to be
separated from what they can do.[9] Thus the strong individual is
characterised by his unique capacity, while the mass of people
cultivate shared, impersonal ways. The important fact to grasp is
that the strong are not free to be weak.

We have just been speaking of mankind generally: all are
composed of more or less efficient will to power. In addition,
Nietzsche has in common with Lawrence a faith in a certain
'metaphysical' distinction of gender. Since the will to power is
primary in Nietzsche, if not in Lawrence, gender is a secondary
consideration to the philosopher. Nor does Nietzsche think of his
distinction of men's and women's personalities as unsurpassable
but, on the contrary, cultural and open to change. Nevertheless,
Nietzsche believes that we had better maintain some age-old
differences. His comments about relations between the sexes are
candidly recommendations and are not presented as biological
'laws'. Another way of putting the matter would be to say that they
are candidly prejudices. They do not seem to me to be indispensable to his thought, for I cannot understand how his doctrines
would be seriously affected, let alone destroyed, if men and
women were held to have potentially the same qualities, including
of course the same creative scope.

However, Zarathustra declares that 'For the woman, the man is
a means: the end is always the child. But what is the woman for the
man?'[10] The answer is that the man is a warrior and a child, one
who fights and plays, so that the woman is his recreation. She is a
bitter recreation preferably, says Zarathustra, but a recreation just
the same. The woman's point of view is that the man gives her
children. The man's point of view is that the woman respects his
creative activity. 'The man's happiness is: I will. The woman's
happiness is: He will.'[11] This does not mean that she should
automatically obey, far from it, but that she is happy when the
man's creative drive is such that she can willingly obey. Lawrence's novels repeatedly deal with this very topic.

Both Nietzsche and Lawrence believed that civilisation cannot be
at its best whenever women's enterprises tend away from repro-

duction and nurturing. A specialised woman might do a 'man's work' instead, by which I do not mean run-of-the-mill jobs but some pioneering activity. Factory work is not 'man's work' in this sense, and neither is accountancy. On the other hand, Marie Curie eminently did man's work.

A man properly desires to create 'beyond himself', as Zarathustra puts it: to create something higher than himself. This might well be a child whose superior value to the father betokens the father's value. A good marriage is in being when a woman supports a man in his self-transcending ambition. 'Marriage,' says Zarathustra, 'that I call the will of two to create the one who is more than those who created it.'[12] Both parents in a good marriage desire such offspring-above-themselves. In order to desire this offspring both the father and the mother must be self-created people. It may happen, of course, that a bad or mediocre marriage, in which neither the man nor the woman is self-created, produces a superior child. For all that, in the best sort of alliance the mother's will flows towards pregnancy and her husband's creativity. Zarathustra's teaching is that a man should make his own path and a woman should choose a man who does so.

Generally that is Lawrence's teaching also, though he regularly confronts obstacles to such a way of life and empathises with his heroines. According to him men have lost their way, becoming ciphers, while women either blindly lead or clamour to become equal ciphers with the men. This is a principal theme in Lawrence from the beginning almost to the end, from *The White Peacock* to *Lady Chatterley's Lover*.

The title of Lawrence's first novel is not so inapt as has sometimes been supposed. Annable, the gamekeeper, remarks to the young narrator, Cyril, that the soul of a woman is like the peacock which the pair of them observe one evening in the Hall churchyard. This bird perches on the neck of an angel, spreads its glimmering tail and defiles its holy pedestal. A little later Annable tells Cyril the story of his marriage. As a young man he was a tolerably contented curate, but a Lady Crystabel lusted after him, married him and abandoned him when she was physically sated. Cyril comments that, at any rate, Lady Crystabel must have been a white peacock, since she could not help her behaviour.

Cyril's remark is not superfluous but to some extent an explanation of the novel. For us much falls into place because of the title. Perhaps the meaning of the design grew clearer to Lawrence himself when (in 1910, at his publisher's insistence) he changed the name from 'Nethermere'. Certainly Lawrence must have appreciated only after the passage of years that his beautiful rustic composition revolved around the theme of man's loss of direction and woman's consequent waywardness.

The young farmer, George Saxton, is handsome, indolent, inwardly soft and purposeless. Cyril's graceful sister, Lettie, rejects George, though he pleads with her to marry him and tell him what to do with his life. He needs a woman to give him a goal. But Lettie rightly maintains that she is not strong enough to guide them both. Instead she marries the rich Leslie Tempest, who has ordinary social ambitions. Leslie's career – as a mine-owner and later a politician – proves to be meaningless to Lettie because it is 'inorganic', unconnected with the actual man. Lettie ends desperately bored: her life is drifting away while her husband goes about his conventional business.

George Saxton marries Meg of the Ram Inn and, despite Meg's sensual loveliness, either accelerates or fails to check his own decline. His status is now that of Meg's husband, father of her children. He ends as a sot, serving a contemptuous woman and heading for an early death. The burden is clear: in this fertile district of 'Nethermere' the young besport themselves with rare intensity so long as the sap is simply rising, but when the time comes for life-defining choices these people turn out to be empty or misguided. Neither George nor Leslie is a pathfinder, and the women, Lettie, Meg and, less significantly, Emily Saxton, are lost because they are bereft of pioneering masculine guidance. *The White Peacock* is a lament for the loss of religious meaning.

'Religious meaning' may seem an odd, arbitrary phrase to use in this connection. Yet the words are fitting, because Lawrence recognised even then, at the outset of his career, that a sense of personal meaning is bound up with a sense of universal meaning. If the world is seen as a collection of mechanical bits and pieces, or if society (Marxianly) blots out the natural world, then the individual is merely a unit. Thus there is a complete difference between a personal meaning and a public, or social, or mechanical *explanation*. The latter is a pale substitute for meaning.

The people of *The White Peacock*, men and women, lack assured individuality. Cyril perhaps has this quality, but the story he tells is not his story. The same theme is amplified and much clarified in *Sons and Lovers*. For the first six months of their marriage Walter and Gertrude Morel each seem lit from within, as it were, by a beacon. Gertrude comes from a 'good old burgher family'[13] and has the haughty pride of her father. This pride in her integrity is Gertrude's beacon. Her personality largely consists in a sturdy, unyielding response to the environment. Everything around her is resisted, or else appropriated. She is the resistant one and is therefore strong. Gertrude is here and the world is there. Note that this is not simply because her bourgeois soul shrinks from the mining community, but fundamentally because her puritan nature must needs dominate the 'world as such'. The antagonism between Gertrude's nature and the 'wilderness of this world', as Bunyan calls it, is tragic and creative. She herself is somewhat intellectual, psychologically astute and receptive. The last-mentioned quality is not a defence mechanism or a form of shyness, but just her strong, inquisitive way of encountering externality.

Gertrude is fascinated by Walter Morel when she first meets him at a Christmas party because he is handsome, excessively physical, unmoral and heedless. 'Mindless', one might pardonably say. He does not resist the world but flows along with it, like an animal. Religion to Gertrude amounts to tragic, unrelenting personal integrity: one resists for the sake of resisting, to the death. Morel's way amounts to a set of sure instincts, like a dog's: he venerates nothing so much as his own impulses. Everything and everyone is to him merely the object of an impulse. He reacts as a dog reacts, basking in affection, or snarling with rage, or going to sleep.

In the early period of their marriage Gertrude remains true to her puritan nature, which is not an ascetic nature but a proud, assertive, oath-keeping sort of personality. At the same time Walter begins to assume the posture of a whipped and defeated dog. His 'fighting back' consists of surliness and fits of violence, for he cannot learn some effective technique with which to combat his wife. Lawrence remarks in the chapter 'The Young Life of Paul' that Morel 'had denied the God in him',[14] implying, I believe, that one's God, or one's version of the universal God, is one's will to power. Thus Morel's will to power naturally still lurks within him, but as a broken, baffled agent.

Here we can align Lawrence's terminology with Nietzsche's. In this vision of the artist one partakes of God. God is 'in' the individual. But the form God takes is evidently peculiar to the individual. Similarly, as we have seen, one's will to power is 'in' one, or constitutes oneself. This personal version of God, or this personal will to power, is what, according to both Nietzsche and Lawrence, one should become. ('How One Becomes What One Is' is the subtitle of Nietzsche's *Ecce Homo*.)

The individual who succeeds in this endeavour has progressively shaken off any ill-fitting, imitative garments he has acquired. He becomes what he is by ridding himself of everything he is not. Likewise the God in Lawrentian man is that man's share of godhood – since God to Lawrence is never absolute or transcendental. Both Nietzsche and Lawrence refute mechanistic interpretations of life by denying not only the machinery of nature but also the First Cause. Absolute being is absolute and harmful fantasy in the eyes of both men. There are only struggling little beings, each one of potential value in his own right. There are no commandments now and, it seems, to Lawrence (as to Nietzsche) the way of Christ is simply a way one might choose. (Of course it has been argued often enough that Jesus wanted such followers, not a Christian Church, not Christian nations, not an empire of Christendom.)

Even the old concept of a moral God is finished in Lawrence's view, since morality may no longer be regarded as a fixed standard for all persons and places. But if God is alternatively apprehended as 'morality', undefined and unformulated, then each moral individual makes his own way to God. God Himself is possibly a meeting point of a myriad private moralities. There is all the difference in the world between a private morality and no morality. Many people have no morality in Lawrence's sense, since to him morality consists in creative transactions between the individual and the environment, and most of us are uncreative.

In *Sons and Lovers* there are snares for the individual who has a creative spark. William, the eldest son, is ensnared when he courts the Streatham girl 'Gypsy', who understands 'nothing but love-making and chatter'[15] and has been confirmed three times through love of the ceremony. Gypsy is certainly a 'white peacock' who means no harm but contrives to kill her fiancé by her soullessness. William is so torn between his own soul, his will to power in other words, and his promise to this girl that he dies of pneumonia. The point is not that William's soul belongs to his mother,[16] but that Mrs Morel has fostered in him a delicate and still-growing structure of selfhood which Gypsy cannot perceive, let alone nurture.

The pattern is developed far more elaborately in the relation of Paul Morel and Miriam Leivers. Paul is an artist who acknowledges the 'God in him' and never frustrates his own lively, observant spirit. On the other hand, Miriam crushes her instincts, since she is driven by fear. Out of fear all must be defined and formalised. Nothing is allowed to reveal itself but is instead subordinated to an ideal. The self or soul of everything – a person, a flower, an animal, a task, a pastime – must be aligned with a prescribed form. An original self is by definition bad.

Miriam is a victim of what Nietzsche calls 'ascetic ideals'. Nietzsche writes that 'in the case of the physiologically deformed and deranged (the *majority* of mortals) . . . these ideals are an attempt to see themselves as "too good" for this world'.[17] For example, says Nietzsche, 'there is no necessary antithesis between chastity and sensuality; every good marriage, every genuine love affair, transcends this antithesis'.[18] But the ascetic idealist may wish to confront any actual marriage with chastity, to compare the confused details of the marriage with a spotless standard.

Miriam is proud of her humility; even her 'joy is like a flame coming off sadness', Paul tells her;[19] she leaves 'no emotion on a normal plane';[20] her body is 'not flexible and living'.[21] When Paul declares that he does not love her, Miriam assumes that he is mistaken.[22] Miriam is Gothic, Paul points out, meaning that she wishes to rise heavenwards like a Gothic arch and preferably never return to earth. Earth is axiomatically bad. The flesh is rendered acceptable only when it is given a firm, conscious meaning and thus commandeered. Fear is the root of this; fear of the body, of course, but mainly just fear. By making something conscious Miriam limits it and seems to control it. An artist such as Paul is not seen as an inconsistent, ever-growing, ever-changing individual but as a category of person who must perforce follow certain artist-rules and correspond minutely to the ideal or image of 'the artist'. He may not enjoy vulgar amusements, for instance.

On the other hand, Clara Dawes has next to nothing to do with ascetic ideals. It is true that she feels guilty after her first act of adultery with Paul, but that is no more than a slight bow towards convention and a far cry from Miriam's reverence for rules. Clara's ten years of self-education and membership of the women's movement are not aspects of an attempt to see herself as too good for this world. She is a rather bitter, rebellious person but not a renegade from life itself. The distinction here is important, since many who are renegades from life see themselves as merely social rebels: sufferings are overwhelmingly ascribed to conditions of society. Clara is not of that numerous persuasion. She and Miriam differ chiefly in that the latter seeks an impossible sphere of static, perfected being, while Clara, despite her bitterness, accepts the actual sphere of becoming.

Mrs Morel is like Clara in this vital respect. The mother's puritanism is a studied attitude towards life, not a yearning for heaven. One must fight as a matter of pride and principle. Hence, of course, the rejection of Morel, who will not grasp that the natural way for a man differs from the natural ways of other animals. Each species has its power or genius and *homo sapiens* should continually *make*, or reinterpret, the environment (compare Rilke) – not in order to blot out the changes, the ups and downs, the pains of living, but merely out of creative zeal.

Most of Lawrence's exemplary characters do not fly straight to a creative destiny like an arrow to its target. The chief exceptions are Birkin, the author's self-projection in *Women in Love*, and Don Ramón in *The Plumed Serpent*. Apart from those two, no one in Lawrence says, with Nietzsche, 'Formula of my happiness: a Yes, a No, a straight line, a *goal* . . .'.[23] Generally Lawrence's characters are distracted, or they start late, or they eventually give up. But the principle remains constant: nothing matters so much as creativity. 'Progress' in the benevolent political and scientific senses is regarded as utter nonsense.

The Rainbow is a portrait of creative ebb and flow amid predominantly hostile conditions in the late nineteenth century. We may not readily accept Lawrence's interpretation of those conditions, yet, on the other hand, his picture might now seem more discerning than the old tales of triumphant progress. His reigning attitude towards the early twentieth century was a strange mixture of anger and chirpiness. Man in his lunatic pride was rushing into the desert of mechanisation, but somehow he would come through. There is something here of Nietzsche's philosophical assumption that great movements of history must work themselves out. Lawrence sometimes thinks in that fashion but, conversely, he often conveys a sense of urgency, even of desperation.

The Rainbow illustrates more clearly than preceding novels the *blindness* of the will to power. Those Brangwen men at the beginning of the book, farmers before 1840, have 'a kind of surety, an expectancy, the look of an inheritor'.[24] This look is not searching, since the inheritance is assured. They are blindly at one with the soil and the seasons. Their will flows with the will of the land. The Brangwen womenfolk of that period yearn for knowledge and spiritual fulfilment. Their will also is blind, for they peer into darkness. Who is creative, the male or the female?

The men are midwives to nature and are therefore comparatively unconscious and personally unfruitful. They have no problems of meaning and prefer darkness to light. For that very reason the women yearn for light, for 'poetry' in the widest, Shelleyan sense of all the grand works of interpretation: Homer, the Dialogues of Plato, the Bible. Such works once made everything fall into place, illuminating even the dullest and nastiest events. That is the kind of light sought by the Brangwen women of the early nineteenth century. Two generations later Anna Brangwen still requires similar enlightenment, because she finds the explanations offered by church and school to be inappropriate to her. She is proud while the other girls at school are, she declares, 'bagatelle'. The schoolmistress has a 'coarsely working nature'[25] and commands Anna, the little aristocrat, to learn thirty lines of *As You Like It*.

In other words, Anna Brangwen forms a self-image which is independent of immediate social influences, for it seems to be part of Lawrence's purpose to demonstrate the self-generating character of such images. We might trace a line of descent for Anna's notion of herself, but the essential feature of such a line must be precisely that it is not mechanical and therefore not a 'cause' in the usual sense.

To consider this matter from Lawrence's own point of view, we should remark that, having resolved to grow into an aristocrat of some sort, the child Anna indeed moulds herself aristocratically – that is, without reference to social expectations. 'Free, proud lady' is her self-definition and therefore her accomplishment, for what could check her advance? She would not bow to an impediment even if she were physically impeded, since stone walls do not a prison make. She might conceivably be an 'imprisoned aristocrat' some day, yet no one could rob her of her nature. It is Lawrence's view (and Nietzsche's) that free people thus create themselves. Social and physical conditions are flimsy entanglements. To those who regard such an attitude as self-deception, Lawrence would certainly have replied – *The Rainbow* makes this clear – that one must cope with social circumstances from the standpoint of one's own freely conceived self. That self is primary, not formed by circumstances but potentially formative of them.

Nothing of note in contemporary culture supports Anna's

definition of herself, since she interprets Christianity so liberally as to be almost a pagan and has no time for science, reform, the march of the British Empire or Victorian respectability. Anna represents an ascending form of life, a way of pride, indifference and individual conquest, while around her people abase themselves either to nostalgia (in the fashion of the Pre-Raphaelites and Ruskin) or to dreams of the future. The present is widely supposed to be a vantage point for looking forward or back, while Anna lives entirely in the present. But she does so by making her own little world in the village of Cossethay.

At eighteen she marries her cousin Will, who appears to her as an outsider, a strange mixture of refinement and uncouthness, distinguished from the local Ilkeston youths. Soon after their wedding Will proves himself to be an escapist, not a cultured man in the adventurous Renaissance sense but one who clings in fear to outworn symbols. He prefers symbols to concrete reality.[26] The lamb of God is God to him, while to Anna it is a living lamb. Lincoln Cathedral is a vast symbol which reassuringly excludes the wild and fecund world. Nevertheless this preference of the husband constitutes his being. It is all there is of him, his entirety, his crippled will to power, and accordingly his way of battling with his wife. Her way of fighting him is often mockery but at her most triumphant it is pregnancy. When she is pregnant she excludes the father. So she builds her domain while Will tends the church, Cossethay Church, beside their house.

Students of Lawrence will have found the foregoing excessively familiar, but it has been necessary to rehearse these matters in order to emphasise that Lawrence is presenting not 'character' in the traditional sense but will to power. That is approximately what he meant in declaring to Edward Garnett that 'The ordinary novel would trace the history of the diamond – but I say, "diamond, what! This is carbon".'[27] The 'this' that is carbon is the portraiture in *The Rainbow*, which can be regarded as a static element only in relation to the ordinary motions of consciousness. The 'carbonaceous' core of character that Lawrence depicts in *The Rainbow* is not actually static. In the letter to Garnett he meant to stress that he viewed the ego not as a coherence of thoughts, feelings and so on, but as something deeper and more stable. More stable, pervasive, consistent, but surely not motionless, since it must move in response to circumstances. In fact the carbon in question can only be will to power. Thus the core of Anna Brangwen is an ever-active will with which she fends off the injunctions and blandishments of the community.

The exercise of will to power is much more evident in the career of Ursula Brangwen, eldest daughter of Will and Anna and properly the 'heroine' of *The Rainbow*. For Ursula's will is far more varied, inclusive and contradictory than that of either her father or her mother. Ursula's personality is unusually rich and productive, because it is composed of conflicting drives which she does not try to harmonise by mendacious means. She has the minimum of bad faith. Such is the quality of a highly creative personality. Anna Brangwen's creativity more or less stops at reproduction, Will Brangwen's at handicrafts and handicraft-teaching. But Ursula tries to reconcile in herself the great spiritual tensions of turn-of-the century Europe.

There are apparent causes of Ursula's nature which are, once again, no causes at all. These are merely predisposing circumstances, notably the child's love-hate relation with her father and a certain isolation from a mother forever preoccupied with the next baby. Like Anna before her, Ursula sees herself as superior to the local children and it never occurs to her that others might have a poor opinion of her. Here once more is the master-morality element of the Brangwens, the tendency (missing in Will Brangwen) to confer value, or discover it, rather than receive it ready-made.

Ursula loves learning partly because she has an aspiring nature. She aspires not to any social standard, for she is above such considerations, but to a scarcely definable criterion which at its zenith assumes the mask of a personal God. Jesus is not Ursula's God, or rather the human, crucified Jesus of the common people is not hers. She regards herself as one of the daughters of men who will one day be taken by a son of God. So she is exceptional, linked with God rather than part of the social nexus. And hers is a godlike God, a fierce, noble divinity, composed of lion and eagle.

Ursula's progress consists more radically than her mother's in rejecting the influences of society. It would be yet more accurate to say that while Anna turns her disdainful back on society, Ursula needs to do battle with society. Finding her own route must include pinpointing the wrongness of the general route. One aspect of the general route is illustrated in the person of Anton Skrebensky, Ursula's lover. He has an aristocratic demeanour but turns out to be glad to be a brick in the social fabric. How accurately in the portrait of Skrebensky Lawrence predicts the tendency of people of all classes to fall into the democratic trap, where only token responsibilities remain!

Likewise Ursula grows out of her love for the teacher Winifred Inger, because Winifred is an uncaring observer. Then University College, Nottingham, seems intellectually exciting at first but quickly proves to be a commercial sham. One studies to enter the world of commerce, not the kingdom of heaven. Or rather, the kingdom of heaven, which university work ought actually to constitute (in the sense not of unrelieved joy but of hallowed meaning), has been supplanted by considerations of trade. Ursula also finds her profession of schoolteaching to be just a mechanical discipline, without zest or human purpose.

Most interesting for our purposes, I suggest, is a jarring conversation Ursula has at the university with a certain Dr Frankstone. This lady, a physics lecturer, opines as follows:

> I don't see why we should attribute some special mystery to life – do you? We don't understand it as we understand electricity, even, but that doesn't warrant our saying it is something different in kind and distinct from everything else in the universe – do you think it does? May it not be that life consists in a complexity of physical and chemical activities, of the same order as the activities we already know in science? I don't see, really, why we should imagine there is a special order of life, and life alone . . . [28]

Ursula frets over these remarks and then, a few days later, gazes at a unicellular creature under her microscope. It moves and Ursula joyously recognises that the creature is moving of its own volition.

> It intended to be itself. But what self? . . . She could not understand what it all was. She only knew that it was not limited mechanical energy, not mere purpose of self-preservation and self-assertion. It was a consummation, a being infinite. Self was a oneness with the infinite. To be oneself was a supreme, gleaming triumph of infinity. [29]

Now here it seems to me that Lawrence, in his zeal to prove his Dr Frankstone wrong, might actually have misrepresented matters. The lecturer is right: life is probably not 'something different in kind and distinct from everything else in the universe'. It is not life alone that is mysterious. Only the strictly mechanical is mechanical. Modern biologists no longer make a hard and fast distinction between the organic and the inorganic, but bring the two together by extending the sphere of the first.

Nevertheless, although Dr Frankstone is technically right, she is appallingly and symptomatically wrong in her desire to abolish mystery or, in other words, to reduce all to measurable factors. The lesson Ursula draws is Lawrence's and Nietzsche's lesson also. It is Nietzsche's as well as Lawrence's because in concluding that 'self was a oneness with the infinite' Ursula rids herself of mechanical interpretation. In one of its senses the infinite is the all, everything that ever has been and ever will be. The infinite is thus vaguely understood to be a grand aggregate of finite things. This is a mechanistic conception of infinity which actually amounts to a monstrous finitude, a whole which is yet remotely circumscribed.

Ursula's radically different insight was expressed in the seventeenth century by Spinoza. 'Every substance', he wrote, 'is necessarily infinite.'[30] His proof of this proposition was that a substance can be limited only by another substance having exactly the same attributes. I may be limited only by another me, not by some other person or process. Similarly, Ursula concludes that any being in its unique self is creatively unlimited. It limitlessly creates itself, out of itself. There can be no check on this process except for the self-imposed check of mechanisation; that is, the false belief that people are essentially social or biological components. People cannot be components, but it has often seemed useful for us to think of them as such. It is clear, also, that according to this Lawrentian or 'Ursuline' doctrine physical death is not contemplated as the absolute end of a being but as transformation. We have encountered this vision in Rilke and here it is necessary only to stress that at all stages of one's being some sort of creation is possible. That is the mode of identity of the self and the infinite.

We now approach another aspect of that doctrine of self-becoming which Lawrence shares with Nietzsche. Ursula's story is so far incomplete because throughout her youth she has merely, if bravely, rejected a number of false solutions. She may not retreat, as her mother did, into the sort of marriage which tends to exclude the larger social world. For Ursula, as for her author, everything should cohere: religion, society, culture, one's vocation and one's most intimate personal relations. Consequently the rainbow which Ursula sees at the conclusion of the novel is nothing more than a hopeful sign: it does not tell her *how* to proceed. This provincial girl may not solve vast problems of life and spirit, yet, at the same time, she may not rest content if no one else is tackling them.

Thus, in writing *Women in Love*, Lawrence, being now ready to tackle such problems himself, gives Ursula the role of argumentative disciple. She becomes the character upon whom he 'tries out' his anguished ruminations. Amusingly enough, she is not even a sympathetic pupil but one who is apt to find her teacher over-solemn and perverse. Through the relation of Birkin and Ursula, Lawrence imagines how a lively, enquiring young woman would greet his own philosophical thoughts. A good deal of the time she is in robust disagreement with them, but of course Lawrence, as Birkin, has no intention of letting Ursula win. Why should he, since her own thoughts are usually at best reservations and at worst uncomprehending insults? Even at the very end she is still convinced that Birkin's desire for 'two kinds of love' ('eternal union' with a man as well as a woman) is 'an obstinacy, a theory, a perversity'.[31]

This means that Lawrence could not accept that his own desire for two kinds of love might be a perversity. Just the same, he realised that it was impossible to explain to his wife, Frieda, why he was not satisfied with her alone. And he would likewise have found it impossible to explain to his former fiancée, Louisa (Louie) Burrows, upon whom Ursula is largely based.[32] Lawrence commonly experienced this kind of difficulty because he ventured to the limits of thought and could not find reasons for his ideas. The point is, however, that Ursula is a yea-sayer, an affirmer of life in all its *natural* forms. She is probably wrong – so we understand – to detect some sort of decadence in Birkin's desires, but she is right to stand on guard against decadence.

She is right also to sense decadence all around her, to be aware of the 'decline of the west'. If this sounds too grand, we should remember that all her life Ursula has recognised and rejected that decline in the forms of her father's nostalgia, her mother's cavalier withdrawal, the education system, the ethics of nationalism (Skrebensky), joyless cynicism (Winifred Inger), the progress of scientific materialism and the inadequacy of the church.

Ursula's younger sister, Gudrun, is yet another focus for Lawrence's investigations, since she greets the decline of the west in an entirely different fashion. To Gudrun that decline is attractive precisely because it smells of dissolution and decay. These two ways of life, Ursula's and Gudrun's, Lawrence, through Birkin, calls 'synthetic creation' and 'destructive creation'. The first term corresponds to what Nietzsche calls 'health', the second to what he calls 'decadence'.

Now here we enter an obscure terrain which Lawrence, at any rate, never bothers to illuminate. On the other hand Nietzsche does unravel these matters and he means, I believe, more or less what Lawrence means. First, it is necessary to recognise that health and decadence (I will use Nietzsche's language for the sake of simplicity) are not mutually exclusive. To the contrary, Nietzsche regarded himself as both healthy and decadent. He makes it plain in the first section of *Ecce Homo* that his own decadence consisted in long experience of morbidity, of actual physical sickness, from which vantage point he examined the attitudes and values of abundant health. That is, he came to know how typical decadents feel, or he knew the groundwork of their feelings. To this physically sick Nietzsche there thus came an intimate knowledge of how certain values inimical to life (nihilistic values) had arisen. Specifically these were and are the Christian moral values which once openly held life in contempt and even now seek to 'amend' life so far as the human race is concerned. This desire for amendment, Nietzsche argues, is ultimately a rejection of one's own personal degeneracy. One establishes two equations: goodness = health, harmony and co-operation; badness = pain, discord and antagonism. The object is to eliminate the second equation from all human affairs.

But this seemingly wholesome way is the way of the decadent, for only a decadent dreams of a 'perfected', which is to say an *inorganic* life. For every living thing is of necessity made up of conflict. So it is just an obvious form of decadence, the form to which we normally give the name, that openly relishes *les fleurs du mal*. We should remember that the fascinating Baudelairean savour has to do with a connection between sex and holiness, sex and heaven, sex and 'purity': in short, sex and death. Early Christians and numbers of medieval people actually preferred the sick to the healthy, since the healthy were too much in love with life to be ready candidates for heaven. The infirm were demonstrably heading for the 'perfection' of the afterlife. Then there is our modern mode of decadence which reaches out for the inorganic, sees people as more or less interchangeable and concentrates upon their purely social worth.

The point is that the typical decadent *depersonalises* himself and others. An individual is then regarded as one of God's scarcely differentiated children, or as a member (a 'unit') of the Church, or else, in modern parlance, as one who 'belongs to society'. His or her body is an assemblage of parts, although it is we who have fragmented the body for medical purposes. One's very 'soul' is a reflection of society. The overriding aim in all this is the seemingly commendable one of keeping sickness and pain at bay. For millenia, in one fashion or another, we have aimed for unmodified joy – as if joy were incompatible with sorrow.

On the other hand, good health should correctly be seen to consist not in the absence of sickness but in power to surmount it. A healthy person, says Nietzsche, makes use of his illnesses and overcomes them, while an unhealthy person yields to them. Similarly a healthy society, such as the Renaissance, is certainly not one in which few are sick (injured, humiliated, and so on), but one which produces flowers from its natural discord. These are not *fleurs du mal* (though it would be a typical decadent's error to think they were) but, for example, the splendid language of a *Tamburlaine*. Thus health and decadence do not necessarily exclude each other. Sometimes indeed, perhaps as a rule, the first needs the second as antagonist. '*From the military school of life.* – What does not kill me makes me stronger.'[33]

Now Lawrence's Birkin coins the phrases 'synthetic creation' and 'destructive creation'. Two rivers flow concurrently throughout the world. One is the 'silver river of life, rolling on and quickening all the world to a brightness'. The other is 'that dark river of dissolution', a 'black river of corruption'.[34] In plain terms Birkin means that human beings at least (for it is not clear if he intends a non-human application as well) create either by merging things (synthetic creation) or by splitting things (destructive creation), by fusion or by fission. The second sort of creative process has been the commoner in our history, but bursts of synthetic creation occur now and then and, in any event, Birkin cannot tolerate the thought of centuries of 'ice-destructive knowledge, snow-abstract annihilation'.[35] These and similar phrases in *Women in Love* have sometimes seemed to critics of Lawrence to be obscure and eccentric, yet their meaning is vital. Birkin is prophesying the end of Apollonian harmony between the senses and the intellect. Such a fate must also mean the end of individuals. The world's future will be either purely sensual in the 'African' way or abstract in the 'northern' way. In both cases individuality and self-determination will vanish. The individualist's route is anyway painful, so it is especially easy to convince a hedonistic people that it is also wrong – 'selfish', 'anti-social' and so forth. We increasingly aim for a life of either unindividualised sensations or impersonal thoughts. Our lives must then become a sequence of tropical ecstasies, or alternatively, for the northern races, painless immersion in streams of theories, scientific symbols, social doctrines – all thoroughly abstract and comfortingly 'unreal'. So it seems imperative (if conceivably futile) that some people, such as Birkin and Ursula, should struggle against the drift of the world, though that drift is in their blood also. These two are themselves nihilists, but seekers after new values as well.

The nihilism of this pair consists of rejecting not value as such, but old and accordingly valueless values. To Lawrence the term 'old value' is a contradiction in terms, since values are necessarily fresh creations. Alternatively, the nihilism of Gudrun and Gerald Crich is hatred of life itself. It is one thing to turn one's back on the Christian-Platonic tradition and quite another to find no sense and no delight in living. But the moral tradition of Socrates and Christ has been with us for so long that we imagine its absence to be a wasteland. Lawrence's point is that we have to go through the wasteland anyhow. And many, perhaps most, will positively welcome the desert.

When he was a boy Gerald Crich killed his brother by means of a so-called accident, and now Gerald is bent on negating every fertile, growing thing. He wishes to replace becoming with being, the freely mobile with the controlled movements of a machine. Unlike his father, Gerald manages the coal mines efficiently, since he has reduced the once muddled activity of mining to smooth-running mechanism. Gerald loves the mechanical *because it lacks internal conflict*. The parts of a machine work together, since the original will to power of each part as raw material has been rendered dormant. Gerald aspires to be the god of the machine, which means of course that he himself longs for oblivion. He has long done his best to substitute a mechanical (a socially recognised and utilitarian) will for his own original will to power – which must perforce be awkward and unruly. Therefore Gerald also wishes to be the god of such as Minette, the masochistic artist's model, and of Gudrun Brangwen, in whom he senses a kindred spirit.

Gudrun shares Gerald's desire for annihilation, or rather she comes to share it in part. At the beginning of the novel Gudrun and Ursula appear to be at one in detesting the shapeless ugliness of their home town of Beldover. But here is the vital difference between the two of them: Ursula continues to reach out for the 'silver river of life' while Gudrun progressively immerses herself in the 'black river of corruption'. Gudrun, the stylish Gudrun, even grows fascinated by the griminess of pit-heads, railway arches and brutish sex. She likes the squalor because it annihilates her: now she has no more self-responsibility, no idiotic 'standards', no aspirations. Thus Gudrun fights against nature, including her own natural (individuated) self.

No doubt the great circuses and forums of ancient Rome were also unnatural, but the Roman citizens built their temples to gods of nature, not to a purely spiritual God and certainly not to machinery. Lawrence implies that people have come to loathe nature because it is unsafe, wasteful, illogical, fecund and, above all, *pluralistic*. Nature takes a myriad forms, each with its own specific value: it is not remotely a 'system'. In our industrialised societies beauty remains, of course, but it is increasingly contrived, hence degenerate. Lawrence never revered wildness in the Gothic manner, since such reverence is just another fashion, but he always recognised the unsystematic diversity of natural things and creatures. In that particular sense wildness must take precedence over man's tamed and systematised little sphere.

Gudrun controls the highland cattle (in Chapter 14, 'Water-Party') not solely because they are male, but because, being bestially, stupidly, unreasoningly male, they are parts of uncontrollable nature. The cattle are humbled, but there remains an eternity of space-time which Gudrun obviously cannot bring to order. What maddens her is that she can control next to nothing and the entire fugitive world is so 'stupid' and unconscious. Gudrun cannot tolerate unconsciousness which always threatens to overwhelm her. Towards the end (in Chapters 29 and 30, 'Continental' and 'Snowed Up') she forms a tacit alliance with the sculptor Loerke because, for instance, he believes that 'art should *interpret* industry'.[36]

Loerke is a pioneer of the process of destructive creation. His coldly conscious desire is to dominate all spontaneous life, which is to say 'life itself'. The unreachable apex of his ambition is to extinguish will to power in Nietzsche's sense of the phrase, replacing it with the mechanical and controllable. Of course this also can be no more than a perverse form of will to power. All creatures (all forms of growth, presumably) should ideally be geometrised or engineered or otherwise robbed of self-generated movement. Here is complete life-hatred, and Gudrun has her considerable share of it. She helps to kill Gerald Crich, in effect, because she knows that he wants to die – specifically amid a white emptiness, a wilderness of snow, where everything is homogenised. He is a murderer, she is a murderer, and the outcome depends on which one is the more urgently bent on self-murder.

It must not be supposed that Ursula and Birkin are simply a joint antitheses and wholly commendable beings. There is a struggle for and Birkin, at any rate, is enticed now and then by images of dissolution. Lawrence is against purity of definition, against neat antitheses and wholly commendable beings. there is a struggle for domination between Ursula and Birkin, though it is a struggle in which each nobly preserves respect for the other's will to power, and indeed for all varieties of will to power. In addition, we should keep firmly in mind that the pairs Ursula–Gudrun and Birkin–Gerald each have a sort of complementariness, a sharing of blood or spiritual need. It was clearly part of Lawrence's purpose to present these four characters as interlocked in a broadly tragic fashion, not opposed in a moralistic fashion.

Ursula is the least contaminated, the most unmixed, and by the end of the novel one is no longer sure that her rare quality is not something of a defect. Even Birkin, the champion of the silver river of life, is drawn towards death and sometimes yearns for an earth emptied of people. To counteract that 'he guesses', as Nietzsche says, referring to the type of Birkin, 'what remedies avail against what is harmful'.[37] Thus he helps to cure himself of the blow on the head from Hermione Roddice by rolling naked in the grass. He cures himself, however, for a life with Ursula which he knows cannot actually prevail over the world-drift. The fact that Ursula does not realise as much, or does not care, suggests what, to Lawrence, was inadequate about the man–woman union *as a solution*.

It is a partial solution only, by which I do not mean that each partner must also have other social or professional 'contacts', or must 'take an interest in society', as we say. According to Lawrence there should be another kind of intimacy as well. Birkin has wanted 'eternal union with a man too'.[38] 'Eternal', mark you, meaning that at the moment of dying the link is reforged between the one about to die and the survivor. Such a link then becomes part of an endless chain. And Birkin has required union not with any man or with one of a select few but, as it has turned out, with Gerald Crich alone. What does this mean? Lawrence thought in the following way. A fruitful relation must be a complete commitment, and a man (if not a woman) needs two such commitments. This cannot be pre-arranged and if it comes about it is a destiny. For a man, intimacy with one woman greatly helps to keep his head above the black river of corruption. A man's corresponding relation with another man also helps, but in a different way. This is made plain in the Introduction to *Fantasia of the Unconscious* (published 1922). There Lawrence says that sex is most important and it means two things: the division into genders and the 'consummating act of coition'. But sex is not by any means enough, for there is also, and primarily, the 'essentially religious or creative motive'. Contrary to what Freud says, this motive is not sexual in its origins and merely (I presume) utilises the individual's peculiar, differentiated sexuality. Thus Michelangelo painted and sculpted in a certain fashion not as a means of sublimating his sexuality, nor yet because he was homosexual *in a generalised sense*, but in consequence of a primary asexual impulse which inevitably utilised his personal sexuality. This happened to be a special mode of homosexuality.

At this stage of his career Lawrence thus asserted that the best sort of creativity comes about – *when* it comes about – as a result of a man's sexual union with one woman and spiritual union with one man. Such he then believed to be the best way of life for all purposes. The judgement was philosophic or religious and so to be used as the criterion of works of art. By implication Lawrence meant that a greatly talented artist will nevertheless be lopsided if he does not follow such a path. And a lopsided artist or philosopher may lead generations astray.

However, this was Lawrence's doctrine for a few years only, specifically the immediate post-war period of *Women in Love*, *Aaron's Rod* and *Kangaroo*. In *The Lost Girl* (begun in 1913 as 'The Insurrection of Miss Houghton' and published in 1920) everything hangs upon the man–woman relation: Alvina Houghton paradoxically, as it might seem, exercises her will to power by submission to Ciccio, while the latter has no need of a special union with a man.

This was the old Lawrentian doctrine to which he would return by the time of *The Plumed Serpent* (1929), but in writing *Women in Love* (published in 1921) he began a brief, interesting period of departure from it.

In the early twenties Lawrence keenly desired intimacy of some sort with a man. The chances are that this requirement had little or nothing to do with sexuality, except in a highly sublimated form. He wanted a partner on the plane of intellectual and spiritual exploration, for which activity he presumed women to be forever unfitted. I maintain that this still-common presumption is wrong, since it is simply traditional and does not allow for *natural* developments which lie within our powers. However, Lawrence's hope was that he and the other man would spontaneously take it in turns to be disciple and leader, according to which one's qualities were best suited to a stretch of terrain. Thus in *Aaron's Rod* it is clear that Lawrence has projected himself into both Rawdon Lilly and the miner-hero, Aaron: that is, into both leader and led; while in *Kangaroo* Lawrence is Somers, a reluctant disciple who betrays his master.

Aaron Sisson leaves his wife and daughters at Christmas 1918. There is nothing much wrong with his marriage in the usual sense, or with his job as a checkweighman at the pit, and he departs for unknown reasons – unknown to him and to us. Roughly speaking, he finds ordinary life just after the war quite futile. Four years of *mechanised* killing have killed off human meaning, or left it flapping feebly in the mud. Aaron is obscurely aware of this historico-psychological fact, though, realistically, he never says as much: it is all too baffling for words.

As he works in the Covent Garden orchestra and later during his spell in Florence, Aaron is looking for someone to tell him how to live. He knows some things already and these are radical departures from widespread 1920s attitudes. Yet he knows them inarticulately, for Aaron is not an especially articulate man. If he could formulate the matter he would say, 'Give thyself, but give thyself not away.'[39] That is to say, do not *finally* yield yourself in love or in any other cause. The message of romantic novels and love-songs is false (argues Lawrence as narrator), since natural things are connected individually with the elements. For example, a lily is 'life-rooted, life-central'.[40] One lily has nothing essentially to do with another lily, and each lily is concerned with its own growth, not with some generalised notion of lily-growth. It is not absolutely clear why human individuals should do likewise, but Lawrence presumably means that the more people move away from this utterly natural mode the more they deteriorate as individuals.

Rawdon Lilly much expands on this basic teaching. He counsels Aaron to stop trying to lose himself in love or political action, the most prominent forms of modern self-evasion. 'There's no goal outside you – and there's no God outside you', Lilly maintains. Aaron should 'unfold' his own destiny, 'as a dandelion unfolds itself into a dandelion, and not into a stick of celery'.[41] But, we might object, dandelion and celery are generically different: are not two human beings more like two dandelions? To this I imagine Lawrence would have replied that, on the contrary, human beings are singular from their very roots – and so, for that matter, are dandelions.

Lilly's 'harangue', as Lawrence calls it, continues in the following way:

> We've exhausted our love-urge, for the moment. And yet we try to force it to continue working. So we get inevitably anarchy and murder. It's no good. We've got to accept the power motive, accept it in deep responsibility, do you understand me? It is a great life motive. It was the great dark power-urge which kept Egypt so intensely living for so many centuries. It is a vast dark source of life and strength in us now, waiting either to issue into true action, or to burst into cataclysm. Power – the power urge. The will-to-power – but not in Nietzsche's sense. Not intellectual power. Not mental power. Not conscious will-power. Not even wisdom. But dark, living, fructifying power. Do you know what I mean?[42]

Two points need discussion here. First, as we know, Nietzsche's sense of will to power is not distinct from Lilly's but is merely larger. Lilly means very roughly what Nietzsche means in *The Will to Power*, though Nietzsche's definition is universal. In 1922 Lawrence could not have known Nietzsche well enough. Second, in genuine contrast to Lawrence, Nietzsche implicitly contends that love is not finally a different urge from power, but a form or a style of power. All urges are ultimately will to power.

Nevertheless, Lawrence had long flirted with the notion that love is part of the power mode. I do not refer to possessive love but to unselfish love, as, for example, when Mrs Morel nurses Paul through his pneumonia. She unfolds herself into the sick youth in her struggle to bring him back from the verge of death, but it is *herself*, her power, that she thus unfolds. She remains distinct from Paul; there is no childish self-identification and no possessiveness. A like assimilation of love to power occurs when Birkin and Ursula love each other and, more transparently, in Alvina's love for Ciccio. Ursula consummates her self, that is, comes into her own will to power, in loving acknowledgement of Birkin's individual power.

In Lawrence's eyes love is naturally a giving of oneself to the other's needs, but it is a voluntary giving of the wholly-formed self, not a submission of a fledgling self whose entire, adolescent mode is givingness. So this giving is also will to power, or alternatively, selfhood. Moreover, the maxim 'Give not thyself away' applies to a woman as well as to a man. At the same time one realises what Lawrence–Lilly means: simply that a civilisation can be built around the undisguised exercise of ordinary power – of domination and submission – and consequently a culture. Likewise a civilisation may be built around the exercise of love, either as eros or agape; as eros in Alexandria, as both eros and agape in the late Middle Ages.

Love as agape is a good part of the theme of *Kangaroo*, since Australia is the matey, masculine, anti-hierarchical country. Lawrence tests out the possibility of agape as a means of taking civilisation forward again after the Great War. Love as eros does not come into the picture and *Kangaroo* is probably the least erotic of Lawrence's novels. Kangaroo (Benjamin Cooley) is scarcely an attractive figure, as the kangaroo is scarcely a handsome animal. Cooley offers Somers what the latter has always missed: absolute, David-and-Jonathan friendship.

> All his life he [Somers] had secretly grieved over his friendlessness. And now at last, when it was really offered – and it had been offered twice before, since he had left Europe – he didn't want it, and he realised that in his innermost soul he had never wanted it.[43]

Of course Lawrence is here, as always, working out his own problem. It might be formulated in the following manner. Lawrence evidently felt a need to be connected positively with the rest of humanity: that is, he felt (as most of us do not feel) potentially cut off from the rest of humanity. I believe that this is the reason for the odd, repeated insistence on spiritual intimacy with a man, commitment to a man. Physical and spiritual intimacy with a woman was not enough, because such a relation meant precisely a final severing of the bond between himself and mankind. After all, Lawrence had enjoyed a male–female connection since birth and it was the vital connection with a father that he had lacked.

He could not be lonely; he was not at all the hermit type, as Nietzsche was up to a point. But more important, Lawrence could not do as people generally do and simply maintain loose, casual links with others. Just as he was unable to take casual mistresses or enjoy sex with strangers, so he was not content with nodding acquaintances, colleagues, drinking pals and so forth. His connections must be fierce and thorough. Nor could he feel any appreciable contact with people in the mass, with social classes, nationalities, races, professional groups. All these were fairly abstract to him. So his tendency was quite different from that of Jesus. Jesus thought of individuals as 'man', while Lawrence contemplated mankind largely through the medium of his personal acquaintances, chiefly indeed through a few loved beings.

Nevertheless, almost the last thing Lawrence wanted was to sacrifice himself to another. Give thyself, but give thyself not away. He had a peculiar sense of his own inviolate separateness. Consequently, when the dying Kangaroo begs Somers 'Say you love me', all the graceless, sincere Somers can affirm is that he has an 'immense regard' for Kangaroo.[44] Somers believes that to tell Kangaroo he loves him would be more than a white lie: it would also be a self-betrayal. At the end he is obliged to betray either Cooley or himself.

Lawrence recognises in this scene (as elsewhere, time and again) that, for all the trust and affection between people, there is in addition a fundamental collision of wills to power. I do not mean a struggle to be boss, but that two selves are two forces, each to be valued as more or as less than the other at any given moment. Perhaps the words 'more' and 'less' are misleading, since they suggest an underlying similarity and a scale of measurement, while Lawrence implies that a force realises itself by distinguishing itself from others. It does not matter whether the distinction involves conquest or submission – provided the submission is self-willed. A submission, no less than a conquest, may be (as in the cases of Alvina Houghton and Ursula Brangwen) a realisation of self. But then it must be a voluntary submission, of which that of the heroine of 'The Woman who rode away' is the extreme instance.

Nearly at the end of *Kangaroo* Somers insists to Jaz (William James): 'Well, I'm the enemy of this machine civilisation. But I'm not the enemy of the deep, self-responsible consciousness in man, which is what I mean by civilisation.'[45] Each individual is responsible to himself primarily, and therefore, if he gives himself, should do so by design. Thus he becomes what he is. In this way Lawrence opposes both the machine civilisation, in which people are functions of the whole, and the unwilling obedience of the slave. Everything, for Lawrence, begins and ends in the processes of the self, the will to power.

For all that, Lawrence sometimes repudiates what he thinks of as a cult of the self, aligning that cult with shallow modernity. At such times Lawrence sees no self other than this cult-self. The reduction of self to a sort of superficial grasping and hectoring is plain in *The Plumed Serpent*. Here Lawrence is confused about the very topic upon which he is usually expert. For once he has muddled the self with an ersatz self, the real being of a human being with the attitudes and desires people form for social purposes. The fact that many people are almost entirely social creatures is neither here nor there.

Don Ramón, the hierophant of *The Plumed Serpent*, explains to the admirable Kate Leslie that regularly having one's own way means 'running about smelling all the things in the street, like a dog that will pick up something'. 'Of myself', Ramón continues, 'I have no way. No man has any way in himself.'[46] Here it will be seen that we are concerned with fancy and caprice, but what have these *necessarily* to do with will? Ramón means that one's conscious, trivial and, in all probability, fashionable desires ought to be subordinated to something nobler and momentous. Yes indeed, but Lawrence is usually aware that such a nobler force is also a force of the self; that 'self-sacrifice' is sacrifice by the self as well as of the self. There is no will other than the will of an individual, since the so-called 'collective will' is an abstraction.

Ramón seeks to bring back the ancient Mexican god Quetzalcoatl, the plumed serpent god, so that the cruel and ponderous spirit of the Mexicans might be leavened. Quetzalcoatl is held to be superior to Christ, because Christ exhorts us to forsake earth for the kingdom of heaven, which is within (a spiritual condition), while the Mexican god unites heaven and earth; spirit and flesh; the bird, the Quetzal, and the snake, the coatl.

So far this corresponds with Lawrence's usual teaching (and with Nietzsche's, since the philosopher held Christ to be the ultimate repudiator of reality), but pervading the novel is an uncharacteristic confusion of self and ego. Lawrence does not see that Kate's submitting to Quetzalcoatl will be either a discovery of her proper, healthy self or else a final betrayal of it. She may not advisedly 'lose herself', as Lawrence suggests she might. Devoting her life to Quetzalcoatl, Kate will discard her tired, European assumptions and so come into her own, or conceivably fly away into madness. Everything depends upon what her indwelling will to power actually wills. The Quetzalcoatl religion is nothing other than Lawrence's image-cluster for the purpose of combating what he sees as three forms of decadence: Christianity, dialectical reason and commercialism. Evidently someone may transcend his customs, beliefs, attitudes and emotions, but not his will to power – which may only be fostered or evaded.

We have observed throughout this chapter that, in Nietzsche's words, one *becomes* what one is. The process is continuous and should not end at any point. The 'what' of what one is is a route, not a terminus. Kate Leslie wants to eliminate whatever she now (at forty) feels to be false: ways of behaving and feeling once adopted foolishly or *faute de mieux* and grown habitual. On the other hand, Constance Chatterley has wandered into a tiresome trap and *Lady Chatterley's Lover* is the story of her escape. Connie illustrates better than most people in Lawrence the haphazard, fateful and inconclusive character of self-becoming. Up to her present age of twenty-seven she has followed the wrong directions – not necessarily a disagreeable procedure. First there was her 'aesthetically unconventional' youth in Europe, including sex as experiment and pointless little thrill; next her marriage to Clifford, quickly and permanently emptied of substance; and then the short *affaire* with Michaelis. The relation with Mellors is itself a journey of many stages amid a barren social and cultural landscape. Lawrence's chief emphasis is upon awakening and metamorphosis. Even so, Mellors' vicissitudes lie mainly in the past and there are now, I suggest, too few signs of development in him. Conversely, Sir Clifford visibly, if peripherally, changes (for the worse, if anything) as the story proceeds.

The novel is about Lady Chatterley, not her lover. She is the mainspring, or rather, since a mechanical metaphor absolutely will not do, she is the burgeoning plant. Unlike Lawrence's earlier heroines, from Lettie to Kate Leslie, Connie scarcely plans a development, hardly envisages her future. For her there is none of Ursula's positive or Gudrun's negative determination. Connie lets things happen, but comes to distinguish with increasing assurance the good things from the bad.

'Good' and 'bad' refer to blossoming and *unnatural* withering, not to morality. Michaelis amounts to a trivial escapade: he is a cocksure fellow who manages to blame Connie for his early ejaculations. Mellors is quite displeasing in personality at first. But Connie accepts her experiences, even when they make her uneasy: she is constantly watchful and responsive. To this extent she exhibits *amor fati*. At the same time she is fairly passive, but above all 'healthy' in Nietzsche's sense of the word. As for Sir Clifford, his self-discovery is a recognition of his essential vulgarity. It is Connie who turns out to be the aristocrat and Clifford who comes into his own as the village gossip (along with Mrs Bolton, his nurse). Part of Lady Chatterley's aristocratic nature and part of her *amor fati* consist in her new-found love of the body, of the flesh, as opposed to the theories and prejudices of society.

She insists to a scarce-comprehending Sir Clifford that the life of the body is better than the 'life of professional corpses'.

The human body is only just coming to real life. With the Greeks it gave a lovely flicker, then Plato and Aristotle killed it, and Jesus finished it off. But now the body is really coming to life, it is really rising from the tomb. And it will be lovely, lovely life in the lovely universe, the life of the human body.[47]

In writing these words Lawrence was perhaps heralding his next and, as it proved, final story, 'The Man Who Died'. The words are unsatisfactory and it is not clear that Lawrence himself recognises the faults in Connie's enthusiasm. The universe is not simply 'lovely', and Connie fails to appreciate that her regard for nature must include an acceptance of its terror as well as its beauty. Nor was there any compelling reason in 1928 – or now, for that matter – to claim that 'the body is really coming to life'. No one knew better than Lawrence how easy it is to confuse all forms of eroticism with the essentially respectful and insouciant loving that he advocated.

This fact is made plain in 'À Propos of *Lady Chatterley's Lover*'.

As late as 1928 Lawrence had not said in uncluttered fictional form what he must always obscurely have felt to be true. At all events, his doctrine still seemed to be perverse and, of course, excessively taken up with 'sex'. Many times in essays (in 'Reflections on the Death of a Porcupine', 'Democracy', 'New Mexico', 'Indians and Englishmen', 'The Crown') and in substantial parts of *Studies in Classical American Literature, Fantasia of the Unconscious* and *Psychoanalysis and the Unconscious* he had argued his strange yet utterly natural and obvious case. Strange because very few had come near to uttering it throughout man's idealistic and nihilistic history. That history with all its weird beliefs, codes and symbolisations also illustrates, by way of contrast, why and how Lawrence's meaning is simply natural and akin to Zarathustra's 'remain true to the earth'.

'The Man Who Died' is a final and audacious assertion in the most heretical terms. Nietzsche's *Ecce Homo* concludes with the words, 'Have I been understood? – *Dionysus versus the Crucified* – ?' Lawrence's story also depicts Christ as the adversary: that is to say, the risen Christ is the antagonist of his former self. Jesus is himself the Antichrist. And Lawrence sees the way of the old, crucified Christ, the actual Christ, as a deadly error.

The crucifixion is presented as something quite other than the preliminary to the saviour's glorification: now it is the gateway to a proper earthly life. Jesus had always believed death to be the joyful access to the Father in heaven, but now he appreciates the ultimate absurdity at the heart of man's condition: that death alone removes the ever-present fear of death which accounts for our ridiculous history. We live absurdly because we are afraid of dying: hence the nonsense of much of our culture. Jesus has 'miraculously' completed the stages of dying except the last, since he was cut down barely alive. Therefore he has known the worst that life can offer and no longer desires the Father or the kingdom of heaven.

The kingdom of heaven no longer matters to him, because every assault upon his senses, painful or delightful, is sufficient unto itself. Christ's emergence into life is more or less credible, or as credible as such an event could be made. The life to which he returns is the life of the birds and beasts. A young cock tied by its leg maintains its will above all, namely to eat and crow and take the hens. Christ does not 'take' a woman in this way, for his mating with the priestess of Isis (who believes him to be Osiris) is gentle, respectful and at her instigation. Jesus is now entirely reborn into a world whose very cruelties, treacheries and concupiscence he wholeheartedly accepts. So he has been transformed from nay-sayer to yea-sayer *par-excellence*. Lawrence assumes that Christ's ministry was a rejection of the actual world of becoming, of the endlessly changing flesh. The resurrected Christ is not God but a *man* who dies and whose *amor fati* now seems well-nigh complete. He is at home in the material world, interpreting and evaluating all he sees, rejecting nothing. Perhaps he is less awesome than Rilke's Angels or Nietzsche's *Übermensch*, but in his completed humanity he is, like them, a measure of our shortcomings.

An important point remains to be made about Nietzsche's 'will to power' and Lawrence's faith in self-realisation. By 'will' Nietzsche expressly does not mean something fleeting, fashionable or conscious in its origins. Lawrence, however, often does use the word 'will' in that everyday sense and so may be misleading. Nietzsche regards the 'self' as a fiction. He argues that each personality (to think only in human terms) comprises a number of competing forces. There is no single subject, no overlord of these forces, but, he asks, does it not rather seem that there is 'a kind of aristocracy of "cells" in which dominion resides? To be sure, an aristocracy of equals, used to ruling jointly and understanding how to command?'[48] So the subject is a multiplicity, not a single agent. It might be helpful here to think of the multiple self as resembling Homer's Greek heroes, each of whom has more or less equal status with the others. Together they form a coherent body of men distinct from their adversaries, the Trojans, from Helen, from the armourers, slaves and so forth.

How could such a 'multicellular' creature be informed by will to power? In fact this will is, as Deleuze puts it, 'the principle of the synthesis of forces'.[49] The will is what synthesises the 'Homeric heroes', so to speak, except that – and this is most important – the synthesising will is not distinct from the 'heroes' themselves. No one other than the heroes holds the heroes together. They are not conscripted or bound by higher authority. However obscure this might seem, it does describe the manner in which a human being (body and 'mind') behaves. One grasps oneself as a coherence, despite the fact that one is a number of distinct and often conflicting activities. And the 'one' who does the grasping does not exist apart from the activities themselves. There is evidently no single, separable, overseeing subject, which means that such a subject is a convenient (perhaps a necessary) abstraction. We must not lose sight of the fact that separate forces are synthesised in the composition of a human individual not for the sake of his mere survival, but for the sake of power. The forces are disposed so as to enhance the individual. He inescapably wishes to grow, expand, assimilate his surroundings. That is why he is properly defined as 'will to power'.

Lawrence, for his part, was often seduced into aligning 'will' with 'ego', no doubt because he was keenly impatient with the ego, with the overweening demands of consciousness. For example, Hermione Roddice in *Women in Love* boasts to Birkin, Gerald and Ursula that as a child she conquered her nervousness by willpower. Birkin angrily tells her that 'such a will is an obscenity'.[50] I presume Birkin means that Hermione should have acknowledged her nervousness as part of herself, not eliminated it. In fact she disowned it, trampled it underfoot. The 'she' who thus disposed of the nervousness was a dissociated will. So Hermione typically limited herself instead of expanding herself by comprehending the experiences that made her feel nervous. Such a will is anything but a personal, creative will.

In this way Lawrence, like Nietzsche, in effect taught that all one's conscious psychic activities should be avowed and none arbitrarily suppressed. The activities would then compose themselves organically and grow through contact with the environment, as natural organisms grow.

6

God and Nietzsche's Madman

The madman—Have you not heard of that madman who lit a
lantern in the bright morning hours, ran to the market place, and
cried incessantly: 'I seek God! I seek God!'—As many of those
who did not believe in God were standing around just then, he
provoked much laughter. Has he got lost? asked one. Did he lose
his way like a child? asked another. Or is he hiding? Is he afraid
of us? Has he gone on a voyage? emigrated?—Thus they yelled
and laughed.

The madman jumped into their midst and pierced them with
his eyes. 'Whither is God?' he cried; 'I will tell you. *We have killed
him*—you and I. All of us are his murderers.'[1]

Nietzsche's tale is about the murder of God, not His non-existence.
This is far from commonplace atheism, for commonplace, heedless
atheism is itself under attack. Unbelievers generally assume that
God was always an illusion, so that our modern repudiation of him
can only increase our freedom. Nietzsche knows, on the contrary,
that a world without God must be a wilderness as well as an
opportunity. Nietzsche assumes that when God 'lived in men's
hearts' He was alive in an exceedingly valuable sense. He was the
Lord of all power and might, but now every sort of authority lies in
the hands of ordinary people. They have nothing to look up to but
themselves, no one to question, and in particular they have no
model of conduct. Human life has lost its moral meaning, but we
still give it a moral interpretation.

The freethinkers who mock the madman have no idea that they
have done away with undisputed goodness. They have separated
God from the moral law, assuming that the latter has a life of its
own. Though Nietzsche's marketplace atheists are nineteenth-
century persons, they are presumably in the same condition as we;
that is, they oscillate between two attitudes, the first a denial of
binding moral rules and the second a horrified reaction to tales of

depravity. On the one hand there is no God, while on the other hand some deeds are unequivocally and objectively wicked. Nietzsche maintains that these two attitudes contradict each other.

I do not know of a better 'post-Christian' argument for the practice of good than that of Iris Murdoch in *The Sovereignty of Good*. We should strive to discern the particular good required by every circumstance: that is Iris Murdoch's existential recommendation, presented as not 'hers' at all but as a more or less mandatory feature of the human condition. The recommendation (or 'injunction') means that we must realistically observe our situations, eschew fantasy, and above all 'unself' ourselves. It seems possible (though Iris Murdoch would certainly not agree) that this view is an internalisation and humanisation of God. He merely dwells in each of us and dictates our behaviour, or would do so if our perceptions were not clouded by selfishness, fashion and immaturity.

We are told that good is transcendent. It is also strictly a concept, since it is confined to the human race and our conceptualising minds. Nevertheless it is sovereign over other concepts, just as whatever praxis we apprehend as good should push aside other possibilities. That is to say, good is not in even the widest sense a 'matter of opinion'. On the other hand, good deeds are always particular and never exactly repeatable. Each good action is of a piece with a precise set of circumstances. Conversely, badness is myopia or blindness: one squints, averts one's gaze, shuts one's eyes, prefers a formula to an observable reality, fails to look 'under the net' (to adapt Iris Murdoch's Wittgensteinian image from her first novel).

Iris Murdoch remarks that 'The ordinary person does not, unless corrupted by philosophy, believe that he creates values by his choices.'[2] We can imagine Nietzsche agreeing with this and then adding that it is only extraordinary people who create values, which are, nevertheless, created. He might further insist that values are made by our interpretations, not our choices. In Nietzsche's eyes evaluation of behaviour is somewhat like reading a poem and pronouncing upon its meaning and quality. There is no unarguably correct reading and no universally accepted criterion of quality.

It is important to add, in this brief rehearsal of some points in *The Sovereignty of Good*, that good behaviour is said to be pretty well indefinable. However, one specific characteristic that comes near to goodness, or points to it, is humility. Those who lack the 'anxious avaricious tentacles of the self'[3] exercise the uncluttered vision that is a large part of goodness. It is true that we usually respect such people on the very rare occasions that we meet them. This is not the result of Christian influence, since, for example, in Classical times people spoke well of Germanicus and Brutus because they betrayed notably little self-interest or pettiness. For all that, goodness is neither the only sort of impressive behaviour nor always, comparatively speaking, especially impressive at all. Here is the place to start trying to define Nietzsche's anticipatory objection to Iris Murdoch's type of argument, his 'leaping over' twentieth-century moralists.

When Nietzsche speaks of the 'genealogy of morals' he refers to the development of slave morality out of master morality. It is the former, of course, that in modern western thinking equates the good with the unegoistic. It is perhaps not widely disputed that our notions of good and evil have had but a limited life in relation to recorded history, let alone to the span of human time on earth. In the ancient world, and especially before about 1000 BC, the good man was always a lordly being who looked down upon 'bad' or slavish folk. Further, aristocratic and warrior codes have persisted down the ages, so that here and there, in Islamic countries, in Japan, in parts of Latin America and among some African tribes, the moral code as we understand it seems an ill-fitting garment. For millenia there have been persons and entire races who prized qualities which we regard as bad: pride, hardness and cruelty. How can we declare, therefore, that good in our sense must be sovereign? How can we determine that good is what human situations invariably demand?

It would be an altogether different matter to argue that one's values, whatever they are, must take precedence over argument and reason. That is an honourable anti-dialectical position. But we are concerned with the belief that efficient perception leads to good or virtually amounts to good. According to this supposition, Homer and Shakespeare saw matters so undistortedly that their productions reveal the inherent wickedness of wicked behaviour and the inherent desirability of goodness. Possibly there is goodness in our modern sense in the *Iliad*, for instance when Achilles gives the body of Hector to Priam in Book xxiv, but it seems doubtful that this is so, and in any event this one 'good' action of Achilles is not the point of the poem. In fact Homer's unblinkered awareness of his Bronze Age society tends to disprove Iris Murdoch's argument. To Homer good means noble-spirited, and this aristocratic quality too co-exists with lucid perceptions.

When we survey some tapestry of events, real or fictional, it is often not the good person who most impresses us but some variety of the bad. Is this because we have been corrupted by art? Perhaps it is the other way round, since it is the uncorrupted child who most admires Achilles in a child's version of the *Iliad*, and the humane adult who has come to regard Achilles as a murderous brute, and may well have been taught to do so. Most of us have no difficulty in agreeing with Aristotle that the main personages of epic and tragedy are awe-inspiring. We are aroused to wonder by Theseus, by Dido and Aeneas, by Orestes, even by such a vicious woman as Clytemnestra and such a maddened killer as Medea. In contexts of this sort humility would make little impact: it would be absolutely unimpressive. Even Antigone is not good so much as heroically self-willed.

Certainly we must conclude that badness is at least as welcome as goodness on stage. Our hospitality to wickedness is more than a respite from the rigours of respectability in everyday life, for it is, among other things, a recognition (in conditions of personal safety, of course) that we prefer the clash of personalities to the plainer harmony of ubiquitous goodness. It is harmony we aim for, but this should preferably be an ultimate harmony of contrasting figures. Indeed to speak of 'harmony' in any other sense is to misuse the word, for what we then mean is monotony. Hence, as we all acknowledge in theoretical discussion, the need for Goneril and Regan as well as Cordelia and Edgar, for Iago alongside Desdemona, for Iachimo as foil to Imogen. We still like to believe that Shakespeare presents moral lessons, whereas his supposed moralising is a minor element subordinate to his shining images of the world. It does not hold the images together and is a component of each play rather than its governing agency. *King Lear* might be said to be an exception to this general Shakespearean rule, yet even *Lear* is a cry of disgust rather than a lesson for us to heed – and still the sombre images predominate.

The question Shakespeare could be said to pose is this: What value would Desdemona have without Iago? Cordelia without Goneril? It is not just that Iago is necessary as an agent in the play *Othello*, but that his viciousness feeds and sustains an economy in which the honour of Othello and Desdemona thrives. The reverse is also true. Desdemona needs Iago as he needs her, since both are locked in a dramatic sphere. But in this regard *Othello* at least adequately represents society: that is to say, the Desdemona qualities always and everywhere require the Iago qualities, as flowers require choking weeds. It is easy to imagine an essential or 'free-floating' Desdemona who seems not to need either the play of which she is inescapably a part or even our daily sphere of mixed vice and virtue. Yet to imagine such a Desdemona is a mental dodge. It is hard to remember that everything is what it is purely in its contexts. Desdemona absolutely could not exist either as an invented character or as a real person in an Iago-less world.

First, she is part of Shakespeare's pseudo-Venetian sphere, but then she is also a fragment of the predatory earth. Structuralist and 'post-structuralist' critics are, if anything, only too well aware that Desdemona, for example, is a series of signs in a formal work. Possibly Schopenhauer and Nietzsche have good claims to be the ultimate founders of such twentieth-century movements as formalism and structuralism. Neither philosopher measures works of art in terms of their similarity to everyday life. In fact neither believes that we have unimpeded access to reality. For both of them the human mind is an architectonic instrument. It cannot but perform two contradictory functions: it constructs whatever it contemplates (Coleridge's 'primary imagination') while recognising the independence of external things. Our knowledge is a series of inventions, fables and codes joined with a recognition that the world at large is unknowably there.

Our familiar and age-old error is to believe that moral attitudes may have priority over life itself. If they fail to do so, that is somehow 'life's fault'. Nietzsche's moral radicalism consists in pointing out that the proclivities of an Iago are as valuable for our species as those of a chaste wife such as Desdemona. Nietzsche writes that 'the evil instincts are expedient, species-preserving, and indispensable to as high a degree as the good ones; their function is merely different'.[4]

Nietzsche's words explain why we exult in the crimes of tragic heroes and heroines. Of course we are appalled as well, but the last reaction we make, if we are worthy critics, is one of ordinary moral censure. If we condemn Medea, this is mainly because our very language forces us to do so: inwardly and inarticulately we are more than half in league with her. In effect this barbarian puts the case for passionate attachment and private honour against civic responsibilities. It is therefore Medea whom we indefensibly admire and the great Jason, her husband, whom we somewhat despise. These valuations are natural rather than moral, simply because Medea places the life-urge of the individual before the abstract good of the community. The latter is the dull, infertile moral goal. So Medea's dreadful killings, according to the central paradox of all tragedy, are affirmations of life as against the mere rules of society and – what is far more bitter – against the decent feelings of humanity as well.

We cannot term Medea 'degenerate', for she is nearly the opposite. Our own yearning for purity is a sign of degeneration, which means the reduction from a complex to a simple form. Man is more complex than other organisms and must healthily embrace a greater diversity of experiences, yet he usually tries to limit his experience, to simplify himself. 'Diversity' cannot mean an Arcadian sort of variety in which creatures and their habitats are constantly beautiful, pacific and undisturbing. It means instead endless collision and appropriation. For this very reason goodness may become a tyranny. Nietzsche expresses this point as follows:

> The 'good man' as tyrant—Man has repeated the same mistake over and over again: he has made a means to life into a standard of life; instead of discovering the standard of life in the highest enhancement of life itself, in the problem of growth and exhaustion, he has employed the means to a quite distinct kind of life to exclude all other forms of life, in short to criticize and select life.[5]

Although this is only an unpublished notebook utterance, it is a mature utterance made in 1888. Nietzsche of course means that the natural world is primary and inescapable and should therefore be the source of our judgement of ourselves. To judge in opposition to it is madness, though as a rule a collective sort of madness. Among our means to life, morality is often important: that is, morality commonly acts as an enhancement of life. Sometimes, however, it acts as a brake or a poison: it retards processes that should plunge ahead, or it kills processes that should live.

We presumably agree with Iris Murdoch that goodness is a concept. Our aim should be not to weaken morality for the sake of self-gratification, but to confine morality to its proper, subordinate place; to recognise that good ought not to be our sovereign concept. Strictly speaking no concept should inevitably prevail over others, but all should be measured against life itself. No doubt we sometimes conceptualise 'life itself', yet we ought to resist the temptation to do so. If we retain images of growth and decay, of energies expending themselves endlessly and pointlessly, then at least we have a grasp of that profusion of forces against which all mere concepts must be measured and found wanting.

That was the attitude to life in the tragic age of the Greeks. It is also Nietzsche's attitude and, in their individual ways, that of Yeats, Rilke, Mann and Lawrence. The philosopher and the four artists are 'immoralists' in this sense: they do not advocate or prefer immorality, but resist the tyranny of the good man. Nor do they resemble Nietzsche's freethinkers who scoff at his madman, for their work echoes the madman's opinion about the 'greatness' of the deed of killing God.

> Is not the greatness of this deed too great for us? Must we ourselves not become gods simply to appear worthy of it? There has never been a greater deed; and whoever is born after us – for the sake of this deed he will belong to a higher history than all history hitherto.[6]

Is this a 'mad' comment in any sense? Nietzsche himself thinks that posterity, namely ourselves, must belong to a 'higher history than all history hitherto'. He plainly assumes that the bulk of posterity will be unaware of their exalted history. A few, and our four authors belong to this category, will rise to their historical task. Let us now briefly concentrate upon the interpretation of that task made by each author.

From beginning to end Yeats assumes that he must justify mankind by aesthetic and legendary means. True, there is a mood of recantation of this attitude in 'The Circus Animals' Desertion', but the mood has vanished again by the end of *Last Poems*. 'Justify' will seem a strange word to use because it implies guilt, but I refer simply to the making of sense and value out of our lives. That, after all, is justification. The value of humanity need not be (and in Yeats's view had better not be) of an ethical character.

Yeats always knows that the history of Ireland began 'Before God made the angelic clan', that Ireland is a 'Druid land'.[7] This means that the Irish repudiate moralistic interpretations. The dialectic is alien to them also, so that neither Socrates nor St Paul lies behind their manner of thought.

> Know that when all words are said
> And a man is fighting mad,
> Something drops from eyes long blind,
> He completes his partial mind,
> For an instant stands at ease,
> Laughs aloud, his heart at peace.

The references in this late poem, 'Under Ben Bulben', are in the main universal, but the viewpoint is naturally Irish. Yeats declares that a man may be at peace just when he is fighting mad. It is enmity that produces a heart at peace, provided the enmity is zestful and fearless. One is reconciled with oneself just when one is utterly at odds with another. Then the 'partial mind' is completed. It seems, therefore, that the very cause of restlessness and self-division is the attempt to love an enemy as if he were not an enemy. To speak more comprehensively, self-division is the result of setting some standard or ideal against one's appetences. Note that in this respect there is a revealing difference between Yeats and Nietzsche. The latter accepts inward struggles as unavoidable and sometimes fruitful, while the former thinks of mental conflict as surpassable in principle and sometimes, happily, in practice. Nietzsche sees nothing automatically wrong with placing an ego-ideal against the day-to-day workings of the ego, *provided that the ideal is one's own invention*. Both men are agreed upon one aspect of this question, namely that ideals imposed by the social group are barren.

Yeats never departed from his early conviction that the modern world of technology, democracy, equality and progress is calculated to induce a sort of narcotic moralism. Our efforts are directed towards peace, the healing of wounds, by which means we foster precisely a frenzy of dissatisfaction. The 'partial mind' or the 'composite' soul, as Yeats presents it, is a product of philosophies and faiths that divide people from what they can do. One has a will to power which must be primary and at any given moment might or might not entail loving one's neighbour. Yeats never speaks of will to power but he means, time and again, that the neighbour is not necessarily to be loved, but to be faced, measured and, whenever possible, respected for what he is. This facing is not a merging of oneself and the neighbour, not a blurring of identities and desires; on the contrary, it is a reckoning of his forces against one's own and might involve combat of some sort.

Despite this acceptance of outer conflict, there is of course in Yeats the determination to make a unity sooner or later. The 'gong-tormented sea' of 'Byzantium' is to be fashioned into works of art or some kind of handiwork (a 'moonlit dome', say, or whatever the 'golden smithies of the emperor' might produce) and that is man's supreme function. This function is aesthetical, so that the true aesthete is anything but an airy avoider of problems. In fact he is one who confronts difficulties and at his best accepts the tragic groundwork of our lives. He does this by looking outwards to the gong-tormented sea and making patterns of what he observes. The turbulence is neither denied nor palliated but organised, made beautiful. The beauty and the torment belong together.

So Yeats does as Nietzsche's madman suggests and sets himself up as a 'god', a god in the sense of a creator. This means an absolute creator, one who assumes that he can 'play with' the world as he wishes, but nevertheless cannot rob it of its earthly character. In Yeats's view no god can do that, and that is why he identifies Christ Himself with Dionysus. However, Yeats falls short by Nietzsche's standards in refusing to see – as one 'born after us' – that he may not expect a return of historical customs. Yeats retains the spirit of revenge, not in the usual modern guise of a desire for progress (that is, the desire to make up for yesterday's injuries) but in the loftier guise of veneration for hierarchy. Thus he resembles Zarathustra's two kings, higher men indeed but ones who are foolishly confident that social hierarchy of an old ceremonious sort will be restored.

And what of Rilke, for on the face of it the *Duino Elegies* are markedly Nietzschean? Rilke joins Nietzsche's madman and might almost be the madman himself in his apparent overweening assumption that nature has need of us, of each one of us individually. Yet Rilke plainly faces the facts he describes in an altogether different spirit from Nietzsche's. The latter emphasises joy: the last two parts of *Thus Spoke Zarathustra*, 'The Intoxicated Song' and 'The Sign', constitute a veritable hymn to joy, and in *Ecce Homo* Nietzsche repeatedly mentions his high regard for *Zarathustra*. Joy is Nietzsche's leitmotiv, since from beginning to end he seems to regard the mood of sheer happiness as man's proper condition from which we are estranged.

Conversely, as we noticed earlier, Rilke is entirely an elegist. His tones are solemn; there is no laughter, either of happiness or of mockery. At the close of the Tenth Elegy the elder Lament embraces the youth and weeps. The youth ascends alone to the mountains of Primal Pain. Pain is emphasised in Rilke, as in no other poet who comes to mind. The result is that the last verse of the Tenth Elegy celebrates a sort of happiness that 'falls', in other words comes to us willy-nilly when we are not reaching out for it, just because we have recognised the ever-present reality and the fecundity of pain.

Some may argue that Rilke is exemplary in deriving happiness from pain, or in regarding the two conditions as having the same roots. They will maintain that Rilke's whole object is the transformation of what we have experienced as sorrow into happiness, an aspiration partly resembling Nietzsche's. It seems to me, however, that the happiness at the end of the *Duino Elegies* is quite distinct from the rapture at the end of *Thus Spoke Zarathustra*.

I suggest that Rilke relishes the human condition as he portrays it: *he enjoys elegy*. He is admittedly no petty individual pretending to be sad or desperate, but at the same time he is content that human beings should forever be divided from the Angels. Angels remind us of all we lack, and Rilke is reconciled to that. We are, so to speak, the 'not-Angels'. That is exactly our state. We are not so much the 'not-animals', since our chief distinction from other species consists of our aspirations. Whatever we are, we aim to be higher, more complete, more fulfilled. No dog can be more than a dog, but every person, according to both Rilke and Nietzsche, wants to be more than a person. Rilke says that this metamorphosis cannot come about. Can we imagine Nietzsche resignedly saying that man is the creature who can never give birth to the *Übermensch*?

The reason for this difference is that, unlike Rilke, Nietzsche unfailingly recognises 'genealogy': that is to say, he knows that attitudes grow, and must grow according to their own natures. Nietzsche might helpfully be likened to one living in the reign of the Emperor Julian (the Apostate) who knows that the weird modern religion of Christianity absolutely cannot be stamped out. It must take its course. Julian tried to abolish Christianity and superficially must have seemed likely to succeed, but a Nietzsche-figure living then would have *known* (not merely guessed) that the Emperor's proscriptions and purges must fail. Or we could say that Nietzsche resembles a man of the early Renaissance who obscurely senses that his period is the 'Renaissance', that Classical literatures are coming back and science will go forward from now on.

So Nietzsche's belief in the *Übermensch* is not a faith or a mere hope, but an awareness that nihilism, the 'uncanniest of all guests',[8] is upon us and that the answer to an absence of values cannot be a reinvigoration of old values. I suppose the reason for this is that values are implicitly accepted only when they first well up from the unconscious. Then they are triumphant, but as soon as they grow fully conscious they begin to lose vitality, and once they are subjected to reasoned examination they may not re-enter via the unconscious. So they lose their original energy, though communities might enforce them for generations or get up fresh crusades in their favour. In this fashion our old values are burnt out: anyone might live by them but in the future no one will unquestioningly believe in them. Therefore, says Nietzsche in effect, new values must come as surely as the development of science after Copernicus. The one who can 'transvalue' the values and so lead us out of nihilism is by definition the *Übermensch*. Therefore he will come. This is not wishful thinking, and it means that someone not unlike a Rilkean Angel will come.

There are three attitudes to life which we should briefly notice here. First there is the popular attitude which might be expressed as follows: 'At present our race is not doing very well and we have no solid grounds for hope. However, if we cling together and behave agreeably to one another, we may have a pleasant enough time and, who knows, human life might improve out of all recognition.' Second there is Rilke's attitude which declares, 'Joy is always fundamentally pain. If we accept this fact and try constantly to fill ourselves with external realities, we shall live as best we can and experience sporadic happiness.' The third voice is Nietzsche's: 'History and genealogy are actual processes, and while we weave fancies around them, they are not in themselves fanciful. Man's life has hitherto been reactive, his culture a consolatory reaction against living. Our reactive ways are now coming to an end and, if we do not perish, we must turn reaction round until it becomes spontaneous action for the very first time. That final revolution may be undertaken only by the overman.'

It might seem that of these three attitudes Rilke's is the most 'realistic', in the sense of the least deceived. In fact there is a good deal of Zarathustra's shadow in Rilke's make-up. The poet's doubts are excessive and addictive. Nietzsche himself believes in doubting everything that can be doubted, but what if one thereby no longer has a goal? The shadow in *Thus Spoke Zarathustra* has lost his goal and would persuade Zarathustra to forsake his also. Zarathustra knows that man is the animal who must have a goal. As a species we are but a bridge to the *Übermensch*: we have no other function. So this one goal of *Übermensch* must be retained, and Zarathustra leaves his shadow behind. Nietzsche of course does the same, while Rilke remains to relish his suffering – or, to be fair, his amalgam of suffering and happiness. Nevertheless, Rilke has shown us what an active as opposed to a reactive human nature would be. He has given us a glimpse of a higher (though in his view unattainable) humanity.

Thomas Mann's response to Nietzsche is significantly different from Rilke's. The poet goes to the heart of the matter, the ontological question, while the novelist stays most astutely and probingly at the ethical level. Rilke asks, 'What is it for human beings to *be*?' Mann asks, 'What is it for people to live decently?' But Mann's moral question is real, not feigned, for unlike other authors he really does not know the answer. Rather, he does not know the answer as an artist, while as an essayist and letter-writer, indeed as an everyday social man, he is almost the perfect type of modern liberal. It is not that the essays explicitly say something different from the works of fiction (though they sometimes do), but that their thoughtful and well-weighed manner detains us in the civilised context of the lecture theatre. So evil remains, for the moment, a topic for discussion and is robbed of its terrifying vigour.

The novels and stories, however, are nothing if not explorations of the borderline between good and evil or, to be exact, blurrings of that borderline. Since such a procedure is commonly judged to be shabby (a sort of equivocation), it is necessary to emphasise once again that Mann's fictional exercises in that kind constitute the substance and value of his work. As an artist, if not elsewhere, Mann is one who knows and most skilfully shows that we cannot separate our vital energies from our unamiable, destructive impulses.

Let us briefly recall the main examples. Tonio Kröger writes well (or writes as well as he does) because he guiltily alienates himself from his fellows; Aschenbach has in the past kept disintegration at bay and thereby failed to acknowledge his own 'evil'; Mynheer Peeperkorn overwhelms both the disputatious decency of Settembrini and the deadlier sword-thrusts of Naphta by his own unmoral life-force; Joseph is a creator because he is self-centred and thinks himself God's darling; Goethe exploits everyone (including himself) and has never heard of a crime he could not have committed; Felix Krull is sympathetic partly because he is somewhat unscrupulous; and, supremely, Leverkühn refuses to love his fellows (either individually or collectively) and thus 'brings back' great music. Perhaps above all we should remember that the devil in *Doctor Faustus* is always right in his arguments. He is also a plain speaker and it is we, the readers, who equivocate.

Now in all these instances Mann might be said to be contemplating evil without taking real atrocity into account. His wicked people are not remotely the equivalent of concentration camp guards. Does this mean, however, that, with the exception of Cipolla in *Mario and the Magician*, they are simply more intelligent and refined? Does that in turn mean that actual guards were just foully stupid, if possibly intelligent in a narrow technical sense? What sort of moral difference is there between the aesthete who contemplates wickedness and the vicious person who does the deeds – as Lord Henry Wotton differs from Dorian Gray in Wilde's story?

Mann is not one of Zarathustra's 'higher men', but he is perhaps 'higher' in another sense, for he has accurate and courageous knowledge of many things and lacks the common impulse towards self-deception in the realm of ideas. He is a *knower* of a high order. Even so, while dealing in the subtlest fashion with the relation between music and social life in *Doctor Faustus*, Mann does not seem finally able to appreciate that this novel as a whole actually depends upon the monstrous Hitler. The narrator, Zeitblom, regularly deplores Hitler's war, but a sort of inverse relation is assumed between the devastation of Europe and Leverkühn's achievements, instead of the 'symbiotic' relation that should surely be noticed. Similarly Mann describes the child-eating hags in *The Magic Mountain* without quite appreciating that their emblematic value is a measure of the value of the novel. The hags are a comment on the world. They are part of a fictional dream but what they represent is real. These creatures are literary devices which collapse even as devices the moment we confine them to the level of devices.

Mann appears to have insisted that evil was the fount of good, or at least a part of good, in the sphere of art. Nevertheless we are bound to assume that we, the 'decent ones', should use evil for art alone. Yet Mann of all people, the creator of Adrian Leverkühn, knows that evil cannot simply be exploited. Therefore might he not have further realised that Leverkühn's triumphant music arises from an underworld of monstrous growths and vapid souls? Leverkühn's last work, 'The Lamentation of Dr Faustus', transcends despair (writes Zeitblom, the narrator), but the work would not have come into being without despair.

For as Nietzsche says, through the medium of Zarathustra, everything is 'chained, entwined together, everything [is] in love'.[9] Nietzsche assumed that *homo sapiens*, though a product of evolution, cannot himself evolve. Our advances in speech and other modes of symbolisation have not taken us towards our proper destiny as human animals. We have merely developed a variety of techniques for reacting to, or against, our environment. Both science and religion are such techniques. Now that our reactive cultures are wearing thin we should yearn for the major advance that Zarathustra calls the 'great noontide'.

Certainly Nietzsche sometimes speaks as if great men and splendid doings have occurred now and then throughout history. Thus there have been such people as Brutus and Mirabeau, noble souls, but the mass of mankind has remained stuck in the spiritual marshlands. Lawrence too, however nicely he distinguishes both fictional and historical personages, makes only one clear-cut distinction of value, namely the gulf between the noble person and the rest. Needless to say, the noble person in Lawrence is not necessarily of high birth. This is how he expresses the matter in *Movements in European History*:

> Some men must be noble, or life is an ash-heap. There *is* natural nobility, given by God or the Unknown, and far beyond common sense. And towards this natural nobility we must live . . .
>
> The hereditary aristocratic class has fallen into disuse. And democracy means the electing of tools to serve the fears and the material desires of the masses. *Noblesse n'oblige plus* . . .
>
> There is nothing to be done, *en masse*. But every youth, every girl can make the great historical change inside himself and herself, to care supremely for nothing but the spark of *noblesse* that is in him and in her, and to follow only the leader who is a star of the new, natural *Noblesse*.[10]

Now what does this *noblesse* mean, for to adduce such a quality is liable to produce sneers or cries of disbelief from many people? Lawrence says that it means fearlessness and generosity. Both are necessary. To be fearless alone, one might as well be Attila. To be really generous is not possible in a constant state of fear.

Lawrence's hope, therefore, is that a sufficient number of youths and girls might resolve as individuals to be generous of spirit and without fear. That is roughly the difference between Lawrence's heroes and heroines and the rest of his personages. Those of 'heroic' stature try not to be frightened or mean. And they know only too well that exactly these ignoble qualities are masked when one joins the procession.

In Lawrence's fiction, however, the matter is subtler still, for there is such a person as Gudrun Brangwen who senses – or even shares – the quality of *noblesse*, yet rejects it, preferring the nihilism of Dresden. But Gertrude and Paul Morel, Ursula, Birkin, Aaron, Lilly, Somers, Kate Leslie, Don Ramón, Constance Chatterley and a few lesser characters in the stories are in the noble category. Such people are not more moral than others, but have more natural nobility.

To Nietzsche, on the other hand, there is no assurance in that direction. Lawrence's wishes will come to nothing, not because human beings are getting worse but because our all-too-human history is ending. It is ending now because we have broken the old connection between us and the rest of the universe. The connection is no longer implicit, as with animals, or mythical, as with our forebears. It is simply a fact which gives us no privileged status. So we ourselves have no preordained value and, accordingly, neither has the world at large.

Nietzsche is vastly more apocalyptic than Lawrence. Between the noble person and others there is an uplifting difference, but it is not difference enough. For that, Nietzsche supposes, we need the 'greatest elevation of the consciousness of strength in man, as he creates the overman'.[11] And such elevation of consciousness will be the *final* step forward, not the evolution of a higher species but man's coming into his own.

Notes and References

The place of publication is London unless otherwise stated.

1 PERSPECTIVES OF NIETZSCHE

1. F. Nietzsche, *Human All-Too-Human (HAH)*, 2 vols, Part I trans. Helen Zimmern, Part II trans. Paul V. Kohn BA (Edinburgh and London: T. N. Foulis, 1909 and 1911) 'Miscellaneous Maxims and Opinions', Part II, No. 29 p. 26.
2. Ibid., Part I, No. 220, p. 199.
3. William Blake, *Poetry and Prose of William Blake* (The Nonesuch Press, 1939) 'The Marriage of Heaven and Hell', p. 187.
4. F. Nietzsche, 'On the uses and disadvantages of history for life', *Untimely Meditations (UM)*, trans. R. J. Hollingdale, intro. J. P. Stern (Cambridge University Press, 1983) p. 81.
5. F. Nietzsche, *The Will to Power (WP)*, trans. Walter Kaufmann & R. J. Hollingdale, ed. Walter Kaufmann (New York: Vintage Books, A Division of Random House, 1967) Section 560, pp. 302f.
6. F. Nietzsche, *The Birth of Tragedy* and *The Case of Wagner (BT and CW)*, trans. with commentary by Walter Kaufmann (New York: Vintage Books, A Division of Random House, 1967) *BT*, Sections 10 to 25.
7. *WP*, Section 480, p. 266.
8. John T. Wilcox, *Truth and Value in Nietzsche: A Study of His Metaethics and Epistemology*, foreword by Walter Kaufmann (Ann Arbor: University of Michigan Press, 1974).
9. Ibid., pp. 156f.
10. For thorough discussion of Nietzsche on 'sublimation' see especially Walter Kaufmann's *Nietzsche: Philosopher, Psychologist, Antichrist* (Princeton University Press, 1968) Part III.
11. F. Nietzsche, *Twilight of the Idols* and *The Anti-Christ (TI and AC)*, trans. with introduction and commentary by R. J. Hollingdale (Harmondsworth, Middlesex: Penguin 1968) *AC*, Section 54, p. 172.
12. *WP*, Section 963, pp. 505f.
13. F. Nietzsche, *On the Genealogy of Morals* and *Ecce Homo (GM and EH)*, *GM* trans. Walter Kaufmann & R. J. Hollingdale, *EH* trans. Walter Kaufmann (New York: Vintage Books, A Division of Random House, 1969) *GM*, Third Essay, p. 160.
14. *HAH*, Vol. I, pp. 13f.
15. Ibid.
16. Ibid., Part I, No. 107, p. 108.
17. F. Nietzsche, *Beyond Good and Evil, Prelude to a Philosophy of the Future*

(BGE), trans. with commentary by Walter Kaufmann (New York: Vintage Books, A Division of Random House, 1966) Section 260, p. 204.

18. Ibid., Section 260, p. 207.
19. Ibid.
20. Ibid., Section 24, p. 35.
21. W. B. Yeats, *The Collected Poems of W. B. Yeats* (Macmillan, 1982) 'The Circus Animals' Desertion', p. 391. (First published in hardback 1933.)
22. Thomas Mann, *The Magic Mountain*, trans. H. T. Lowe-Porter (Secker & Warburg, 1971) Chapter 6, 'Snow', p. 496.
23. F. Nietzsche, *Philosophy in the Tragic Age of the Greeks (PTG)*, trans. with introduction by Marianne Cowan (Chicago: Regnery Gateway, 1962) p. 31.
24. *EH*, Section 3, p. 274.
25. *PTG*, pp. 51f.

2 YEATS AND ARISTOCRACY

1. W. B. Yeats, *Autobiographies* (Macmillan, 1973) p. 78. (First published in this edition 1955.)
2. *The Collected Poems of W. B. Yeats (CP)*, (Macmillan, 1969) 'The Choice', p. 278.
3. George Orwell, 'Yeats', *Collected Essays* (Secker & Warburg, 1961) p. 182. (Essay first published in 1943.)
4. W. B. Yeats, *Explorations* (New York: Macmillan, 1962) p. 368.
5. W. B. Yeats, *Essays and Introductions* (New York: Macmillan, 1961) p. 424.
6. Otto Bohlmann, *Yeats and Nietzsche: An Exploration of Major Nietzschean Echoes in the Writings of William Butler Yeats* (Macmillan, 1982) p. 1.
7. *Letters of W. B. Yeats*, ed. Allan Wade (Rupert Hart-Davis, 1954) p. 379.
8. F. Nietzsche, *Thus Spoke Zarathustra (Z)*, trans. and intro. by R. J. Hollingdale (Harmondsworth, Middlesex: Penguin, 1961) 'Of Self-Overcoming', p. 137.
9. *BGE*, 'What is Noble', Section 257, p. 201.
10. *WP*, Section 842, p. 444.
11. *CP*, 'The Seven Sages', p. 271.
12. *WP*, Section 431, p. 235.
13. See A. Norman Jeffares, *A New Commentary on the Poems of W. B. Yeats* (Macmillan, 1984) p. 12.
14. *Autobiographies*, p. 52.
15. Ibid., p. 60.
16. Ibid., p. 522.
17. Richard Ellmann, *The Identity of Yeats* (Faber & Faber, 1964) p. 64. (First published by Macmillan, 1954.)

18. *BT*, Section 5, p. 52.
19. See A. J. P. Taylor, *English History 1914–1945* (Oxford University Press, 1965) p. 56, and Robert Kee, *Ireland: A History* (Weidenfeld & Nicolson, 1980) pp. 153ff.
20. See Joseph Hone, *W. B. Yeats 1865–1939* (Harmondsworth, Middlesex: Penguin, 1971) p. 303. (First published by Macmillan, 1943.)
21. *GM*, Second Essay, Section 7, p. 69: 'Tragic terrors ... were intended as festival plays for the gods.'
22. T. R. Henn, *The Lonely Tower* (Methuen, 1965) p. xxii.
23. Richard Ellmann, *The Identity of Yeats*, p. xviii.
24. *Autobiographies*, 'Estrangement', p. 475.
25. This argument briefly recurs, but it is present in concentrated form in 'David Strauss: The Confessor and Writer', in *Untimely Meditations*.
26. 'Cathleen Ni Houlihan', in *The Variorum Edition of the Plays of W. B. Yeats*, ed. Russell K. Alspach, assisted by Catherine C. Alspach (Macmillan, 1966) p. 229.
    EH, p. 258.
28. See Nancy Cardozo, *Maud Gonne: Lucky Eyes and a High Heart* (Victor Gollancz, 1979) p. 407.
29. *CP*, 'Mohini Chatterjee', p. 279.
30. *Pages from a Diary Written in Nineteen Hundred and Thirty* (Dublin, 1944) p. 55.
31. *CP*, 'A Prayer for My Daughter', p. 211.
32. *A Vision* (Macmillan, 1962) p. 295.
33. Ibid.
34. *CP*, 'The Phases of the Moon', p. 185.
35. *A Vision*, pp. 126ff.
36. *EH*, 'Why I am So Clever', p. 255.
37. *CP*, 'Two Songs From a Play', p. 239.
38. Quoted by Richard Ellman in *The Identity of Yeats*, p. 109.
39. *WP*, Section 275, p. 157.
40. Ibid.
41. *WP*, Section 881, p. 470.
42. F. Nietzsche, *Daybreak: Thoughts on the Prejudices of Morality (D)*, trans. R. J. Hollingdale, intro. by Michael Tanner (Cambridge University Press, 1982) Section 206, p. 126.
43. Ibid., Section 308, p. 156.
44. Ibid., Section 360, p. 167.
45. *TI*, 'Maxims and Arrows', 38, p. 27.
46. Ibid. 'What the Germans Lack', 4, p. 62.
47. See ibid., 'The Problem of Socrates', 5, p. 31.
48. Ibid., 10, p. 33.
49. See *Essays and Introductions* (New York: Macmillan, 1961) pp. 292f.
50. *AC*, Section 11, p. 121.
51. F. Nietzsche, *The Gay Science (GS)*, trans. with commentary by Walter Kaufmann (New York: Vintage Books, A Division of Random House, 1974) Book One, Section 55, p. 117.
52. Ibid., Book Two, Section 98, p. 150.

53. Ibid.
54. Ibid., Book Three, Section 270, p. 219.
55. Z, Part One, 'Of Reading and Writing', p. 67.

3 RILKE'S ANGELS AND THE *ÜBERMENSCH*

1. *AC*, Section 3, p. 116.
2. Z, Part One, 'Of the Priests', p. 117.
3. *GS*, Book Three, No. 143, p. 191.
4. Z, Part One, 'Zarathustra's Prologue', 3, p. 41.
5. *EH*, 'Thus Spoke Zarathustra', 6, p. 304.
6. Z, Part One, 'Zarathustra's Prologue', 4, p. 43.
7. Ibid., p. 44.
8. Ibid., Part Four, 'The Intoxicated Song', p. 332.
9. Walter Kaufmann, *From Shakespeare to Existentialism: An Original Study* (Princeton, NJ: Princeton University Press, 1980) p. 225. (First published by the Beacon Press in 1959.)
10. Ibid., p. 226.
11. Ibid., p. 228.
12. Ibid., p. 229.
13. Ibid., p. 233.
14. Ibid., p. 239.
15. Ibid., p. 251.
16. *Selected Letters of Rainer Maria Rilke 1902–1926*, trans. R. F. C. Hull (Macmillan, 1946) pp. 66f.: letter No. 70 of 9 July 1904.
17. Ibid., p. 230: letter No. 105 of 15 March 1913.
18. All quotations from the *Elegies* are taken from *Duino Elegies*, German text with English trans., intro. and commentary by J. B. Leishman & Stephen Spender (Chatto & Windus, 1981). (First published by The Hogarth Press, 1939.)
19. *GS*, Book Three, No. 224, p. 211.
20. Rainer Maria Rilke, *The Notebook of Malte Laurids Brigge*, intro. by Stephen Spender (Oxford University Press, 1984) p. 221.
21. *GS*, Book Three, Section 109, p. 168.
22. Romano Guardini, *Rilke's Duino Elegies: An Interpretation*, trans. K. G. Knight (Darwin Finlayson, 1961) p. 103.
23. *Duino Elegies*, p. 124.
24. *Letters*, p. 250: letter of 28 June 1915.
25. Ibid., p. 355: letter of 20 February 1922.
26. *The Notebook of Malte Laurids Brigge*, Introduction, p. ix.
27. *GS*, Book Three, Section 270, p. 219.
28. *Letters*, p. 338.
29. Ibid.
30. Joan Stambaugh, *Nietzsche's Thought of Eternal Return* (Baltimore and London: Johns Hopkins Press, 1972) p. xi.
31. *Duino Elegies*, p. 142.

32. Romano Guardini, op. cit., p. 299.
33. *Nietzsche: Unpublished Letters*, trans. and ed. Karl F. Leidecker (Peter Owen, 1960) p. 132: letter to Brandes of 10 April 1888.
34. Z, Part Four, 'The Cry of Distress', p. 254.
35. F. A. Lea, *The Tragic Philosopher: A Study of Friedrich Nietzsche* (New York: Philosophical Library, 1957). See the last chapter.
36. *AC*, Section 29, p. 141.
37. Z, Part Four, 'The Leech', p. 263.
38. Ibid., p. 266.
39. Gilles Deleuze, *Nietzsche and Philosophy*, trans. Hugh Tomlinson (Athlone Press, 1983) p. 165. (First published by Presses Universitaires de France, 1962.)
40. Z, Part Four, 'Retired from Service', p. 273.
41. Ibid., 'The Ugliest Man', p. 277.
42. Ibid., 'The Voluntary Beggar', p. 280.
43. Ibid., 'The Shadow', p. 285.
44. Ibid., 'The Greeting', p. 293.
45. Ibid.
46. Ibid., 'The Intoxicated Song', p. 326.
47. Martin Heidegger, *Nietzsche*, Vol. II, *The Eternal Recurrence of the Same*, trans. with notes and analysis by David Farrell Krell (San Francisco: Harper & Row, 1984) pp. 135f. The four volumes of Heidegger's *Nietzsche* were in the main originally lectures given at Freiburg between 1936 and 1940.

4 MANN: BEYOND GOOD AND EVIL

     Thomas Mann, *Joseph and his Brothers*, trans. H. T. Lowe-Porter (Secker & Warburg, 1981) Prelude, p. 24.
2.   Ibid., p. 287.
3.   Ibid., p. 27.
4.   *BGE*, Section 52, p. 66.
5.   *Joseph and His Brothers, Young Joseph*, 'In the Pit', p. 385.
6.   Ibid., *Joseph the Provider*, 'I Will Go and See Him', p. 1139.
7.   *The Letters of Thomas Mann 1889–1955*, selected and trans. Richard & Clara Winston (Harmondsworth, Middlesex: Penguin, 1975) p. 184.
8.   The happiness of Mann's childhood and youth is affirmed in Richard Winston's *Thomas Mann: The Making of An Artist, 1875–1911* (Constable, 1982). For the originals of the characters of *Buddenbrooks* see Chapter 7 of that work.
9.   See Rainer Maria Rilke, 'Thomas Mann's *Buddenbrooks*', trans. Henry Hatfield, in *Thomas Mann: A Collection of Critical Essays* (Englewood Cliffs, NJ: Prentice-Hall, 1964).
10. Thomas Mann, 'Tonio Kröger', in *Stories of Three Decades*, trans. H. T. Lowe-Porter (Secker & Warburg, 1946) p. 103.
11. Ibid., p. 132.

12. Ibid., Preface, p. vi.
13. Ibid., 'Death in Venice', p. 431.
14. Ibid., p. 385.
15. Ibid., p. 386.
16. Ibid.
17. Ibid.
18. *GS*, No. 351, p. 293.
19. See Richard Winston, *Thomas Mann: The Making of an Artist*, Chapter 17.
20. *BT*, Section 20, p. 123.
21. Ibid., p. 130.
22. Thomas Mann, *The Magic Mountain*, trans. H. T. Lowe-Porter (Secker & Warburg, 1971) Chapter 5, 'Soup Everlasting', p. 200.
23. Ibid., Chapter 4, 'Necessary Purchases', p. 98.
24. Ibid.
25. Ibid., Chapter 5, 'Freedom', p. 221.
26. Ibid., p. 222.
27. *Thomas Mann: Diaries 1918–1939*, selection and foreword by Herman Kesten, trans. Richard & Clara Winston (André Deutsch, 1983) p. 96: diary entry for 21 May 1920.
28. *The Magic Mountain*, 'Encyclopaedic', p. 246.
29. Ibid., p. 242.
30. Ibid., p. 266.
31. See *Letters*, p. 121: letter of 5 January 1925 to Herbert Eulenberg, who had mentioned Mann's 'secret love' for Peeperkorn. Mann replies, 'I did not think it was all that secret.'
32. *The Magic Mountain*, 'Vingt Et Un', p. 566.
33. Ibid., 'Of the City of God', p. 398.
34. *Z*, 'Zarathustra's Prologue', 3, p. 42.
35. *WP*, 21, p. 17.
36. Thomas Mann, 'Goethe's *Faust*', in *Essays of Three Decades*, trans. H. T. Lowe-Porter (Secker & Warburg) p. 23.
37. *PTG*, p. 51.
38. Thomas Mann, *Lotte in Weimar*, trans. H. T. Lowe-Porter (Secker & Warburg, 1940) Chapter 9, p. 340.
39. Ibid., Chapter 7, p. 234.
40. Ibid., Chapter 7, p. 270.
41. *Letters*, p. 406: letter of 6 November 1948 to Erika Mann.
42. Ibid., p. 465: letter of 7 June 1954 to Erika Mann.
43. *Stories of Three Decades*, Preface, p. vii.
44. *Diaries*, p. 17: entry for 29 December 1918.
45. T. E. Apter, *Thomas Mann: The Devil's Advocate* (Macmillan, 1978) p. 134.
46. Thomas Mann, *Confessions of Felix Krull Confidence Man*, trans. Denver Lindley (Secker & Warburg, 1955) Part Three, Chapter 5, p. 294.
47. Thomas Mann, *Doctor Faustus*, trans. H. T. Lowe-Porter (Secker & Warburg, 1969) Chapter 25, p. 239.
48. Ibid., p. 237.

49. Ibid., Chapter 19, p. 155.
50. *EH*, 'Why I am So Wise', p. 222.
51. Thomas Mann, 'Nietzsche's Philosophy in the Light of Recent History', in *Last Essays*, trans. Richard & Clara Winston and Tania & James Stern (Secker & Warburg, 1959) pp. 145f.
52. Ronald Hayman, *Nietzsche: A Critical Life* (Weidenfeld and Nicolson, 1980) p. 64.
53. *Last Essays*, p. 142.
54. *Doctor Faustus*, Chapter 46, p. 491.
55. Ibid., Chapter 34, p. 386.
56. Ibid., Chapter 45, p. 477.
57. Ibid., Chapter 47, p. 499.
58. *Diaries*, pp. 254f.: entry for 16 January 1936.
59. 'Nietzsche's Philosophy in the Light of Recent History', *Last Essays*, p. 174.
60. *WP*, Book Two, pp. 192f.
61. See Chapter 1 above (note 7): *WP*, Section 480, p. 266.
62. *D*, Book II, Section 103, p. 103.

5 LAWRENCE: HOW ONE BECOMES WHAT ONE IS

1. *UM*, 'Schopenhauer as Educator', p. 129.
2. *WP*, Book Four, 'Discipline and Breeding', Section 1067, p. 550.
3. Arthur Schopenhauer, *The World as Will and Representation*, trans. G. F. J. Payne, 2 vols (New York: Dover Publications, 1966) Vol. II, p. 197.
4. Martin Heidegger, *Nietzsche*, Vol. I, *The Will to Power as Art*, trans. with notes and analysis by David Farrell Krell (San Francisco: Harper & Row, 1979) p. 61.
5. See Chapter 1 above.
6. Albert Einstein in *The Times*, 28 November 1919.
7. *WP*, Section 619, pp. 332f.
8. Gilles Deleuze, *Nietzsche and Philosophy*, p. 49.
9. On this aspect see Gilles Deleuze, op. cit., especially 'Active and Reactive', Section 10.
10. *Z*, Part One, 'Of Old and Young Women', p. 91.
11. Ibid., p. 92.
12. Ibid., 'Of Marriage and Children', p. 95.
13. D. H. Lawrence, *Sons and Lovers* (Phoenix Edition, William Heinemann, 1974) p. 7. (First published 1913.)
14. Ibid., p. 63.
15. Ibid., p. 131.
16. Lawrence himself gives this false impression in the famous letter to Garnett of 14 November 1912: 'William gives his sex to a fribble, and his mother holds his soul.' (*The Letters of D. H. Lawrence*, General Editor James T. Boulton, Vol. I, 1901–13, ed. James T. Boulton (Cambridge University Press, 1979) letter 516, p. 477.) The novel

itself does not quite bear out Lawrence's remark, but rather suggests that the real split is between William's sense of honour as a betrothed man and his personal needs.

17. *GM*, Third Essay, Section 1, p. 97.
18. Ibid., p. 98.
19. *Sons and Lovers*, p. 152.
20. Ibid., p. 153.
21. Ibid.
22. See *Sons and Lovers*, pp. 221f.
23. *TI*, 'Maxims and Arrows', No. 44, p. 27.
24. D. H. Lawrence, *The Rainbow*, intro. by Richard Aldington (Phoenix Edition, William Heinemann, 1961) p. 1. (First published 1915.)
25. Ibid., p. 95.
26. Concerning the original of Will, namely Alfred Burrows, see *Lawrence in Love: Letters to Louie Burrows*, ed. with intro. and notes by James T. Boulton (University of Nottingham, 1968) especially the Introduction, pp. ix ff.
27. *Letters*, Vol. II, letter 732, p. 183.
28. *The Rainbow*, 'The Bitterness of Ecstasy', p. 440.
29. Ibid., p. 441.
30. Benedict de Spinoza, 'The Ethics', in *Works of Spinoza*, Vol. II, trans. and intro. by R. H. M. Elwes (New York: Dover Publications, 1951) Part I, p. 48.
31. D. H. Lawrence, *Women in Love* (Phoenix Edition, William Heinemann, 1961) p. 473. (First published 1921.)
32. See James T. Boulton's Introduction to *Lawrence in Love*.
33. *TI*, 'Maxims and Arrows', 8, p. 23.
34. *Women in Love*, p. 164.
35. Ibid., p. 246.
36. Ibid., p. 415.
37. *EH*, p. 224.
38. *Women in Love*, p. 473.
39. D. H. Lawrence, *Aaron's Rod* (Phoenix Edition, William Heinemann, 1979) p. 161. (First published 1922.)
40. Ibid., p. 162.
41. Ibid., p. 286.
42. Ibid., p. 288.
43. D. H. Lawrence, *Kangaroo* (Phoenix Edition, William Heinemann, 1966) p. 104. (First published 1923.)
44. Ibid., pp. 344f.
45. Ibid., p. 256.
46. D. H. Lawrence, *The Plumed Serpent* (Phoenix Edition, William Heinemann, 1955) p. 69. (First published 1926.)
47. D. H. Lawrence, *Lady Chatterley's Lover*, intro. by Richard Hoggart (Harmondsworth, Middlesex: Penguin, 1961) p. 245. (First published 1928.)
48. *WP*, Book Three, 'Principles of a New Evaluation', No. 490, p. 270.
49. Gilles Deleuze, op. cit., p. 50.
50. *Women in Love*, p. 131.

6 GOD AND NIETZSCHE'S MADMAN

1. *GS*, Book Three, No. 125, p. 181.
2. Iris Murdoch, *The Sovereignty of Good* (Routledge & Kegan Paul, 1970) p. 97.
3. Ibid., p. 103.
4. *GS*, Book One, No. 4, p. 79.
5. *WP*, Book Two, No. 354, pp. 194f.
6. *GS*, Book Three, No. 125, p. 181.
7. *CP*, 'To Ireland in the Coming Times', pp. 56f.
8. *WP*, Book One, No. 1, p. 7.
9. *Z*, Part Four, 'The Intoxicated Song', p. 332.
10. D. H. Lawrence, *Movements in European History*, intro. by James T. Boulton (Oxford University Press, 1981) pp. 320f. (First edition published by Oxford University Press, 1921. This edition first published in hardback, 1971.)
11. *WP*, Book Four, 'Discipline and Breeding', No. 1060, p. 546.

Bibliography

The place of publication is London unless otherwise stated.

Apter, T. E., *Thomas Mann: The Devil's Advocate* (Macmillan, 1978).

Bergsten, Gunilla, *Thomas Mann's Doctor Faustus: The Sources and Structure of the Novel*, trans. Krishna Winston (Chicago and London: University of Chicago Press, 1969). (First published 1963.)

Bohlmann, Otto, *Yeats and Nietzsche: An Exploration of Major Nietzschean Echoes in the Writings of William Butler Yeats* (Macmillan, 1982).

Cardozo, Nancy, *Maud Gonne: Lucky Eyes and a High Heart* (Victor Gollancz, 1979).

Cleugh, James, *Thomas Mann: A Study* (Martin Secker, 1933).

Copleston, Frederick, *Friedrich Nietzsche: Philosopher of Culture* (Search Press, 1975).

Daleski, Herman M., *The Forked Flame: A Study of D. H. Lawrence* (Faber & Faber, 1965).

Danto, Arthur Coleman, *Nietzsche as Philosopher* (New York: Macmillan, 1965).

Deleuze, Gilles, *Nietzsche and Philosophy*, trans. Hugh Tomlinson (Athlone Press, 1983). (First published as *Nietzsche et la philosophie* by Presses Universitaires de France, 1962.)

Einstein, Albert, quoted in *The Times*, 28 November 1919.

Ellmann, Richard, *The Identity of Yeats* (Faber & Faber, 1964). (First published by Macmillan, 1954.)

Ellmann, Richard, *Yeats: The Man and the Masks* (Oxford University Press, 1979). (Previous editions New York: Macmillan, 1948; London: Faber & Faber, 1961.)

Freeman, Mary, *D. H. Lawrence: A Basic Study of His Ideas* (University of Florida, 1955).

Guardini, Romano, *Rilke's Duino Elegies: An Interpretation*, trans. K. G. Knight (Darwin Finlayson, 1961).

Hatfield, Henry, (ed.), *Thomas Mann: A Collection of Critical Essays* (Englewood Cliffs, NJ: Prentice-Hall, 1964).

Hayman, Ronald, *Nietzsche: A Critical Life* (Weidenfeld & Nicolson, 1980).

Heidegger, Martin, *Nietzsche*, Volume I, *The Will to Power as Art; Nietzsche*, Volume II, *The Eternal Recurrence of the Same*, both volumes trans. with notes and analysis by David Farrell Krell (San Francisco: Harper & Row, Volume I 1979, Volume II 1984). German edition in four volumes based on lecture courses at Freiburg, 1936–40.

Heller, Eric, *The Ironic German: A Study of Thomas Mann* (Secker & Warburg, 1958).

Hendry, J. F., *The Sacred Threshold: A Life of Rainer Maria Rilke* (Manchester: Carcanet New Press, 1983).

Henn, T. R., *The Lonely Tower* (Methuen, 1965).

Hollingdale, R. J., *Nietzsche: The Man and His Philosophy* (Routledge & Kegan Paul, 1965).

Hollingdale, R. J., *Thomas Mann: A Critical Study* (Rupert Hart-Davis, 1971).

Hone, Joseph, *W. B. Yeats 1865–1939* (Harmondsworth, Middlesex: Penguin, 1971). (First published by Macmillan, 1943.)

Hough, Graham, *The Dark Sun* (Duckworth, 1968).

Jaspers, Karl, *Nietzsche: An Introduction to the Understanding of His Philosophical Activity* (Tucson: University of Arizona Press, 1965). (First published in German, 1936.)

Jeffares, A. Norman, *A New Commentary on the Poems of W. B. Yeats* (Macmillan, 1984). (First edition 1968.)

Kaufmann, Walter, *From Shakespeare to Existentialism* (Princeton, NJ: Princeton University Press, 1980). (First published by Beacon Press, 1959.)

Kaufmann, Walter, *Nietzsche: Philosopher, Psychologist, Antichrist* (Princeton, NJ: Princeton University Press, 1968). (First edition 1950.)

Kee, Robert, *Ireland: A History* (Weidenfeld & Nicolson, 1980).

Lanvin, Janko, *Nietzsche: A Biographical Introduction* (Studio Vista, 1971).

Lawrence, D. H., *Aaron's Rod* (Phoenix Edition, William Heinemann, 1979). (First published 1922.)

—, *The Collected Short Stories* (Club Associates by arrangement with William Heinemann, 1974).

—, *Fantasia of the Unconscious* and *Psychoanalysis and the Unconscious* (William Heinemann, 1922).

—, *Kangaroo* (Phoenix Edition, William Heinemann, 1966). (First published 1923.)

— *Lady Chatterley's Lover*, intro. by Richard Hoggart (Harmondsworth, Middlesex: Penguin, 1961). (First published 1928.)

—, *Lawrence in Love: Letters to Louie Burrows*, ed. with intro. and notes by James T. Boulton (University of Nottingham, 1968).

—, *The Letters of D. H. Lawrence*, General Editor James T. Boulton (Cambridge University Press). Eight volumes are planned and the first appeared in 1979.

—, *The Lost Girl*, ed. John Worthen (Cambridge University Press, 1981). (First published 1920.)

—, *Movements in European History*, intro. by James T. Boulton (Oxford University Press, 1981). (First published 1921.)

—, *Phoenix II: More Uncollected Writings*, ed. Warren Roberts & Harry T. Moore (William Heinemann, 1968).

—, *The Plumed Serpent*, intro. by Richard Aldington (Phoenix Edition, William Heinemann, 1955). (First published 1926.)

—, *The Rainbow*, intro. by Richard Aldington (Phoenix Edition, William Heinemann, 1961). (First published 1915.)

—, *Sons and Lovers* (Phoenix Edition, William Heinemann, 1974). (First published 1913.)

—, *The White Peacock*, ed. Andrew Robertson (Cambridge University Press, 1983). (First published 1911.)

—, *Women in Love*, intro. by Richard Aldington (Phoenix Edition, William Heinemann, 1961). (First published 1921.)

Lawrence, Frieda, *Not I, but the Wind* . . . (New York: Viking Press, 1934).

Lea, F. A., *The Tragic Philosopher: A Study of Friedrich Nietzsche* (New York: The Philosophical Library, 1957).

Leavis, F. R., *Art and Thought in Lawrence* (Chatto & Windus, 1976).

Leavis, F. R., *D. H. Lawrence, Novelist* (Chatto & Windus, 1955).

McIntosh, Christopher, *The Rosy Cross Unveiled: The History, Mythology and Rituals of an Occult Order*, foreword by Colin Wilson (Wellingborough, Northamptonshire: The Aquarian Press, 1980).

Magee, Bryan, *The Philosophy of Schopenhauer* (Clarendon Press, 1983).

Mann, Thomas, *Buddenbrooks*, trans. H. T. Lowe-Porter (Secker & Warburg, 1970).

—, *Confessions of Felix Krull Confidence Man*, trans. Denver Lindley (Secker & Warburg, 1955). (First published 1954.)

—, *Thomas Mann: Diaries 1918–1939*, selection & foreword by Herman Kesten, trans. Richard & Clara Winston (André Deutsch, 1983).

—, *Doctor Faustus*, trans. H. T. Lowe-Porter (Secker & Warburg, 1969). (First published 1947.)

—, *Essays of Three Decades*, trans. H. T. Lowe-Porter (Secker & Warburg).

—, *Joseph and His Brothers*, trans. H. T. Lowe-Porter (Secker & Warburg, 1981). (First published in England by Secker & Warburg in five volumes. Originally published 1933–43.)

—, *Last Essays*, trans. Richard & Clara Winston and Tania & James Stern (Secker & Warburg, 1959).

—, *The Letters of Thomas Mann 1889–1955*, selected and trans. Richard & Clara Winston (Harmondsworth, Middlesex: Penguin, 1975). (First published in Great Britain by Secker & Warburg, 1970.)

—, *Lotte in Weimar*, trans. H. T. Lowe-Porter (Secker & Warburg, 1940). (First published 1939.)

—, *The Magic Mountain*, trans. H. T. Lowe-Porter (Secker & Warburg, 1971). (First published 1924.)

—, *Past Masters and Other Papers*, trans. H. T. Lowe-Porter (Martin Secker, 1933).

—, *Stories of Three Decades* (Secker & Warburg, 1946). This volume includes 'Tonio Kröger', 'Death in Venice' and 'Mario and the Magician'.

Mason, Eudo C., *Rilke* (Edinburgh: Oliver & Boyd, 1963).

Mason, Eudo C., *Rilke and the English Speaking World* (Cambridge University Press, 1961).

Moore, Harry T., *The Priest of Love: A Life of D. H. Lawrence* (Heinemann, revised edition 1974).

Morgan, George A., *What Nietzsche Means* (New York: Torch Books, 1965). (First published by Harvard University Press, 1941.)

Mügge, M. A., *Friedrich Nietzsche* (T. Fisher Unwin, 1908).

Murdoch, Iris, *The Sovereignty of Good* (Routledge & Kegan Paul, 1970).

Nicholls, R. A., *Nietzsche in the Early Work of Thomas Mann* (Berkeley: University of California Press, 1955).

Nietzsche, Friedrich, *Beyond Good and Evil: Prelude to a Philosophy of the Future*, trans. with commentary by Walter Kaufmann (New York: Vintage Books, A Division of Random House, 1966).

—, *The Birth of Tragedy* and *The Case of Wagner*, trans. with commentary by

Walter Kaufmann (New York: Vintage Books, A Division of Random House, 1967).

—, *Daybreak: Thoughts On the Prejudices of Morality*, trans. R. J. Hollingdale, intro. by Michael Tanner (Cambridge University Press, 1982).

—, *On the Future of Our Educational Institutions* and *Homer and Classical Philology*, trans. and intro. by J. M. Kennedy (T. N. Foulis, 1909).

—, *The Gay Science*, trans. with commentary by Walter Kaufmann (Vintage Books, A Division of Random House, 1974).

—, *On The Genealogy of Morals*, trans. Walter Kaufmann & R. J. Hollingdale and *Ecce Homo*, trans. with commentary by Walter Kaufmann (New York: Vintage Books, A Division of Random House, 1967).

—, *Human, All-Too-Human*, two volumes, intro. by J. M. Kennedy, Vol. I trans. Helen Zimmern, Vol. II trans. Paul V. Kohn (Edinburgh and London: T. N. Foulis, 1909 and 1911).

—, *A Nietzsche Reader*, selected and trans. R. J. Hollingdale (Harmondsworth, Middlesex: Penguin, 1979).

—, *Philosophy in the Tragic Age of the Greeks*, trans. with intro. by Marianne Cowan (Chicago: A Gateway Edition, Regnery Gateway, 1962).

—, *Selected Letters of Friedrich Nietzsche*, trans. A. N. Ludovici, ed. and intro. by O. Levy (Soho Book Company, 1985).

—, *Thus Spoke Zarathustra: A Book for Everyone and No One*, trans. with intro. by R. J. Hollingdale (Harmondsworth, Middlesex: Penguin, 1980).

—, *Twilight of the Idols* and *The Anti-Christ*, trans. with intro. and commentary by R. J. Hollingdale (Harmondsworth, Middlesex: Penguin, 1978).

—, *Unpublished Letters*, trans. and ed. Karl F. Leidecker (Peter Owen, 1960). (First published by Philosophical Library USA, 1959.)

—, *Untimely Meditations*, trans. R. J. Hollingdale, intro. by J. P. Stern (Cambridge University Press, 1983).

—, *The Will to Power*, trans. Walter Kaufmann & R. J. Hollingdale, ed. with commentary by Walter Kaufmann (New York: Vintage Books, A Division of Random House, 1968).

Orwell, George, *Collected Essays* (Secker & Warburg, 1961).

Parkin, Andrew, *The Dramatic Imagination of W. B. Yeats* (Dublin: Gill & Macmillan; New York: Barnes & Noble, 1978).

Pasley, Malcolm, (ed.), *Nietzsche: Imagery and Thought* (Methuen, 1978).

Pfeffer, Rose, *Nietzsche Disciple of Dionysus* (Lewisburg: Bucknell University Press, 1972).

Rilke, Rainer Maria, *Duino Elegies*, German text with English trans., intro. and commentary by J. B. Leishman & Stephen Spender (Chatto & Windus, 1981). (First published by The Hogarth Press, 1939.)

Rilke, Rainer Maria, *The Notebook of Malte Laurids Brigge*, intro. by Stephen Spender (Oxford and New York: Oxford University Press, 1984).

Rilke, Rainer Maria, *Selected Letters of Rainer Maria Rilke 1902–1926*, trans. R. F. C. Hull (Macmillan, 1946).

Sagar, Keith, *The Art of D. H. Lawrence* (Cambridge University Press, 1966).

Salter, William Mackintosh, *Nietzsche the Thinker: A Study* (New York: Frederick Ungar Publishing Company, 1968).

Schopenhauer, Arthur, *The World as Will and Representation*, trans. E. F. J.

Payne, 2 vols (New York: Dover Publications, 1966). (This translation first published in Colorado: The Falcon's Wing Press, 1958.)

Spinoza, Benedict de, *The Chief Works of Benedict de Spinoza*, Vol. II, trans. with intro. by R. H. M. Elwes (New York: Dover Publications, 1951).

Stambaugh, Joan, *Nietzsche's Thought of Eternal Return* (Baltimore and London: Johns Hopkins Press, 1972).

Stock, A. G., *WB Yeats: his poetry and his thought* (Cambridge University Press, 1961).

Taylor, A. J. P., *English History 1914–1945* (Oxford University Press, 1965).

Thatcher, David S., *Nietzsche in England 1890–1914* (Toronto and Buffalo: University of Toronto Press, 1970).

Wilcox, John T., *Truth and Value in Nietzsche*, foreword by Walter Kaufmann (Ann Arbor: University of Michigan Press, 1974).

Winston, Richard, *Thomas Mann: The Making of an Artist 1875–1911*, afterword by Clara Winston (Constable, 1982).

Wood, Frank, *Rainer Maria Rilke: The Ring of Forms* (Minneapolis: University of Minnesota Press, 1958).

Yeats, W. B., *Autobiographies* (Macmillan, 1955).

—, *The Collected Poems of W. B. Yeats* (Macmillan, 1982). (First edition 1933.)

—, *Explorations* (Macmillan, 1962).

—, *Letters of W. B. Yeats*, ed. Allen Wade (Rupert Hart-Davis, 1954).

—, *Memoirs*, ed. Denis Donoghue (Macmillan, 1972).

—, *On the Boiler* (Irish University Press facsimile, 1939).

—, *The Variorum Edition of the Complete Plays of W. B. Yeats*, ed. Russell K. Alspach, assisted by Catherine Alspach (Macmillan, 1966).

—, *A Vision* (Macmillan, 1962). (First edition printed privately, 1925.)

Zwerdling, Alex, *Yeats and the Heroic Ideal* (New York University, 1965; London: Peter Owen, 1966).

Index